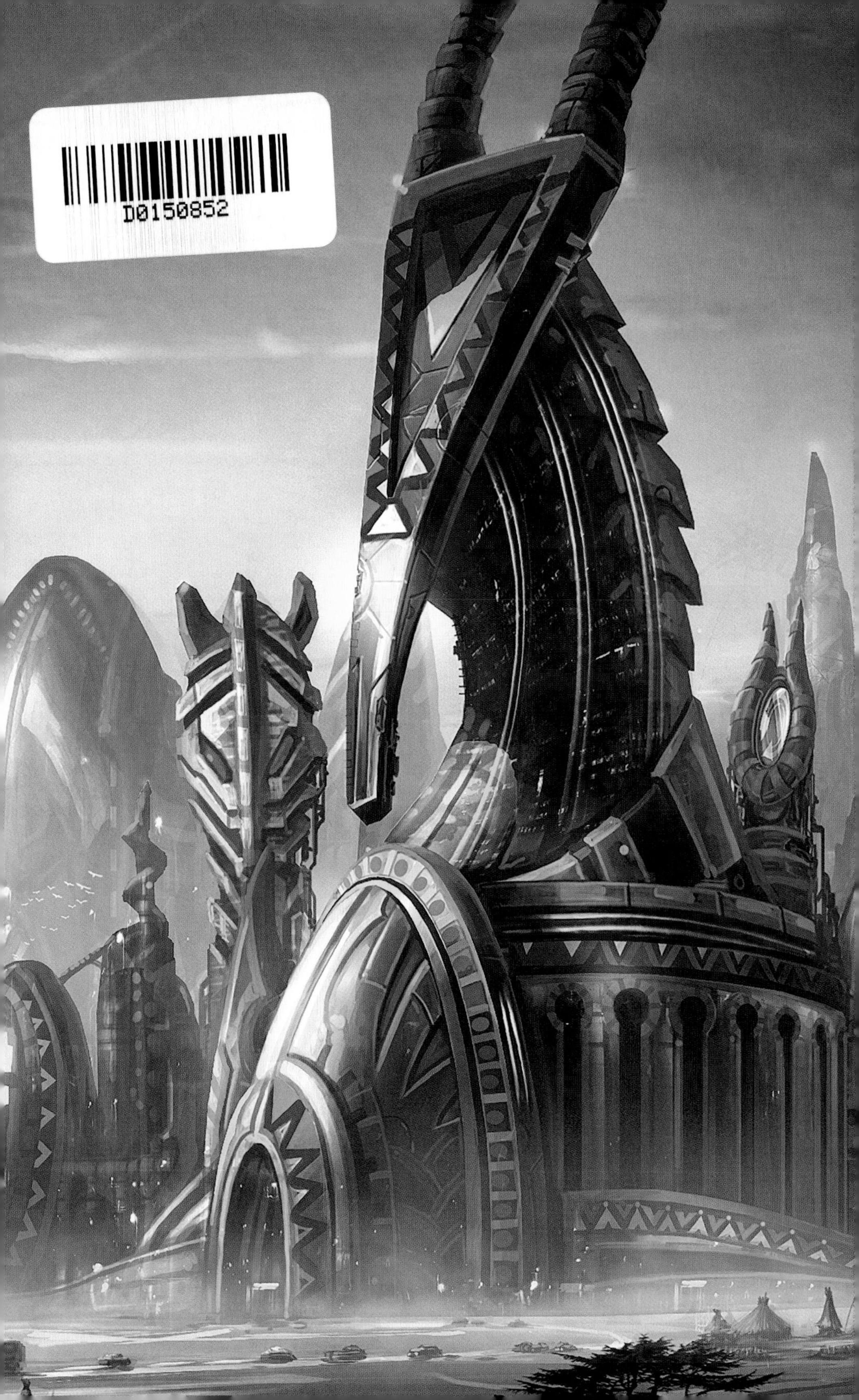

THE OVERWATCH LEGACY
RISE OF THE OMNICS

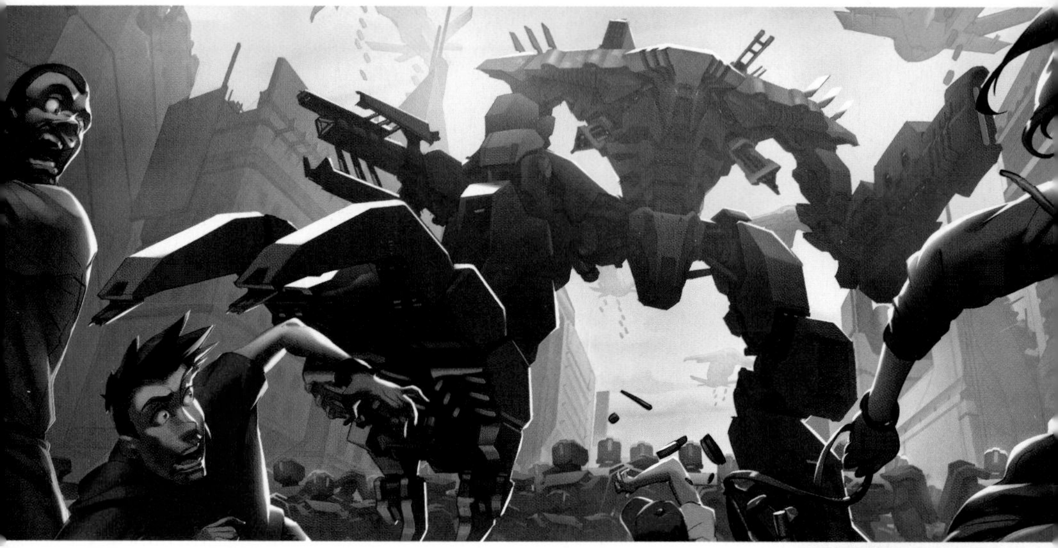

Before there was Overwatch, there was the Omnica Corporation. This revolutionary company figured out a way to mass-produce humanoid robots called omnics. All around the world, Omnica constructed omniums—massive, automated factories, which created omnics to fit all sorts of needs and situations. The omniums churned out these robots by the thousands.

But then the omniums started to break down. After an investigation revealed evidence of corporate fraud, Omnica was shut down. Their massive, once-active factories stood empty.

But before long, the omniums woke up. They launched a military campaign against all humans by building an army of omnic warriors.

The Omnic Crisis had begun. No one knew exactly why the omniums were set on destroying humans, and no country's army could figure out how to shut them down again. The omnics kept attacking and attacking, and they adapted to any strategy used against them.

Humans had to adapt, too. They needed a new kind of hero.

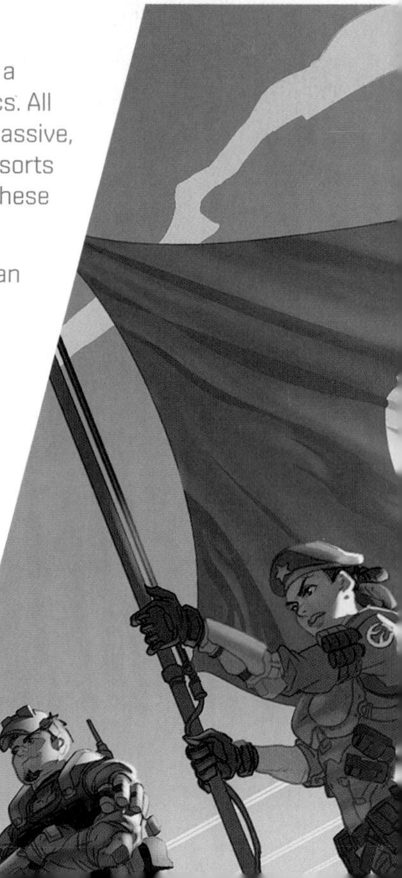

AN ELITE TEAM

It seemed no one country could permanently take down the omniums on its own—the brute strength of an army wasn't working against the omnics. So, the United Nations came up with a new strategy. They recruited a small group of individuals—soldiers, scientists, adventurers, and oddities—each with unique talents and gifted minds. These soldiers were the founding members of Overwatch. The Overwatch agents targeted the omnics in a series of dangerous secret missions, destroyed the omnics' command and control protocols, and ended the Omnic Crisis.

The war was over, but Earth was still in chaos. Overwatch stayed in operation as a global peacekeeping force, and grew even bigger. Its new agents performed heroic rescues, cleaned up polluted environments, and made great strides in medical care. Overwatch became a shining symbol of hope to an entire generation!

But then everything changed . . .

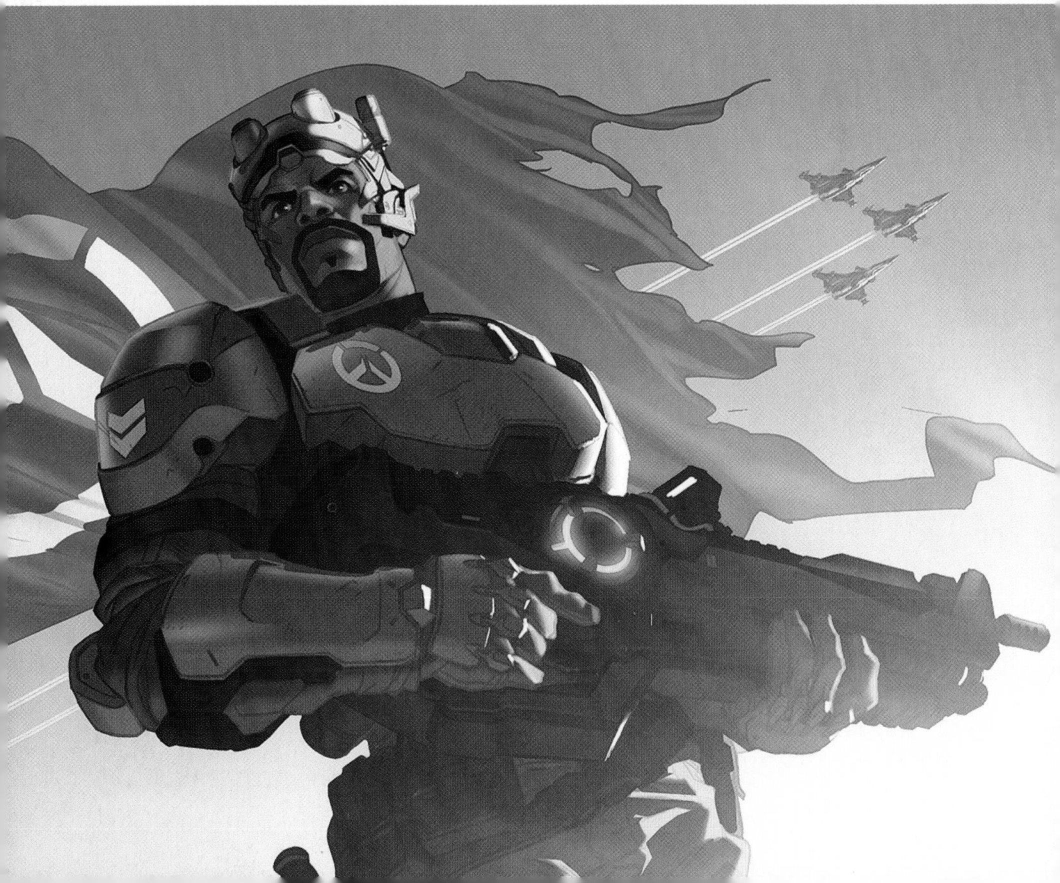

THE OVERWATCH LEGACY
THE FALL

Almost two decades after Overwatch saved humanity, scandals hit the organization. Overwatch's top-secret division, Blackwatch, was exposed to the public alongside stories of corruption, abuse of power, and shady dealings. The public started to turn against the global peacekeeping force, and a series of high-profile mission failures gave the United Nations an easy excuse to shut down Overwatch. But the final blow came when the Overwatch headquarters in Switzerland was destroyed in a battle between Overwatch commander Jack Morrison and Blackwatch commander Gabriel Reyes.

The world moved on. Cities like Numbani were built, where omnics and humans lived together in peace. But in other parts of the world, tensions built between humans and omnics who had trouble trusting each other after the war. Whispers spread of corporations and governments working together to take advantage of citizens. Villains that Overwatch once captured—like Doomfist—escaped. The mysterious Talon organization was gaining even more power. Everything Overwatch had fought against was creeping back . . .

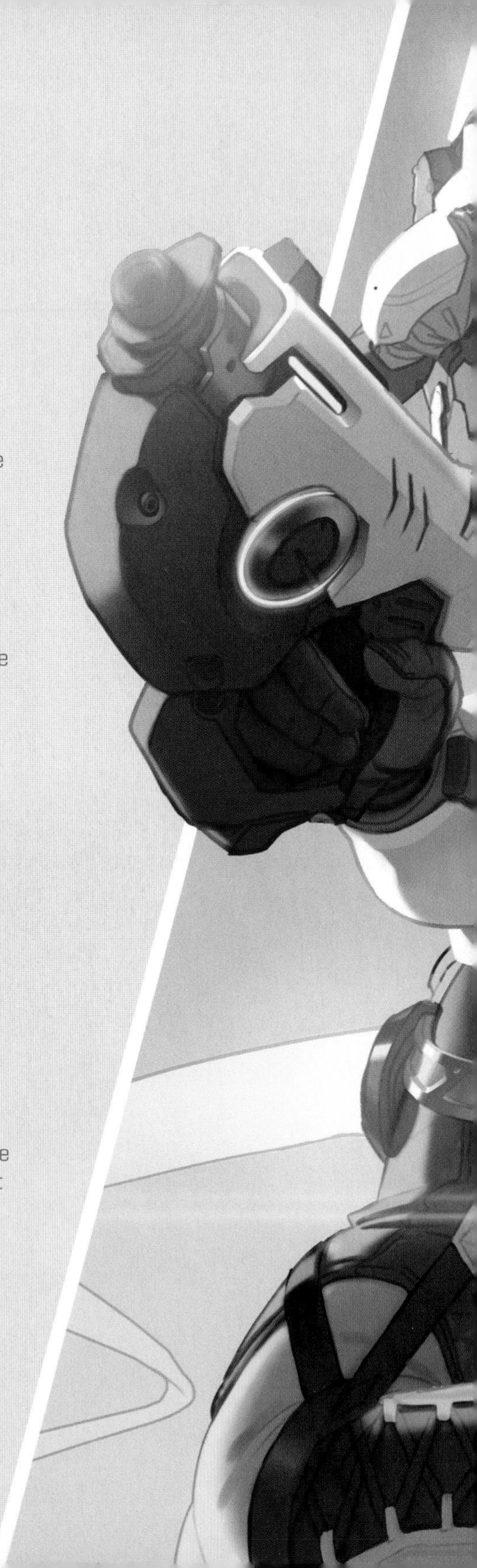

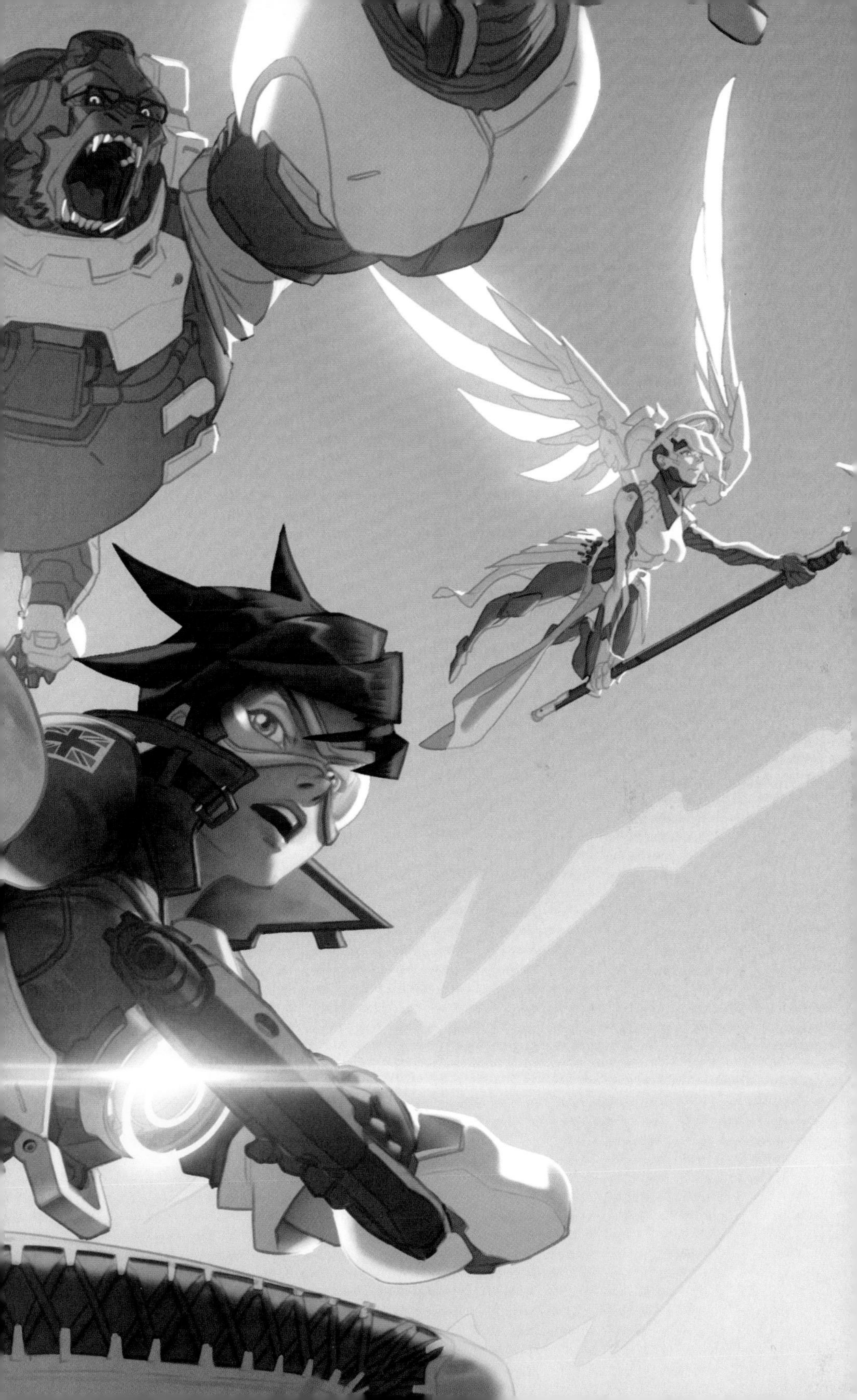

THE OVERWATCH LEGACY
THE RESURGENCE OF TALON

No one took advantage of Overwatch's absence more than the Talon organization. Before the fall of Overwatch, Doomfist, a Talon leader, almost succeeded in thwarting an Overwatch strike team. He was imprisoned in a maximum-security facility for years, where he waited patiently for the events he'd set in motion to play out.

Widowmaker assassinated Tekhartha Mondatta, an omnic spiritual leader and symbol of peace for the coexistence of humans and machines. Sombra and Reaper joined her in a mission to assassinate Katya Volskaya in Russia—which failed, but gave Sombra a chance to pursue her own agenda. Every success increased Talon's influence and propelled Earth ever closer to catastrophe.

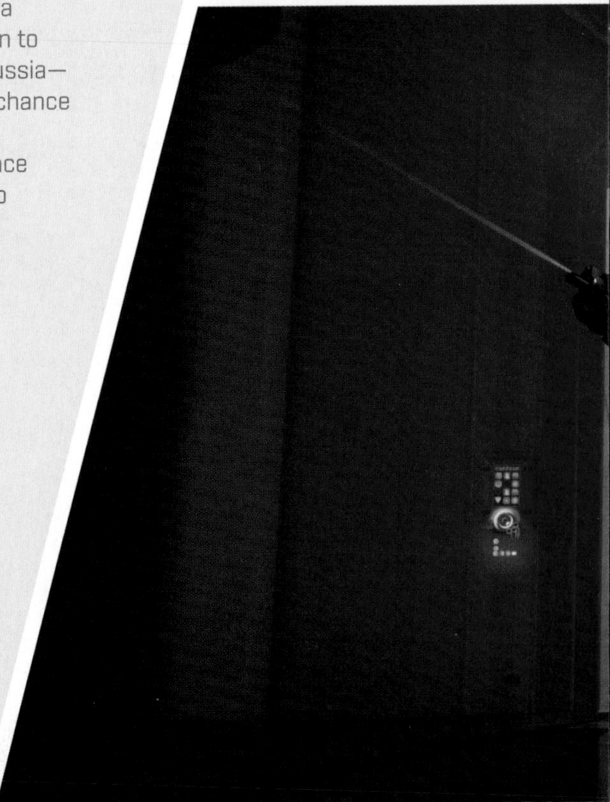

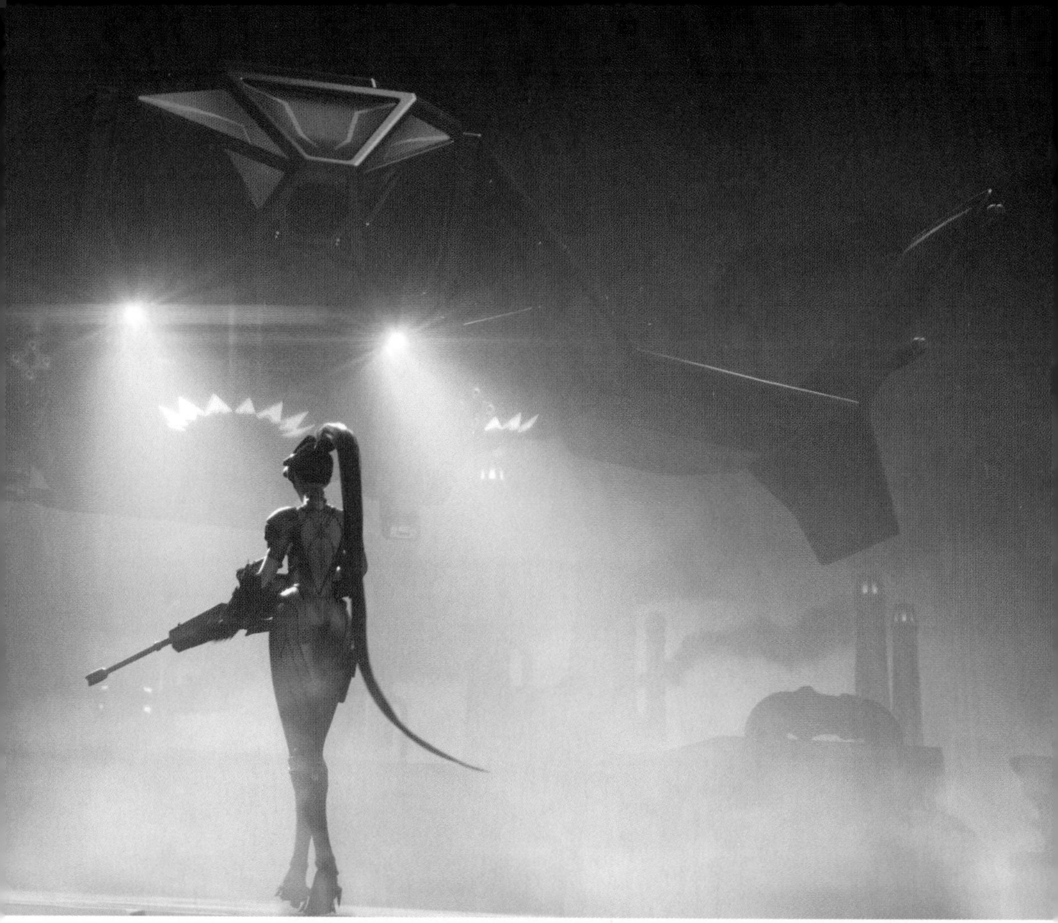

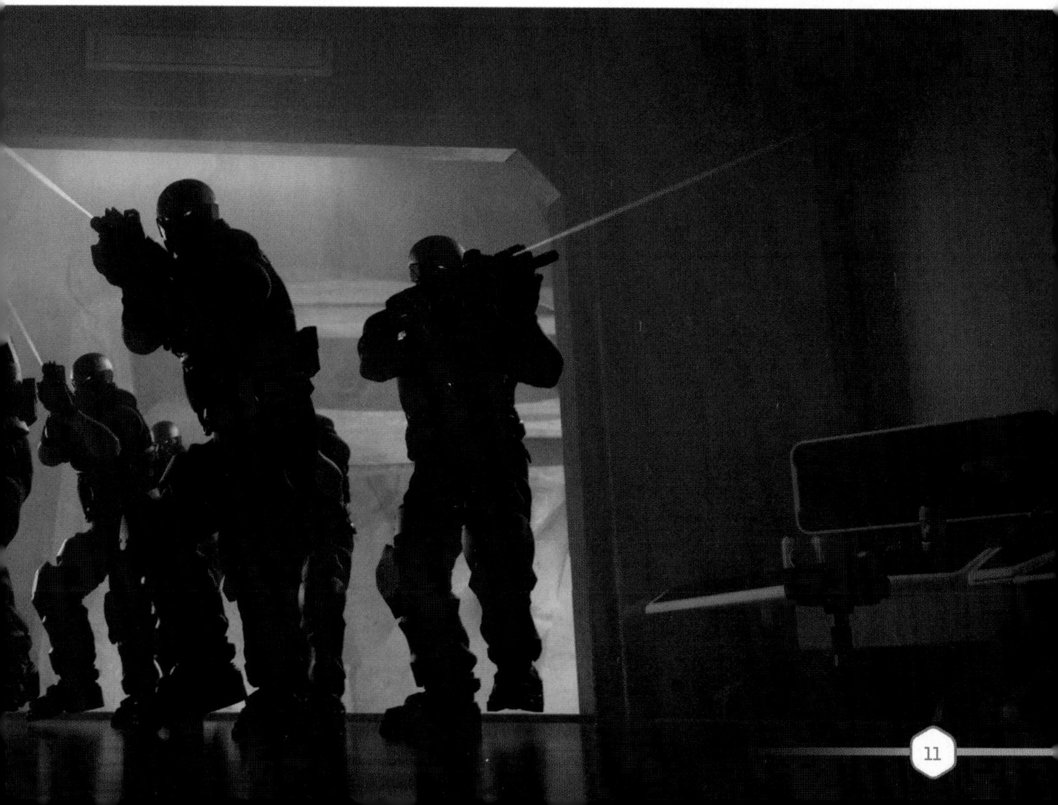

THE OVERWATCH LEGACY
RECALL

Winston, a former member of Overwatch, witnessed terrible events from his lab in Watchpoint: Gibraltar. The world still needed heroes and Winston knew that Overwatch could set things right!

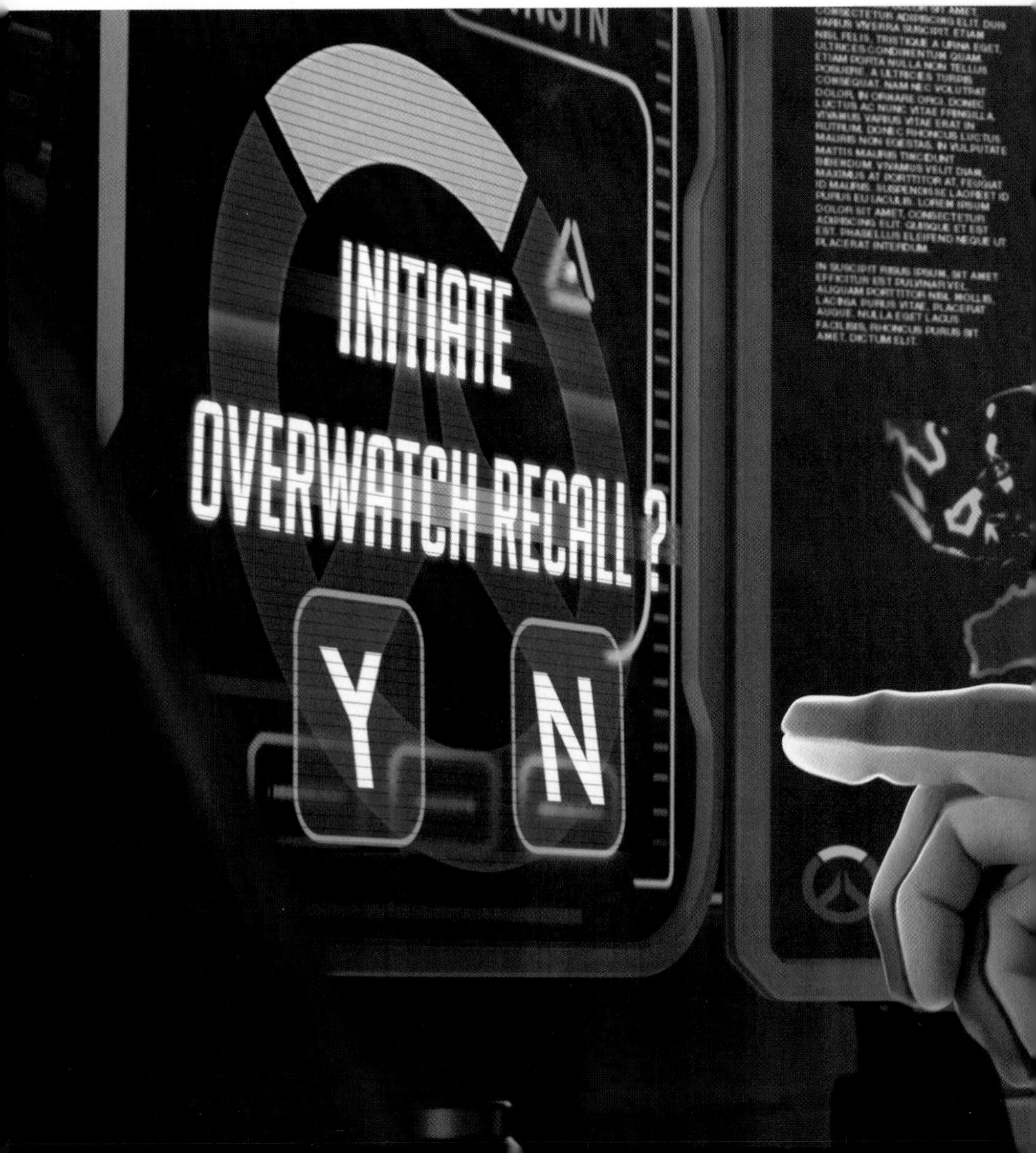
INITIATE
OVERWATCH RECALL ?
Y
N

But reviving Overwatch was against the law, and any official activity was banned by a resolution known as the Petras Act. Athena, an artificial intelligence that assisted Overwatch, initially advised against Winston from initiating the Overwatch recall, but Winston knew that Overwatch could still be the heroes the world needed.

Before he could activate the recall, Reaper and a squadron of Talon troops broke into Winston's laboratory at Watchpoint: Gibraltar. While his troops fought Winston, Reaper attempted to infect Athena with a virus that would give him access to the names and locations of all former Overwatch agents. In his primal rage, Winston defeated Reaper and his forces and stopped the virus before Talon could get the entire database. But the message was clear—if Talon was after Overwatch, it was the time to act. Winston activated the Overwatch recall, despite the risk. Hope was on the way!

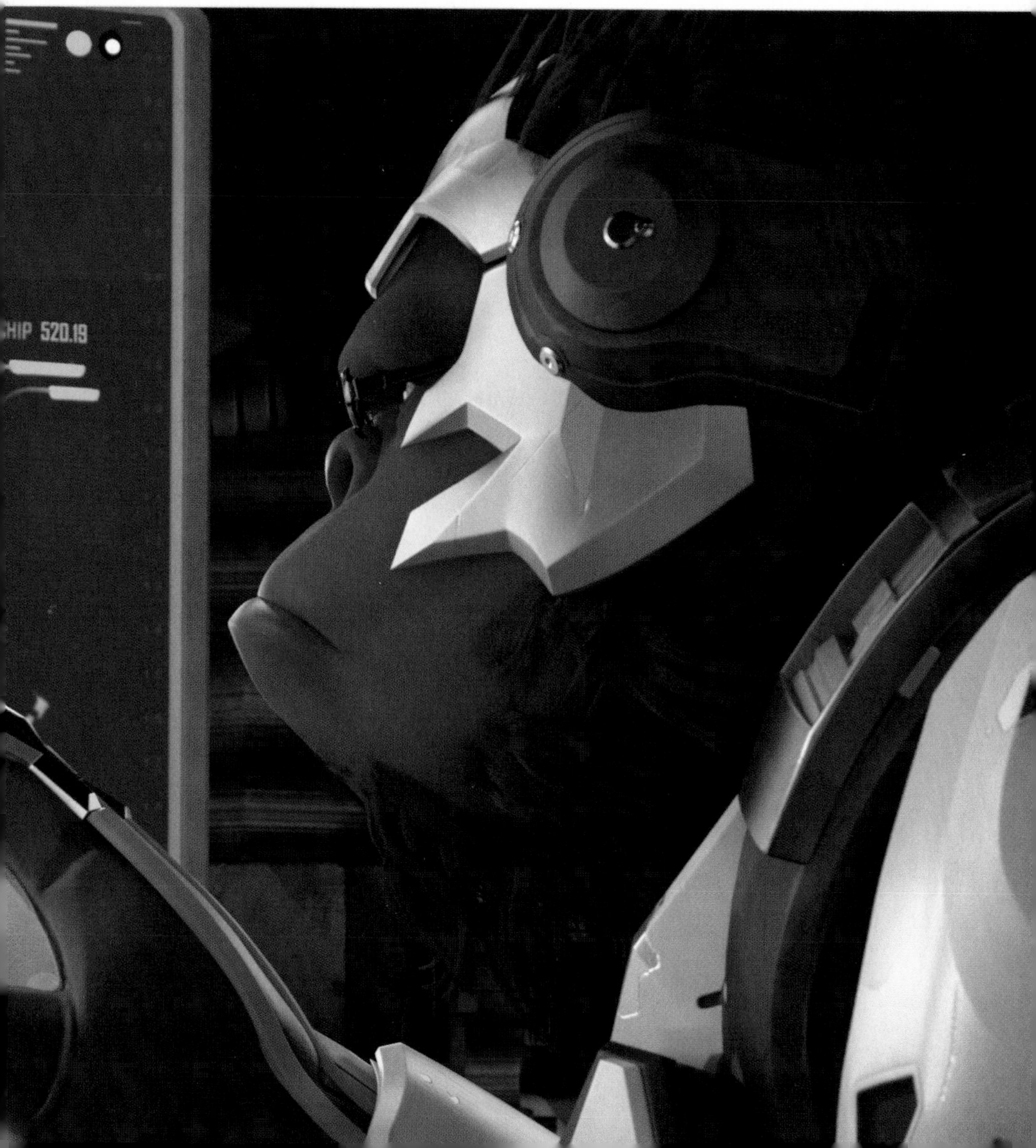
HIP 520.19

Tracer joined Winston in a flash. Though she had failed to stop Widowmaker's assassination of the Tekhartha Mondatta in King's Row, Tracer was determined to prevent such loss of life from happening again. Reunited, Winston and Tracer protected museum visitors from Reaper and Widowmaker, and briefly prevented them from stealing Doomfist's gauntlet.

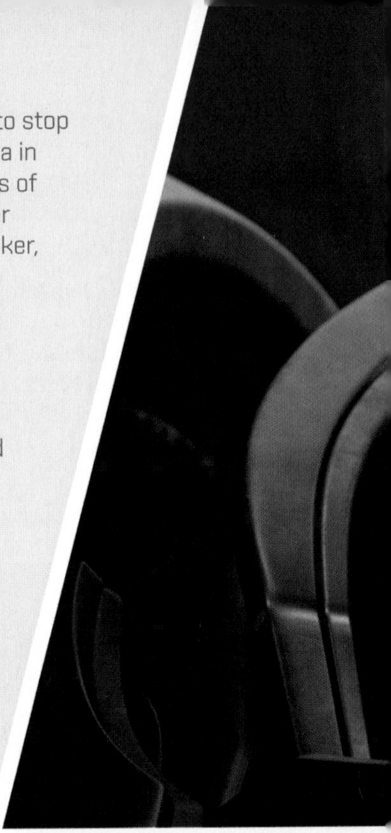

Mei, an Overwatch climate scientist, finally woke from nine years in cryostasis to find Winston's message. With her friendly drone, Snowball, she began her long journey to join the Overwatch team. Reinhardt, inspired by the memory of his old mentor from the Crusaders, accepted the call and was accompanied by his squire, Brigitte. The call to arms continues to reach across the globe, hoping to inspire old agents to take up the mantle once again.

Overwatch even inspired a whole new generation of heroes! Many people were already fighting for Earth: Lúcio used his music to save communities and change lives. D.Va's gaming skills made her perfectly suited to pilot a mech and protect her home. Zenyatta traveled the world guiding others toward harmony and protecting the innocent. Efi Oladele and her robotic creation, Orisa, were keeping the peace in Numbani. Even opportunists like Junkrat and Roadhog were changing the world . . . in their own way.

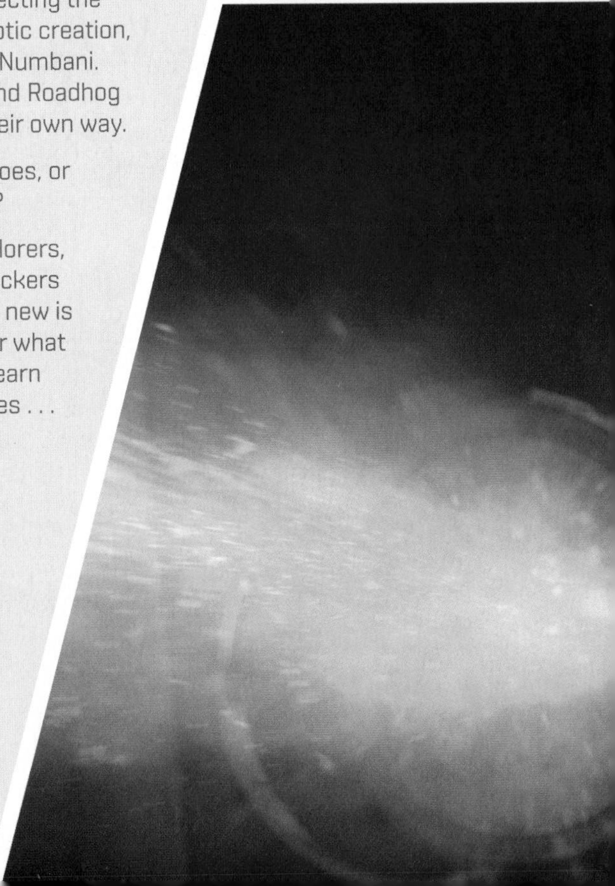

Will the world welcome these heroes, or send them back to the shadows?

Earth is full of scientists and explorers, bounty hunters and criminals, hackers and omnics. Every day, someone new is taking up a cause and fighting for what they believe in. Keep reading to learn who will fight against these heroes . . . and who will save the world!

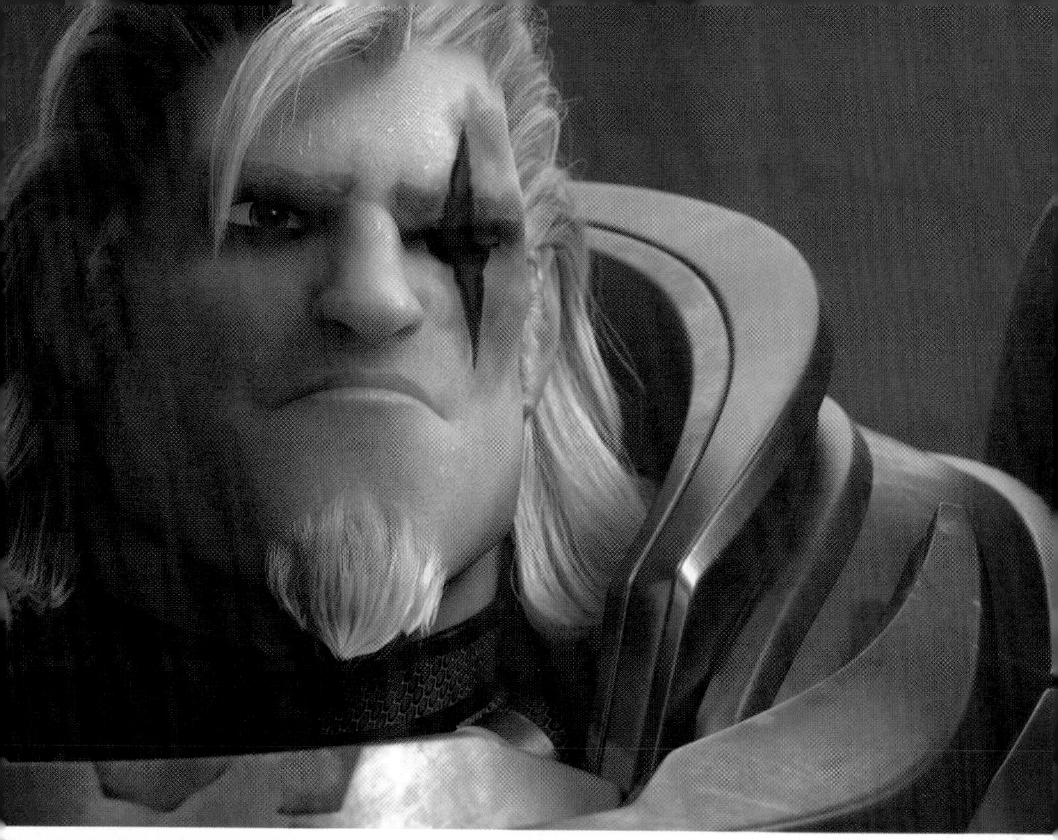

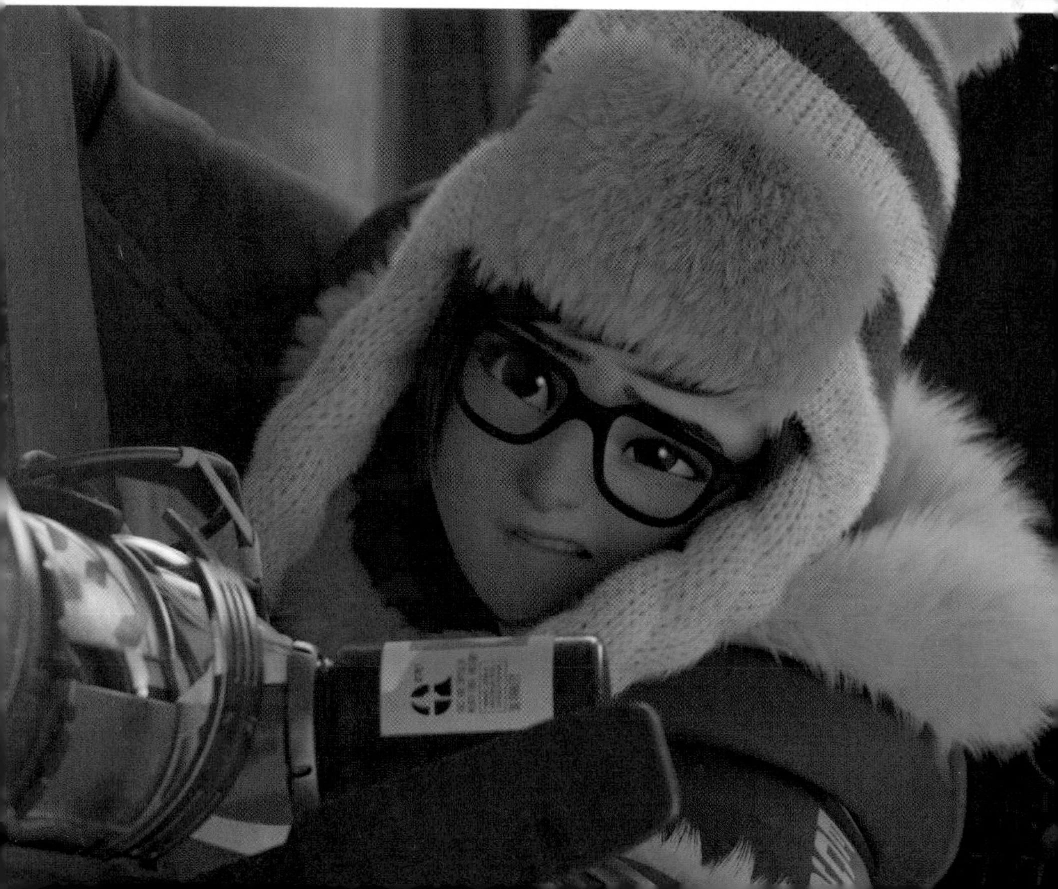

DAMAGE HEROES

Damage heroes are agile, versatile, and they sure do pack a punch! They have less health than other heroes, so they usually need stealth, speed, or shielding to skirt enemy lines and land powerful blows on their opponents. They can be used in many ways, but are best at the following:

-They can scout ahead and spy on the enemy.

-They focus on stopping the opposing team's advancement.

-They can approach enemy teams from behind and eliminate the weakest opponents first.

-They guard key locations.

These heroes aren't easy to defeat; you never know when one of them is going to swoop in from the sky or appear in a blink of an eye!

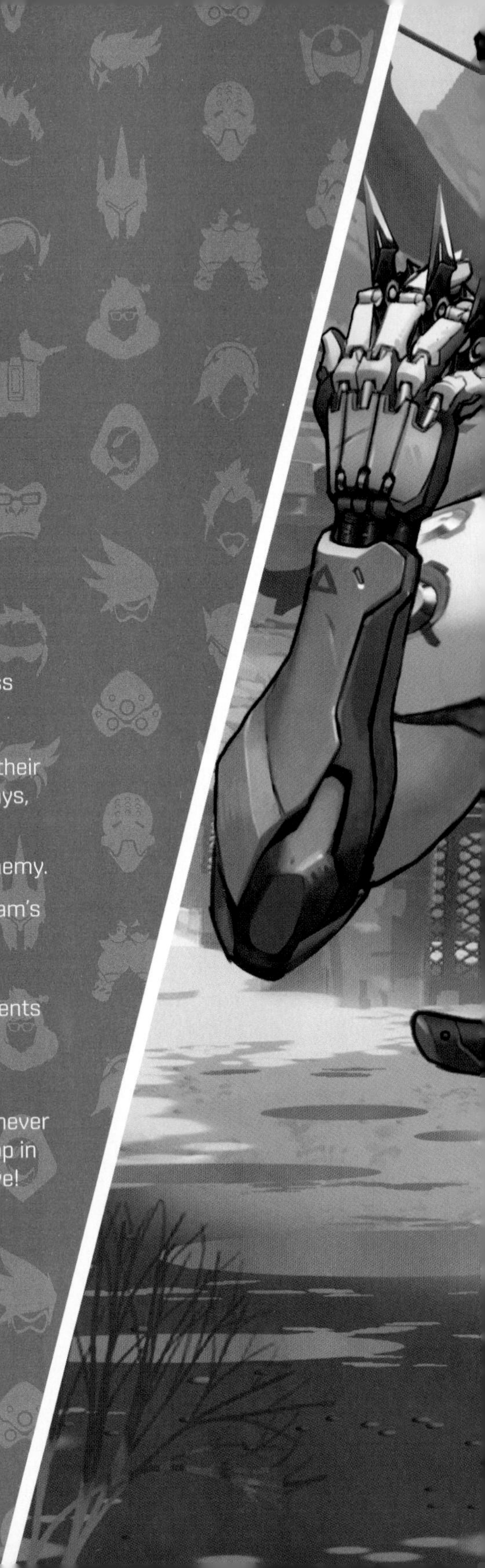

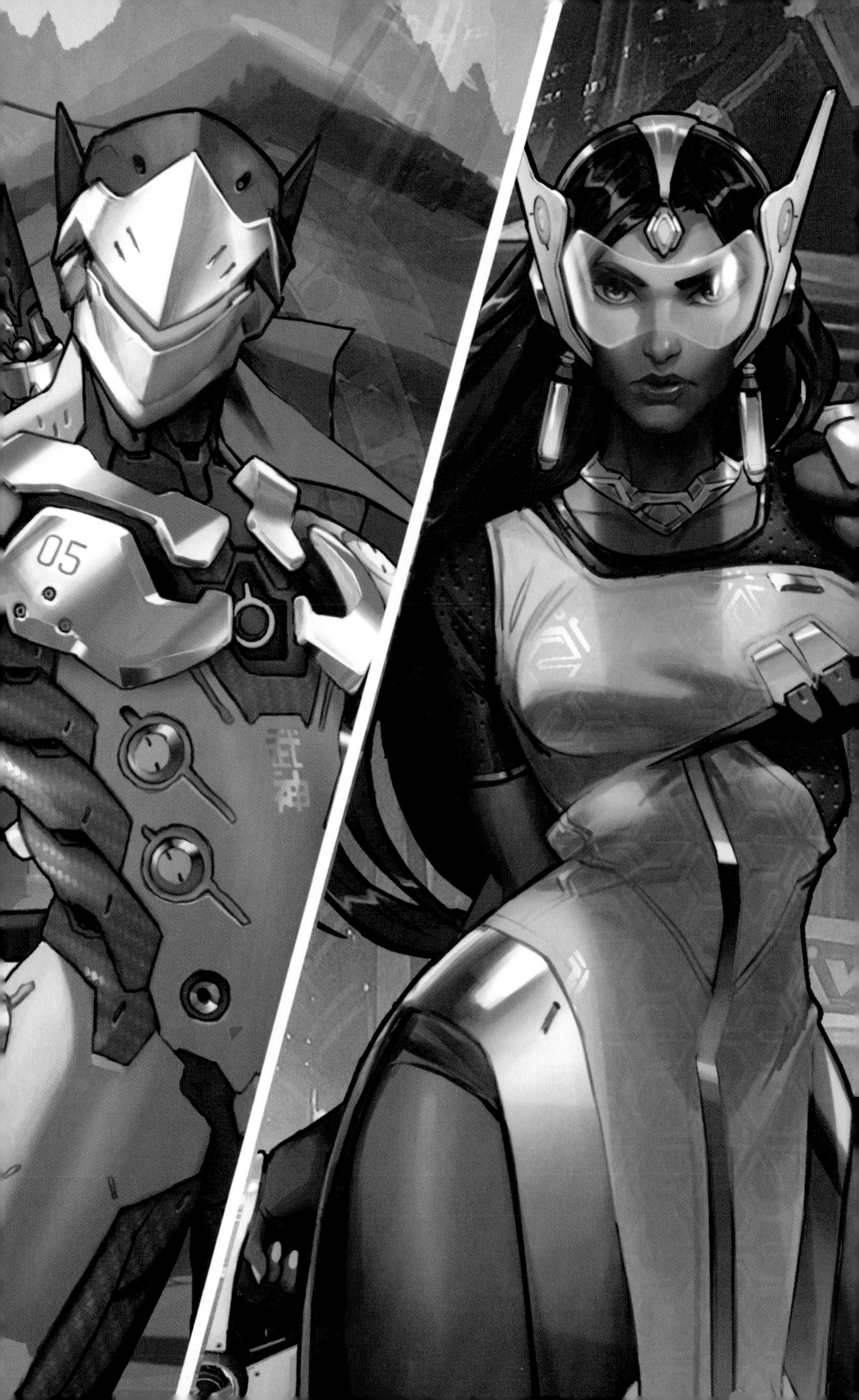
05

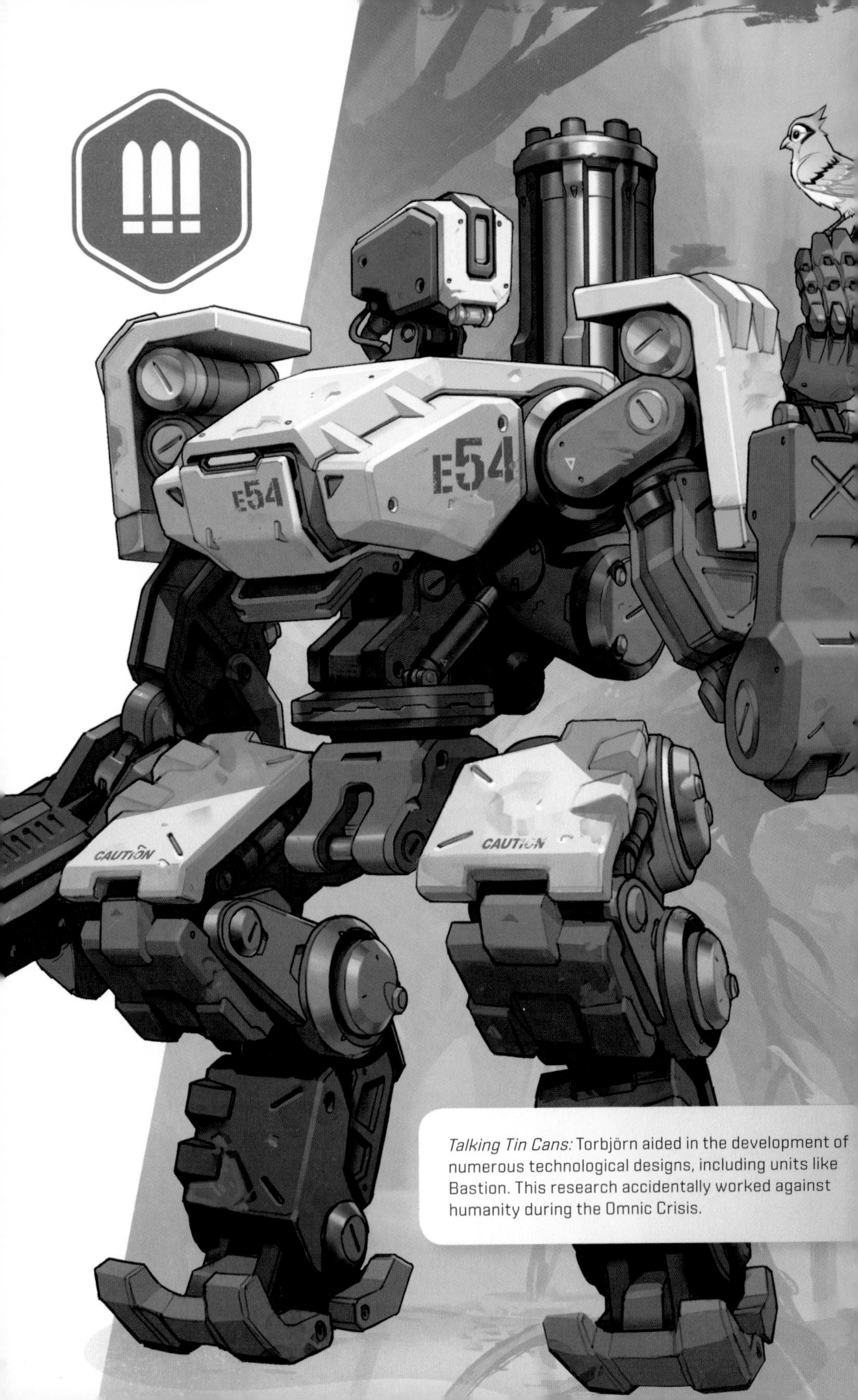
E54
E54
CAUTION
CAUTION

Talking Tin Cans: Torbjörn aided in the development of numerous technological designs, including units like Bastion. This research accidentally worked against humanity during the Omnic Crisis.

BASTION

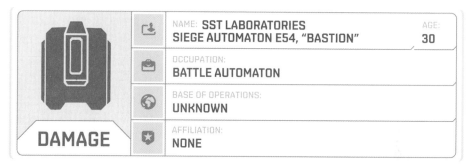

	NAME: **SST LABORATORIES SIEGE AUTOMATON E54, "BASTION"**	AGE: **30**
	OCCUPATION: **BATTLE AUTOMATON**	
	BASE OF OPERATIONS: **UNKNOWN**	
DAMAGE	AFFILIATION: **NONE**	

BIOGRAPHY

Humans originally created Bastion robot units to help keep the peace. Each unit came packed with power—and the ability to quickly transform into a Gatling gun! But during the Omnic Crisis, they were turned against the humans and became a major force in the robot army.

After the war, nearly all the Bastion units were destroyed, and those that weren't were left broken down, forgotten for over a decade. While Bastion sat dormant in the wilderness, vines and roots grew over it, and animals nested in it. Then one day, it reactivated.

With its combat programming nearly wiped out, this gentle giant began to wander the Earth, curious about nature and living creatures. It prefers to live in the wild, away from humans. Because when Bastion is threatened, its core programming kicks in, and then, watch out! It will use its abilities to eliminate anything in its path.

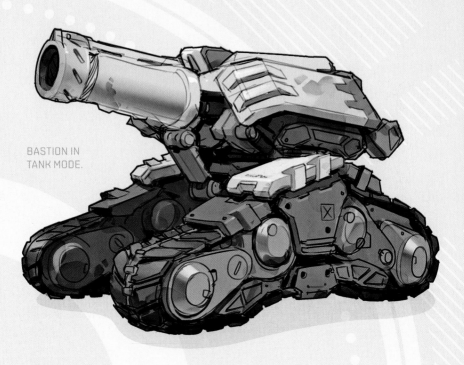

BASTION IN TANK MODE.

ULTIMATE ABILITY— CONFIGURATION: TANK:

Bastion can transform into a tank that delivers major damage with its powerful long-range cannon. But it can't stay in this form for very long.

CONFIGURATION: RECON:

Bastion is fully mobile in this mode and can use its submachine gun to fire steady bursts at medium range.

CONFIGURATION: SENTRY:

When Bastion stands still, it can unleash a hail of bullets with a Gatling gun.

RECONFIGURE:

This ability allows Bastion to quickly switch from Recon mode to Sentry mode during battle.

SELF-REPAIR:

Bastion can restore its own health, but it can't move or fire a weapon while the repair is happening.

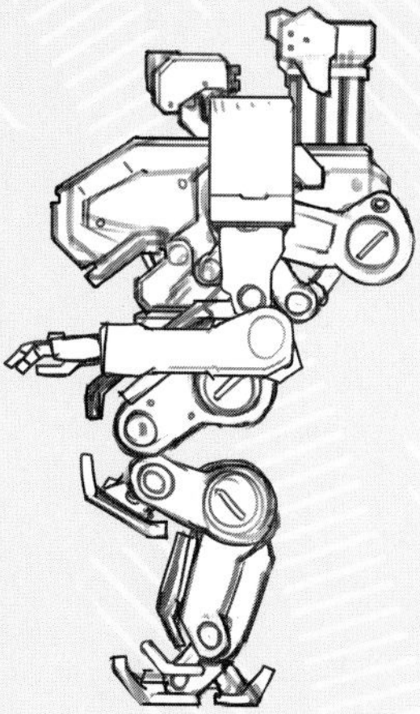

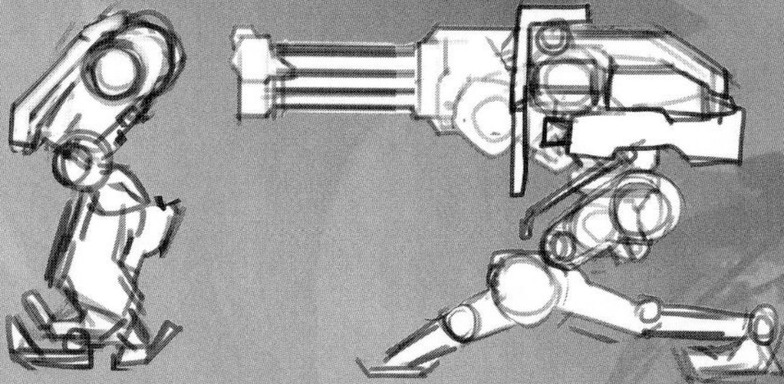

A ROBOT WHO LIKES BIRDS AND CHIPMUNKS? IT'S TRUE. BASTION HAS A SOFT SPOT FOR NATURE.

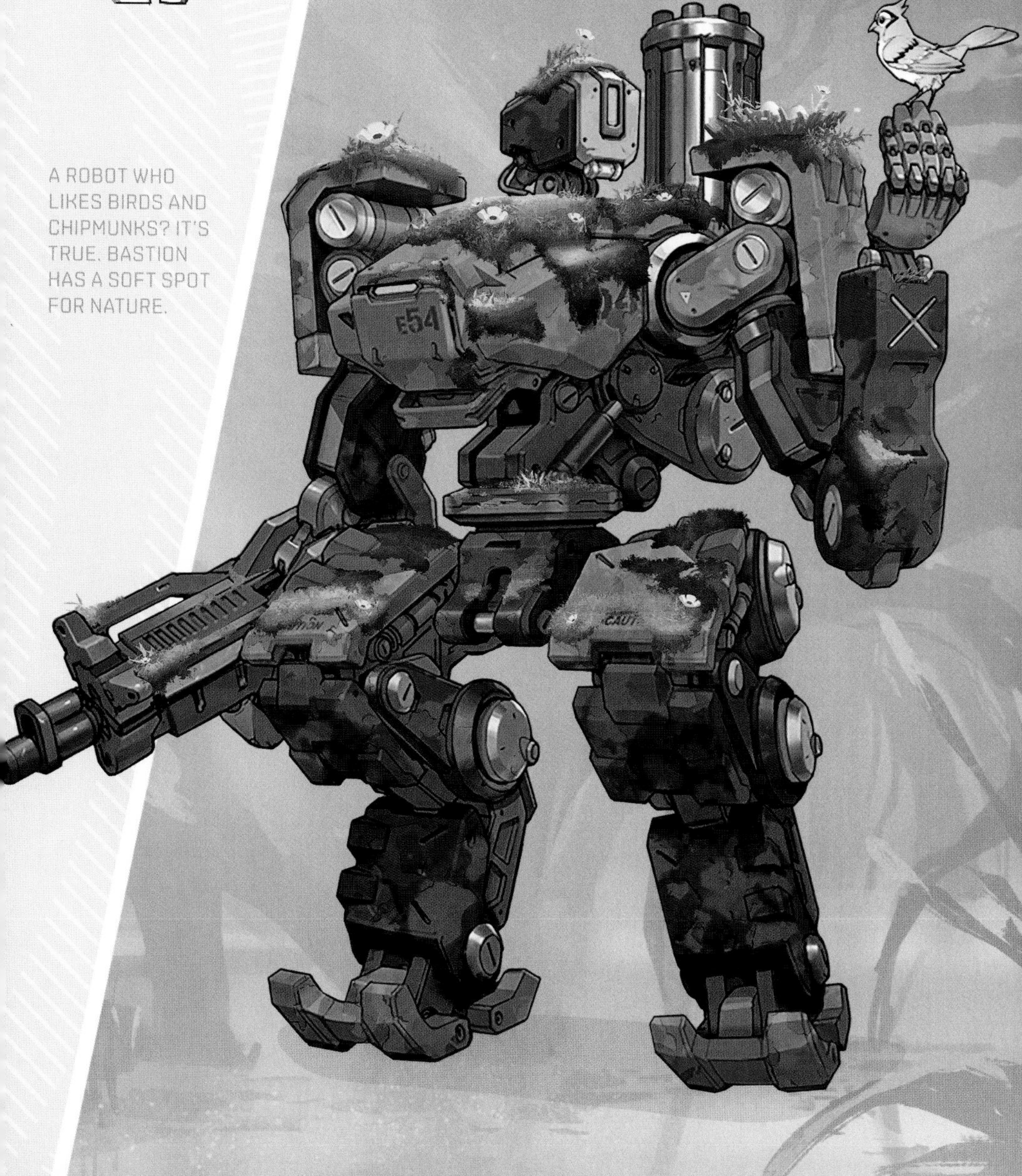

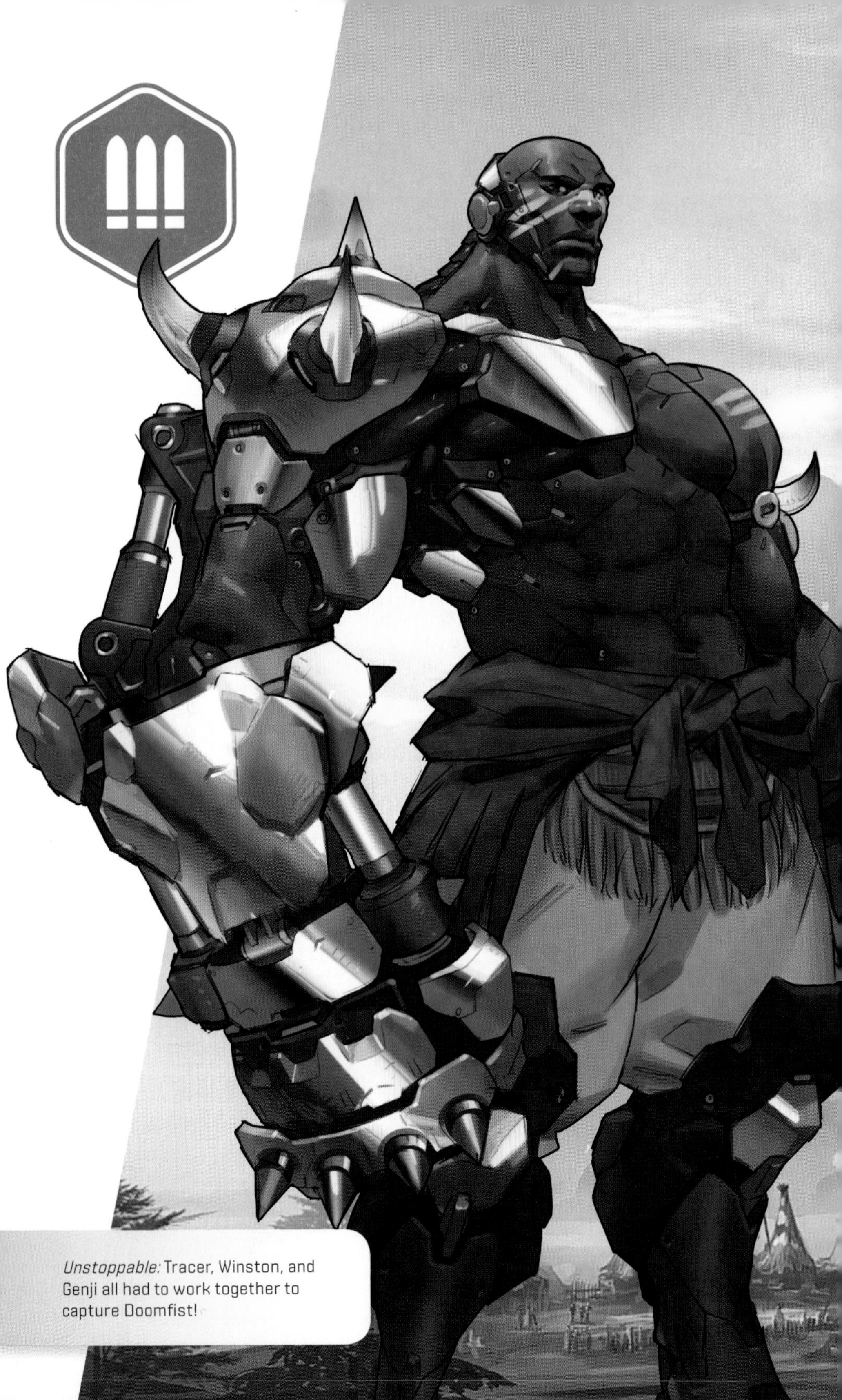

Unstoppable: Tracer, Winston, and Genji all had to work together to capture Doomfist!

HERO PROFILE

DOOMFIST

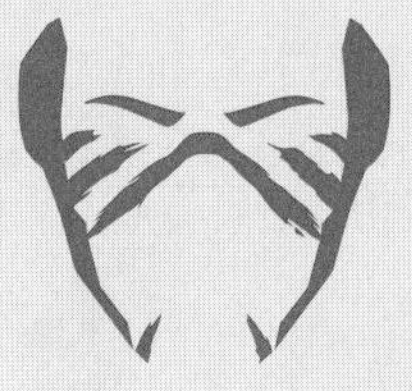

DAMAGE

NAME: AKANDE OGUNDIMU	AGE: 45
OCCUPATION: MERCENARY	
BASE OF OPERATIONS: OYO, NIGERIA	
AFFILIATION: TALON	

BIOGRAPHY

Akande Ogundimu, martial arts expert and heir to a prosthetic technology company, is actually the latest in a line of people to carry the "Doomfist" name and gauntlet. By betraying the previous Doomfist and rising through the ranks of the Talon organization, Ogundimu became one of the most powerful people in the world, until a team of Overwatch heroes imprisoned him in a maximum-security facility. Now he's back on Talon's leadership council, stronger than ever, and ready for a fight. Can the world survive his next big plan?

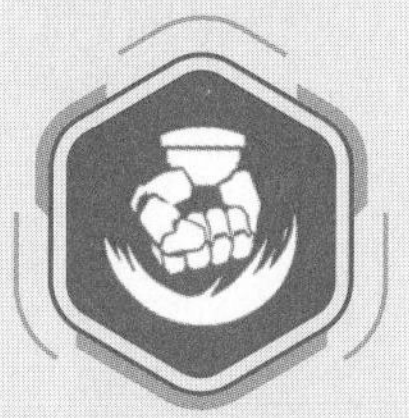

ULTIMATE ABILITY—METEOR STRIKE:

Doomfist rises far above the battle, then crashes to the ground to decimate a wide area.

HAND CANNON:

Doomfist's knuckles fire short-range bursts.

SEISMIC SLAM:

Doomfist leaps forward to smash the ground and knock enemies toward him.

RISING UPPERCUT:

A fierce jump knocks opponents into the air and lifts Doomfist high above the ground.

ROCKET PUNCH:

After charging up, Doomfist lunges forward and knocks enemies backward, dealing extra damage if they hit a wall.

THE BEST DEFENSE...(PASSIVE):

Energy from Doomfist's attacks is converted into shields that protect him from harm.

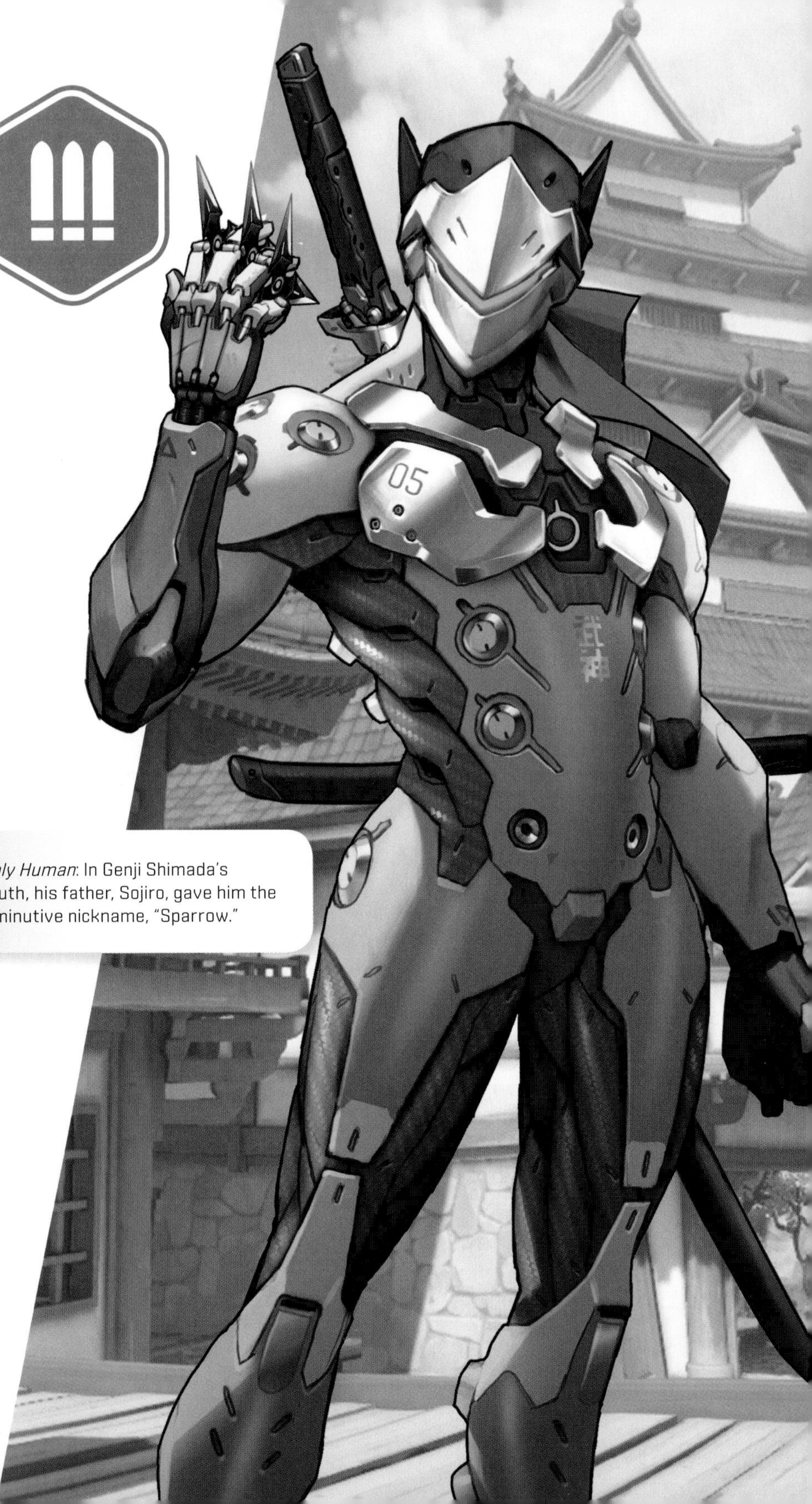
05

Only Human: In Genji Shimada's youth, his father, Sojiro, gave him the diminutive nickname, "Sparrow."

HERO PROFILE
GENJI

		NAME: **GENJI SHIMADA** / AGE: **35**
		OCCUPATION: **ADVENTURER**
		BASE OF OPERATIONS: **SHAMBALI MONASTERY, NEPAL**
DAMAGE		AFFILIATION: **SHIMADA CLAN** (FORMERLY), **OVERWATCH** (FORMERLY), **BLACKWATCH** (FORMERLY)

BIOGRAPHY

Part man, part machine, Genji started out as a human; he was the youngest child of the leader of the Shimada clan. When his brother, Hanzo, nearly killed him, Overwatch saved him with cutting-edge technology: cyberization, which gave him faster speed, better agility, and superior ninja skills. Now he has the body of a cyborg but the soul of a human. To find peace with his new form, he became a student of the omnic monk Zenyatta.

ULTIMATE ABILITY—DRAGONBLADE:
Genji can use his katana—a long Japanese sword—for short periods. Every blow he strikes with it is a success.

SHURIKEN:
This ninja can hurl three throwing stars quickly in a straight line, or even faster in a wider spread.

DEFLECT:
With lightning-quick swipes of his smaller sword, he can send projectiles shooting back at his opponent.

SWIFT STRIKE:
He can race forward, slashing through foes in his path.

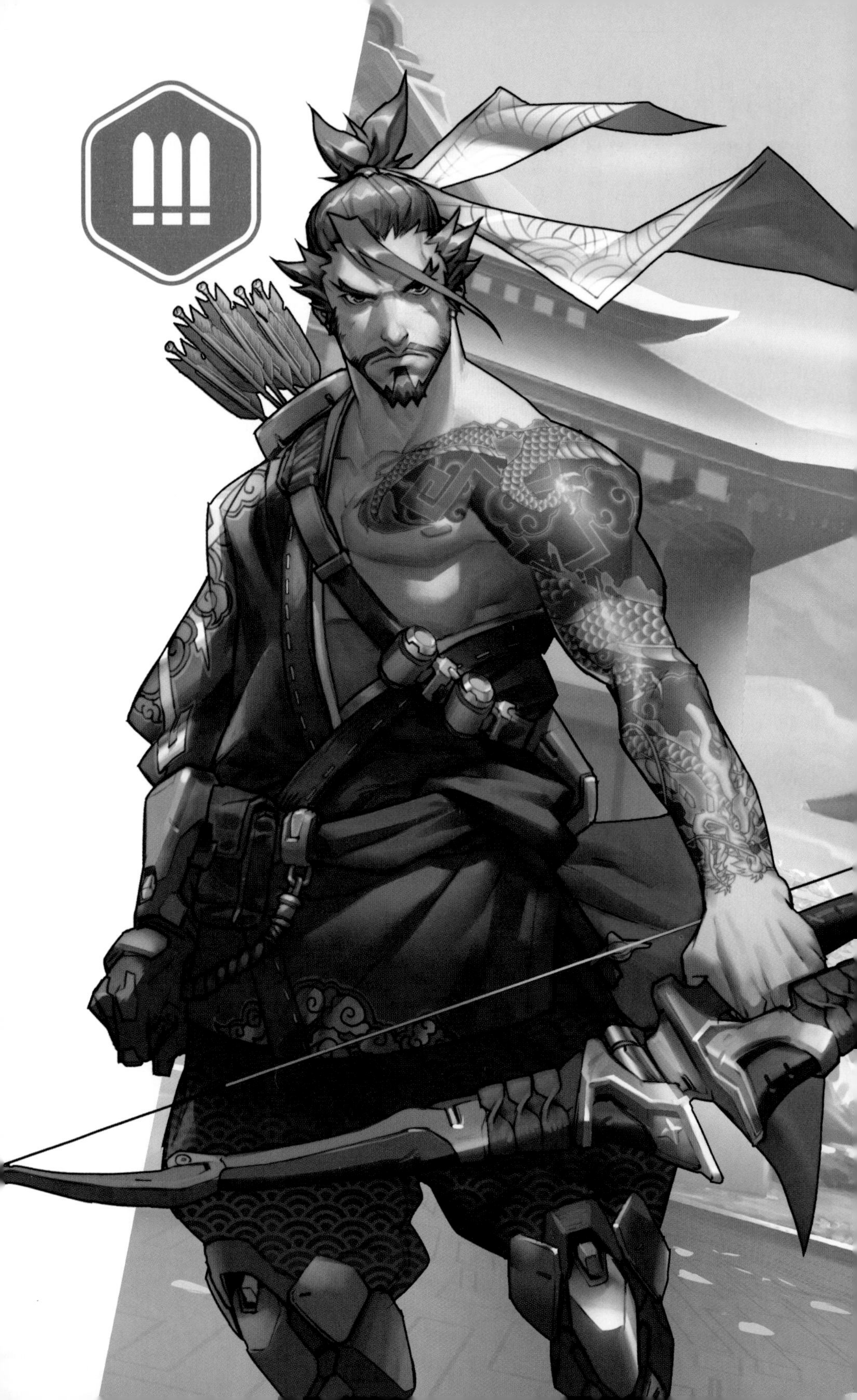

HANZO

NAME:	**HANZO SHIMADA**	AGE: **38**
OCCUPATION:	**MERCENARY, ASSASSIN**	
BASE OF OPERATIONS:	**HANAMURA, JAPAN** (FORMERLY)	
AFFILIATION:	**SHIMADA CLAN** (FORMERLY)	

DAMAGE

BIOGRAPHY

Hanzo is not your ordinary ninja—he can summon the power of a dragon in battle, a gift reserved for the Shimada family. The Shimada family was established centuries ago, a clan of assassins whose power grew over the years, enabling them to build a vast criminal empire. They trained Hanzo in martial arts, swordsmanship, and archery. In his darkest moment, Hanzo confronted his younger brother, Genji, on orders from the clan elders. After the epic battle, Hanzo believed he had killed his own brother. He has since left the clan and now travels the world as a lone warrior.

ULTIMATE ABILITY—DRAGONSTRIKE:
Unleash the dragon! When Hanzo summons a spirit dragon, it can travel through walls to reach his enemies.

STORM BOW:
Hanzo shoots an arrow at his opponent.

SONIC ARROW:
This arrow contains a tracking device to pinpoint enemies.

STORM ARROWS:
The next six arrows Hanzo fires shoot instantly, but deal less damage.

LUNGE:
Hanzo can perform a double jump to reach greater heights.

WALL CLIMB (PASSIVE):
By jumping at walls, Hanzo is able to scale them with ease.

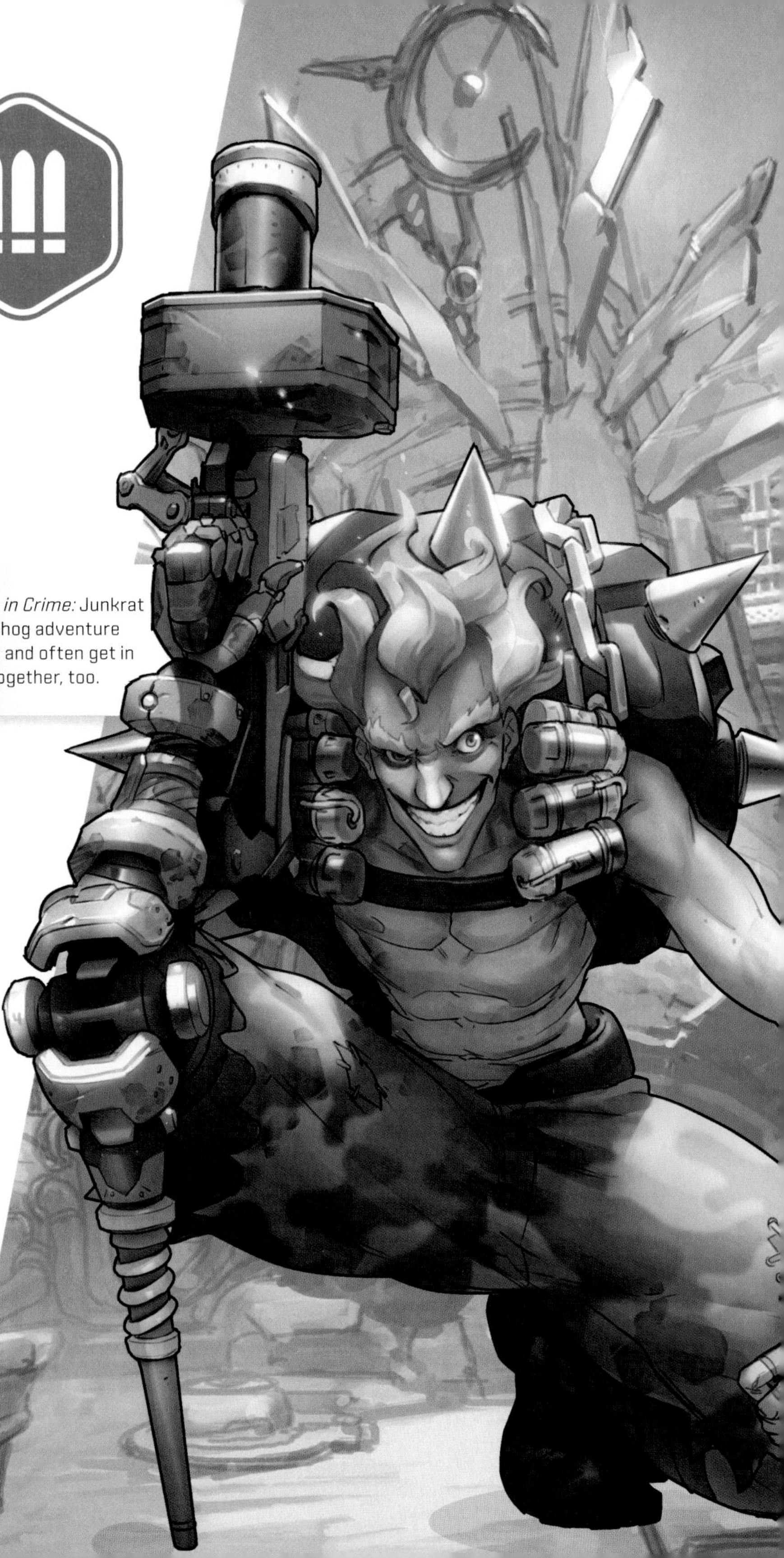

Partners in Crime: Junkrat and Roadhog adventure together, and often get in trouble together, too.

HERO PROFILE
JUNKRAT

	NAME: **JAMISON FAWKES**	AGE: **25**
	OCCUPATION: **ANARCHIST, THIEF, DEMOLITIONIST, MERCENARY, SCAVENGER**	
	BASE OF OPERATIONS: **JUNKERTOWN, AUSTRALIA** (FORMERLY)	
DAMAGE	AFFILIATION: **JUNKERS** (FORMERLY)	

BIOGRAPHY

Junkrat grew up in the Australian Outback. After the war, large parts of the Outback were nearly destroyed, transformed into a wasteland poisoned by radiation from the detonation of the Australian omnium. The people who stayed in the Outback, like Junkrat, survived by scavenging the ruins. Junkrat loves explosives and, even though the radiation has made him a little off-balance, he's a successful thief. He wreaks havoc with his bodyguard, Roadhog.

ULTIMATE ABILITY—RIP-TIRE:
This motorized tire bomb can roll over walls and obstacles.

FRAG LAUNCHER:
Grenades shot by the Frag Launcher can bounce to reach their target.

CONCUSSION MINE:
Junkrat can trigger a Concussion Mine to damage enemies and knock them back—or propel himself through the air.

STEEL TRAP:
This giant trap latches on to unsuspecting enemies and doesn't let go.

TOTAL MAYHEM (PASSIVE):
If Junkrat gets taken out, he leaves a good-bye present: five grenades.

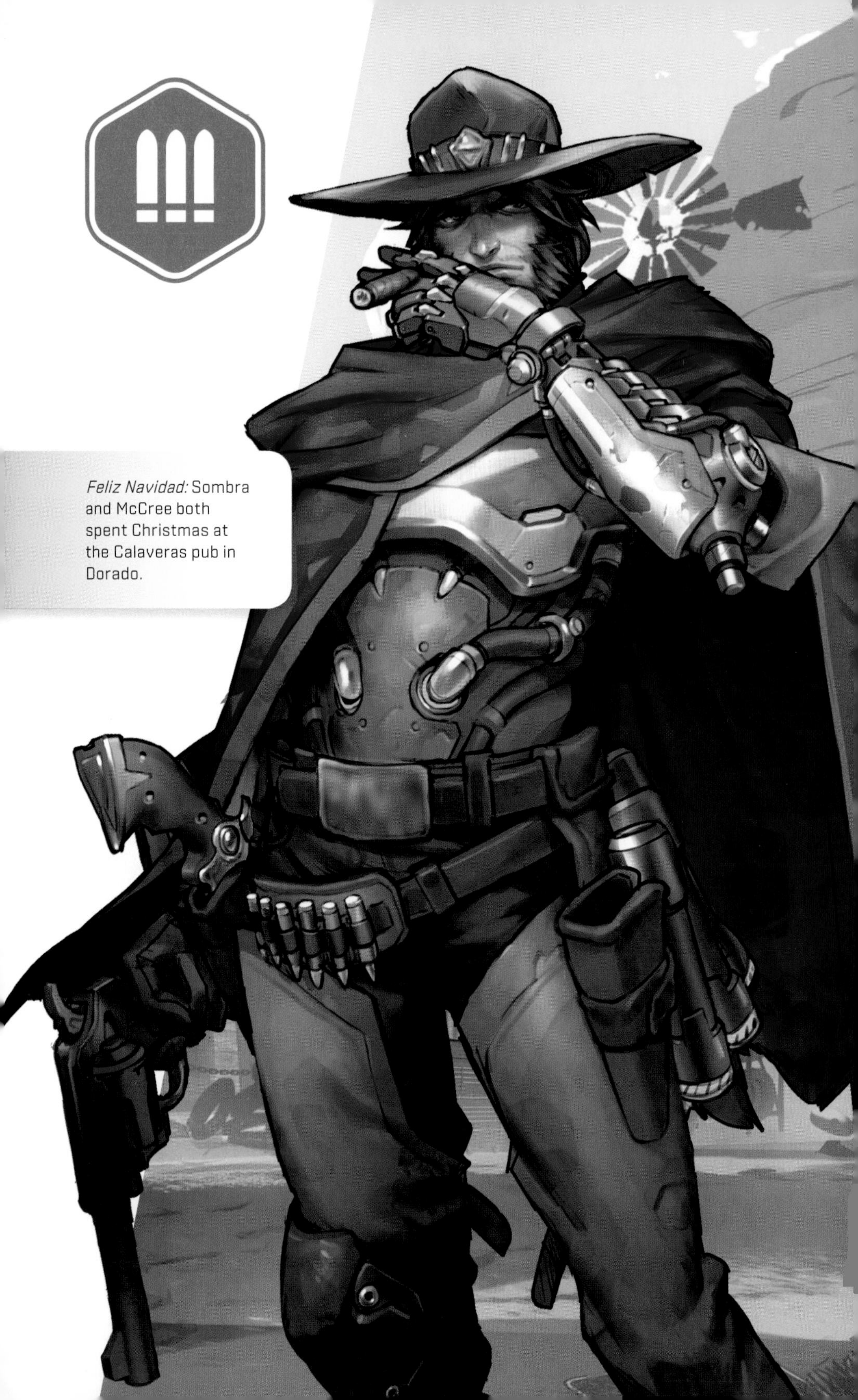

Feliz Navidad: Sombra and McCree both spent Christmas at the Calaveras pub in Dorado.

HERO PROFILE
McCREE

NAME:		AGE:
JESSE McCREE		**37**
OCCUPATION:		
BOUNTY HUNTER		
BASE OF OPERATIONS:		
SANTA FE, NEW MEXICO, USA		
AFFILIATION: **DEADLOCK GANG** (FORMERLY), **OVERWATCH** (FORMERLY), **BLACKWATCH** (FORMERLY)		

DAMAGE

BIOGRAPHY

This expert marksman was one of the original members of the Deadlock Gang until he was captured by an Overwatch sting operation. Gabriel Reyes, a member of the operation, gave him a choice: either go to prison or join his team. McCree went with him and worked undercover on missions, such as the assault on Antonio's base in Venice.

Now McCree works on his own as a bounty hunter, but still finds time to be a hero! When a group of Talon operatives hijacked a hypertrain using old Blackwatch tactics, he intervened. A few good shots later and McCree had saved the passengers—but to keep Talon from attacking again, he gave them what they wanted: a strange glowing box. Still a wanted fugitive, McCree's back to keeping his head down when he can.

ULTIMATE ABILITY—DEADEYE:
When McCree takes the time to aim, he knows that every one of his shots will hit its target.

PEACEKEEPER:
This cowboy can empty his trusty six-shooter, nicknamed "Peacekeeper," in mere seconds.

COMBAT ROLL:
McCree can dodge danger and load his Peacekeeper at the same time.

FLASHBANG:
This hand grenade can stun several enemies at once.

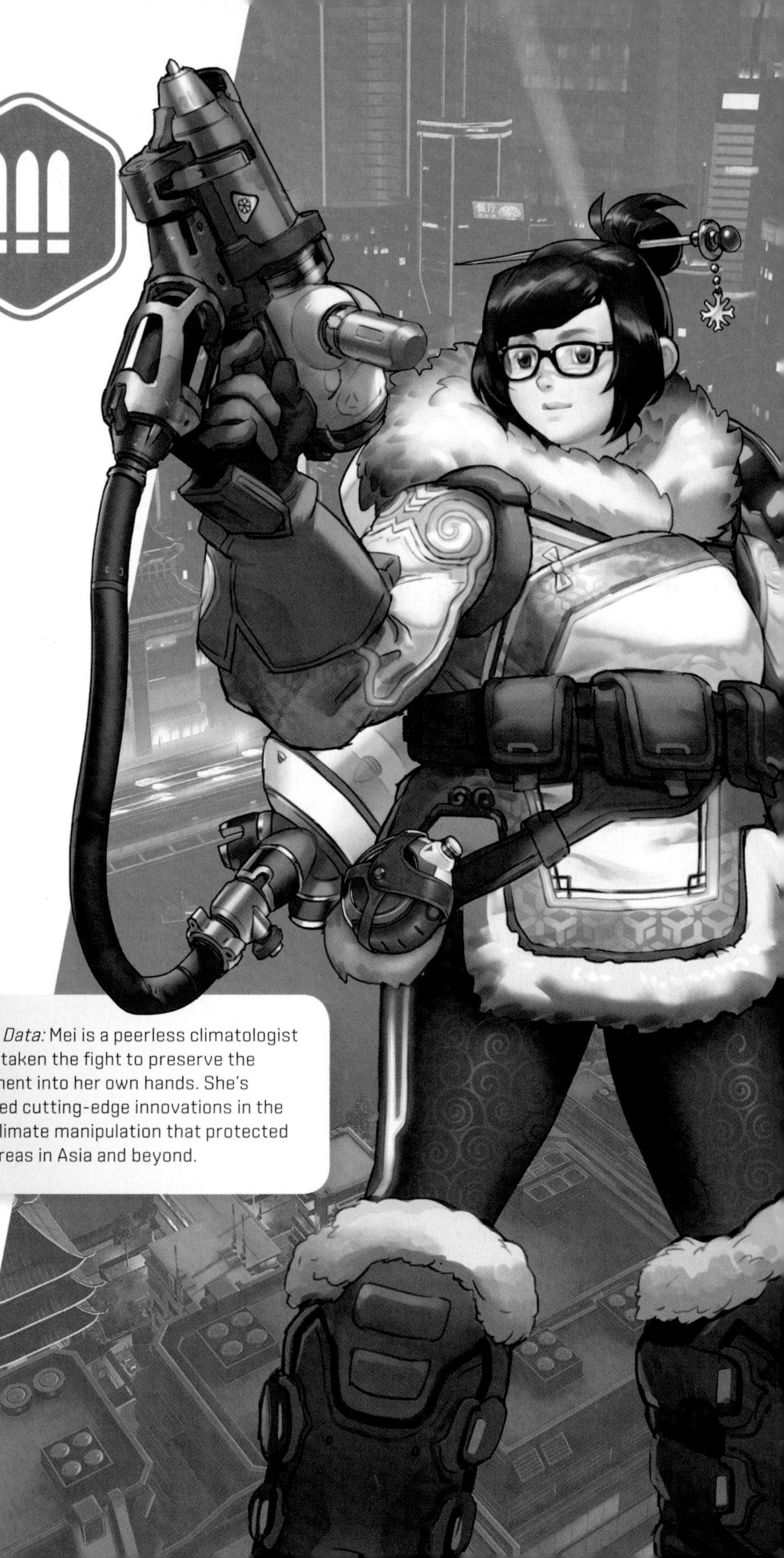

Valuable Data: Mei is a peerless climatologist who has taken the fight to preserve the environment into her own hands. She's introduced cutting-edge innovations in the field of climate manipulation that protected at-risk areas in Asia and beyond.

HERO PROFILE
MEI

	NAME: **MEI-LING ZHOU**	AGE: **31**
	OCCUPATION: **CLIMATOLOGIST, ADVENTURER**	
	BASE OF OPERATIONS: **XI'AN, CHINA** [FORMERLY]	
DAMAGE	AFFILIATION: **OVERWATCH** [FORMERLY]	

BIOGRAPHY

Mei was trained as a climatologist—a scientist who studies weather patterns over time—and she joined a team of Overwatch scientists studying climate change. Unfortunately, a polar storm hit the Ecopoint: Antarctica, leaving the scientists stranded. To survive, they froze themselves in cryostasis, a kind of hibernation. Years later, Mei awoke and escaped, by using an endothermic blaster she built from odds and ends around base. Now she travels the world with a refined version of this technology, hoping to someday save the planet.

ULTIMATE ABILITY—BLIZZARD:
Mei can create an instant blizzard with a weather-modification drone that blasts opponents with gusts of wind and snow. It can slow them down—or freeze them solid.

ENDOTHERMIC BLASTER:
This handheld device can shoot streams of frost at close range, or it can shoot out medium-range icicles.

CRYO-FREEZE:
When Mei needs to heal, she can surround herself with a block of thick ice. She can't take any damage in this mode, but she can't move or use abilities, either.

ICE WALL:
This enormous wall of ice can block attacks and hide Mei from her enemies.

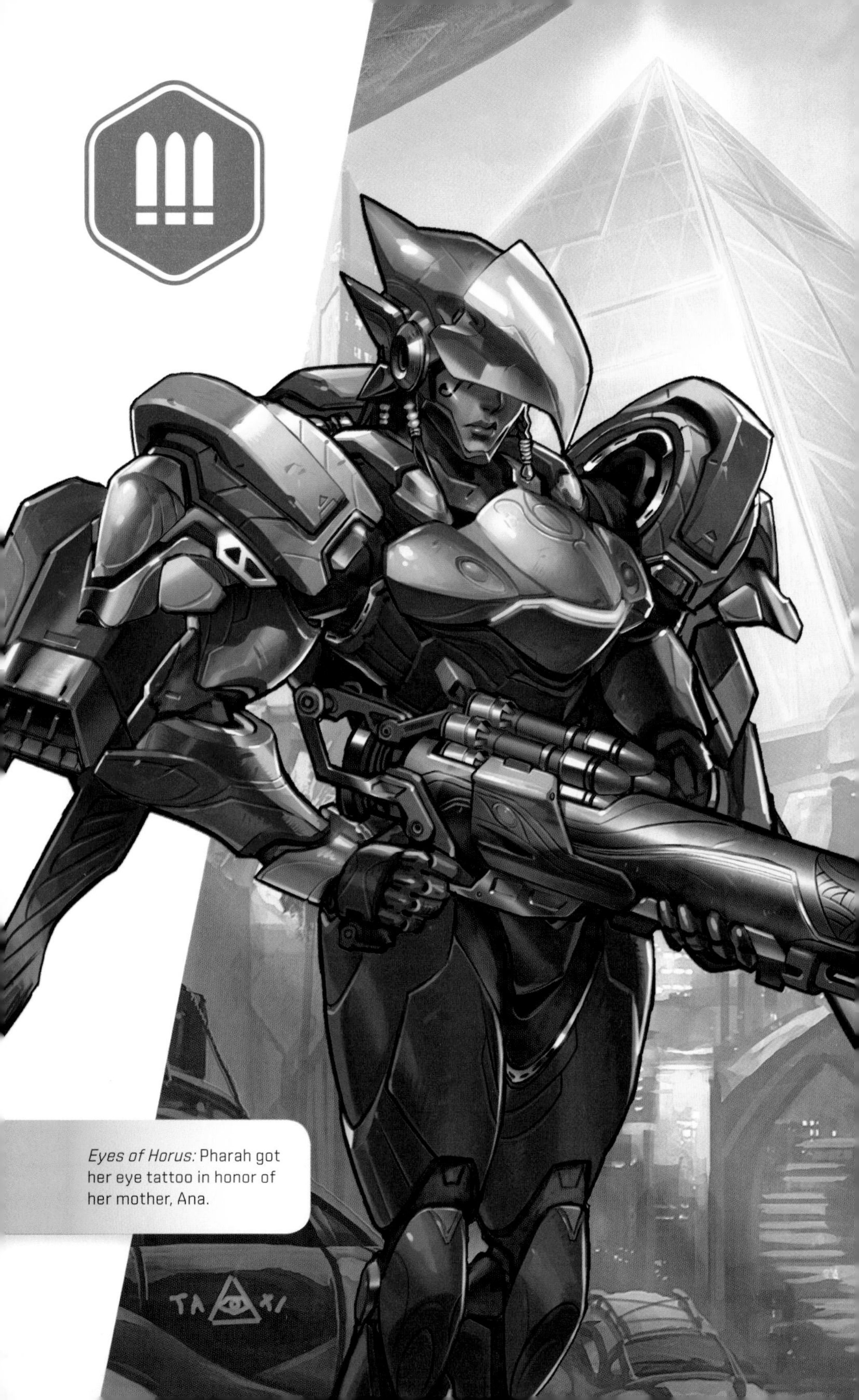
TA XI

Eyes of Horus: Pharah got her eye tattoo in honor of her mother, Ana.

HERO PROFILE

PHARAH

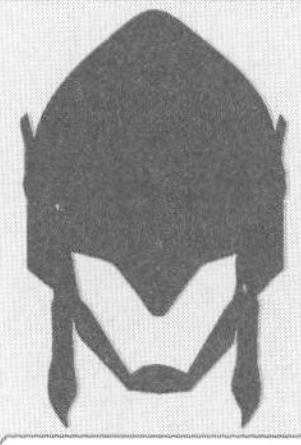

DAMAGE

NAME: **FAREEHA AMARI**	AGE: **32**
OCCUPATION: **SECURITY CHIEF**	
BASE OF OPERATIONS: **GIZA, EGYPT**	
AFFILIATION: **HELIX SECURITY INTERNATIONAL**	

BIOGRAPHY

When you see Pharah on the battlefield, you'll be in awe of her amazing combat suit. But the suit is only part of her story—underneath the armor beats the heart of a champion.

This soldier began life as a young girl named Fareeha. She dreamed of following in the footsteps of her mother, an Overwatch agent. When Fareeha was old enough, she joined the Egyptian army and quickly worked her way through the ranks. Known for her courageous leadership, Fareeha was a natural for Overwatch—but the organization was disbanded before she could join.

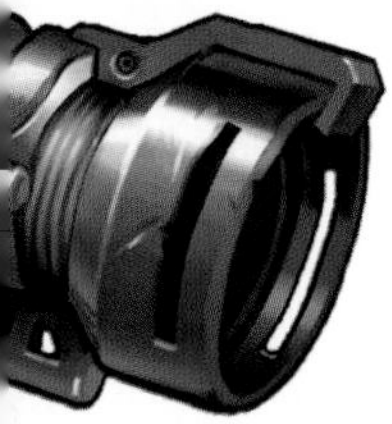

Fareeha went to work for Helix Security International, defending its secret artificial intelligence research facility beneath the desert sands. There, she received training with a mechanical combat suit, the Raptora Mark VI.

Known by the call sign "Pharah," she continues to guard the top-secret facility. But she still dreams of fighting the good fight.

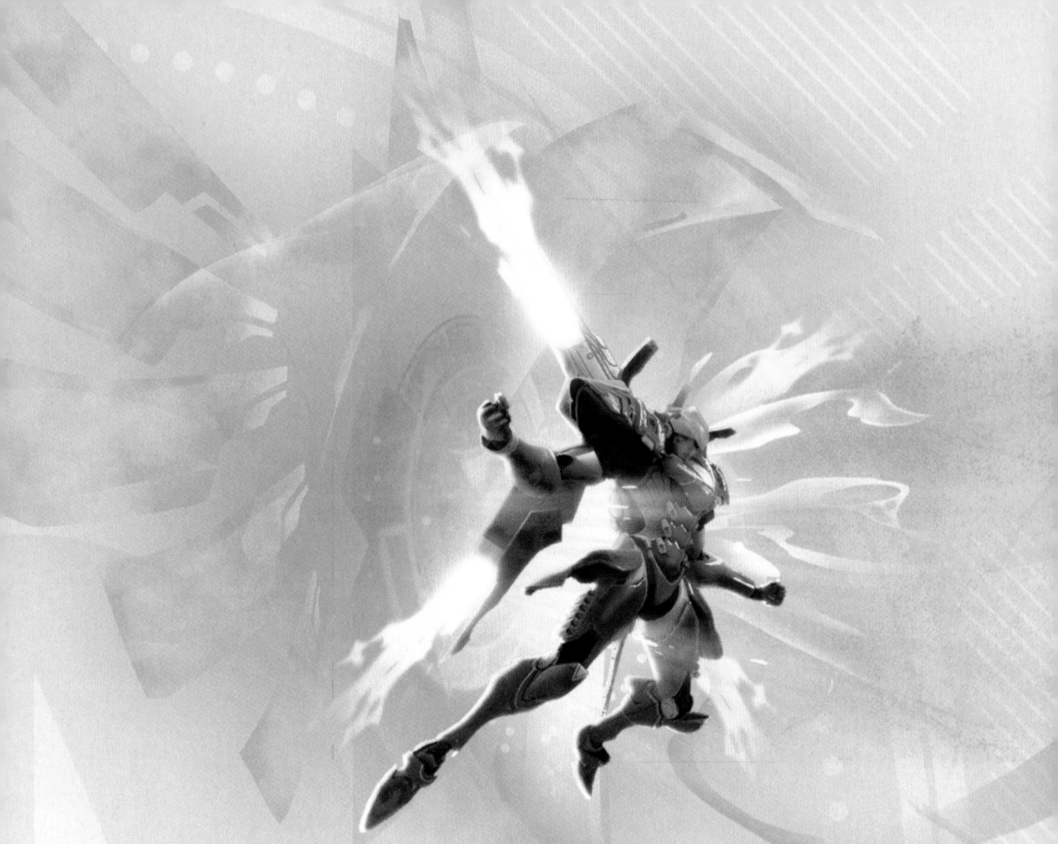

THE RAPTORA MARK VI
SUIT LIGHTS UP WHEN
PHARAH USES BARRAGE.

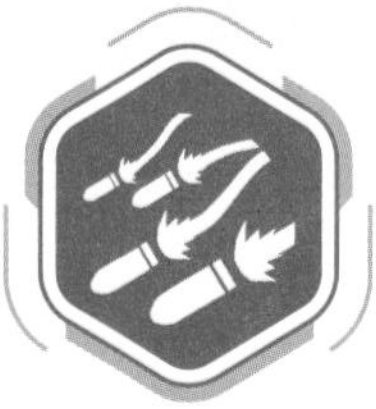

ULTIMATE ABILITY—BARRAGE:
Her combat suit can fire a continuous salvo of mini-rockets to destroy groups of enemies before they even know what hit them.

ROCKET LAUNCHER:
Her main weapon can launch rockets that deal major damage in a wide range.

JUMP JET:
Thanks to thrusters in her suit, Pharah can soar high into the air.

CONCUSSIVE BLAST:
Pharah can let loose a wrist rocket that will knock back any opponent it hits.

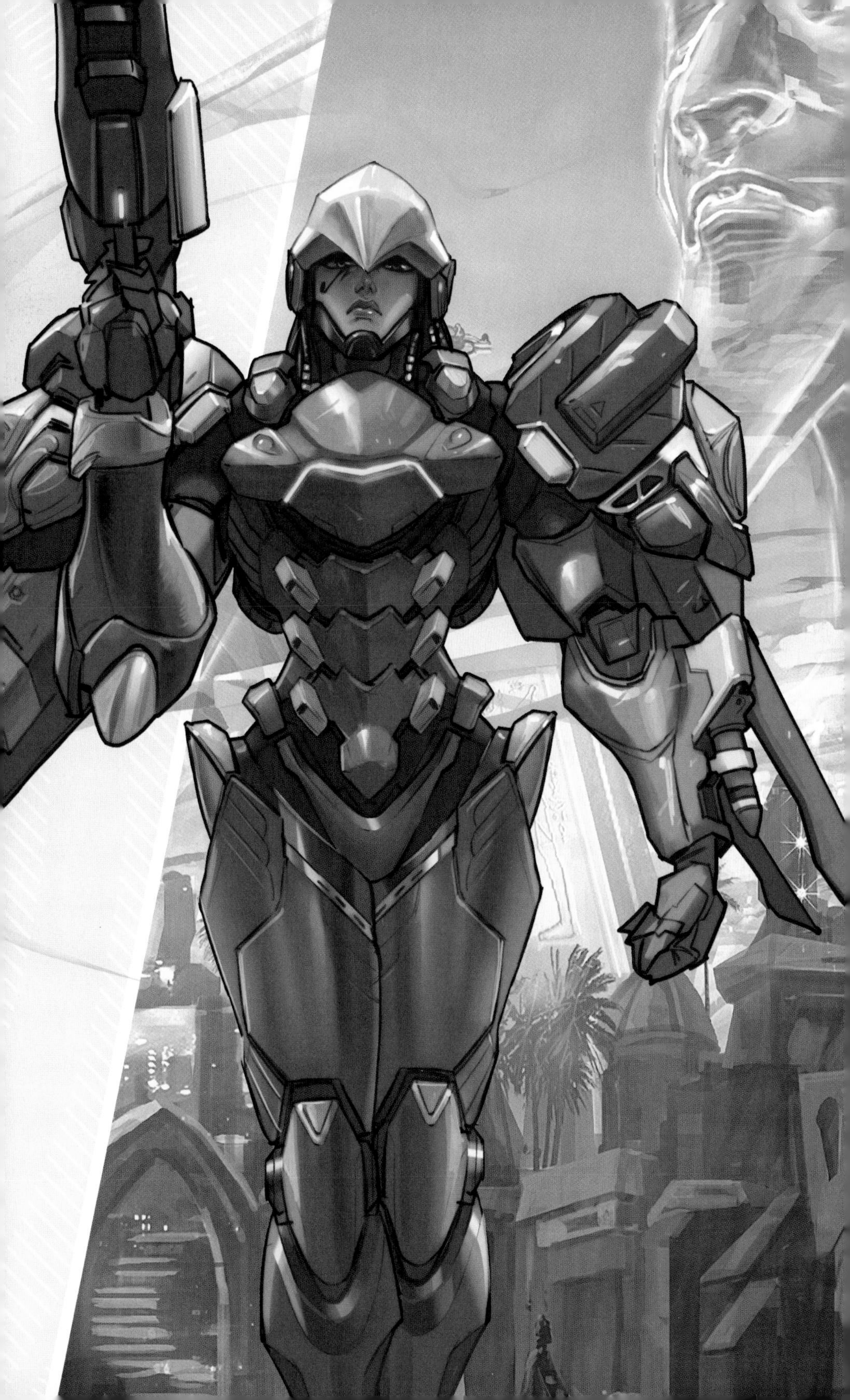

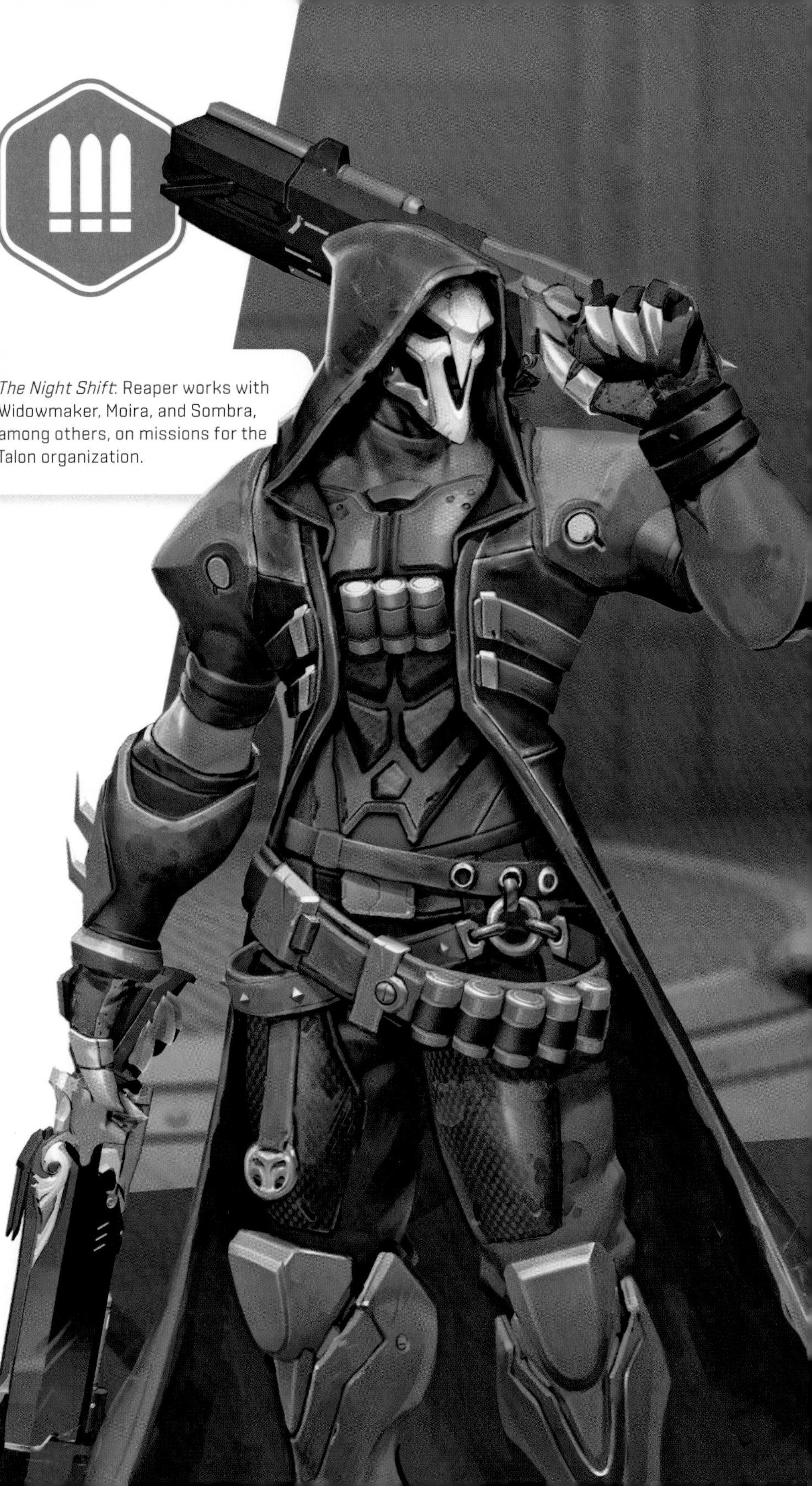

The Night Shift: Reaper works with Widowmaker, Moira, and Sombra, among others, on missions for the Talon organization.

HERO PROFILE
REAPER

	NAME: **GABRIEL REYES**		AGE: **58**
	OCCUPATION: **MERCENARY**		
	BASE OF OPERATIONS: **UNKNOWN**		
DAMAGE	AFFILIATION: **TALON, OVERWATCH** (FORMERLY)**, BLACKWATCH** (FORMERLY)		

BIOGRAPHY

Reaper was once Gabriel Reyes, hero and commander of Blackwatch, Overwatch's covert ops division. The fall of Overwatch and his personal conflict with Jack Morrison culminated in an explosive battle, and most believed he was dead. Now reemerging as the terrorist, Reaper, he's joined the Talon organization, making it his mission to hunt down all remaining members of Overwatch.

ULTIMATE ABILITY—DEATH BLOSSOM:
Reaper can empty his twin Hellfire Shotguns before opponents have a chance to react.

HELLFIRE SHOTGUNS:
These shotguns can do serious damage to opponents, especially at close range.

WRAITH FORM:
Reaper can become a shadow for a short period of time and pass through his enemies. He won't take any damage, but he also can't fire his weapons or use his other abilities.

SHADOW STEP:
After marking a destination, Reaper can disappear and reappear in that location.

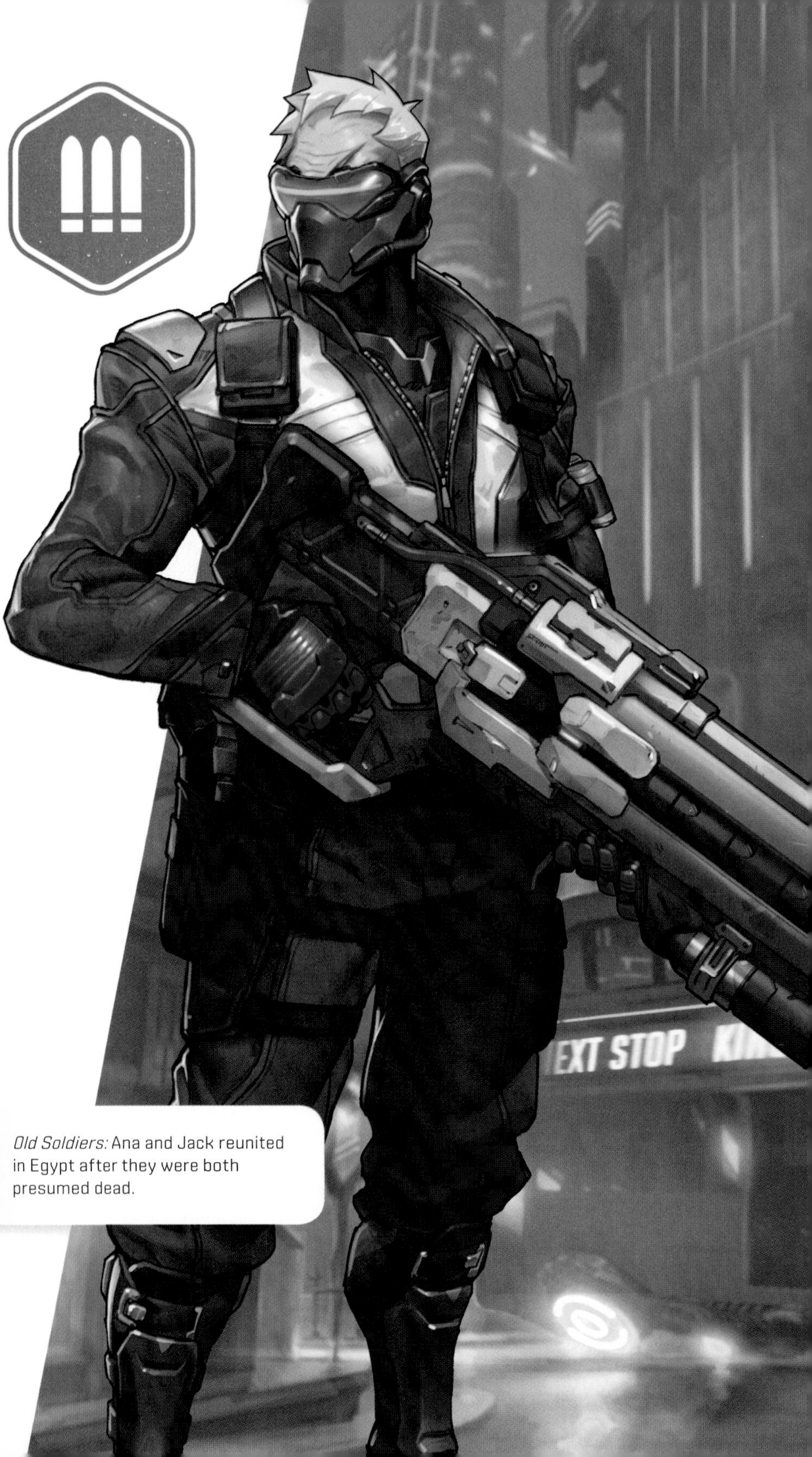
EXT STOP

Old Soldiers: Ana and Jack reunited in Egypt after they were both presumed dead.

SOLDIER: 76

	NAME: **JACK MORRISON**		AGE: **N/A**
	OCCUPATION: **VIGILANTE**		
	BASE OF OPERATIONS: **UNKNOWN**		
DAMAGE	AFFILIATION: **OVERWATCH** [FORMERLY]		

BIOGRAPHY

Before becoming Overwatch's strike commander, Jack Morrison was trained in America's "soldier enhancement program" and physically augmented beyond the abilities of a normal human. His battle with Gabriel Reyes left Overwatch's headquarters destroyed and both of them presumed dead . . . until he reappeared, hidden behind a mask and armed with stolen Overwatch equipment. Now this lone soldier fights to expose the truth behind the fall of Overwatch.

ULTIMATE ABILITY—TACTICAL VISOR:
This eye visor can lock on to a target with incredible precision.

HEAVY PULSE RIFLE:
This rifle remains steady while unleashing fully automatic pulse fire.

HELIX ROCKETS:
Tiny rockets spiral out of the Pulse Rifle in a single burst.

SPRINT:
Soldier: 76 has the ability to rush forward at top speed so he can avoid conflicts—or quickly enter them.

BIOTIC FIELD:
This energy emitter will restore the health of Soldier: 76 as well as the health of any of his teammates within the field.

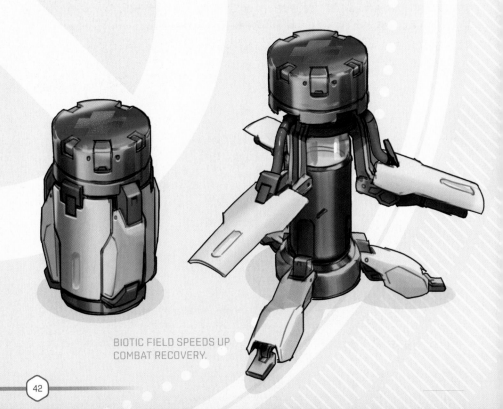

BIOTIC FIELD SPEEDS UP
COMBAT RECOVERY.

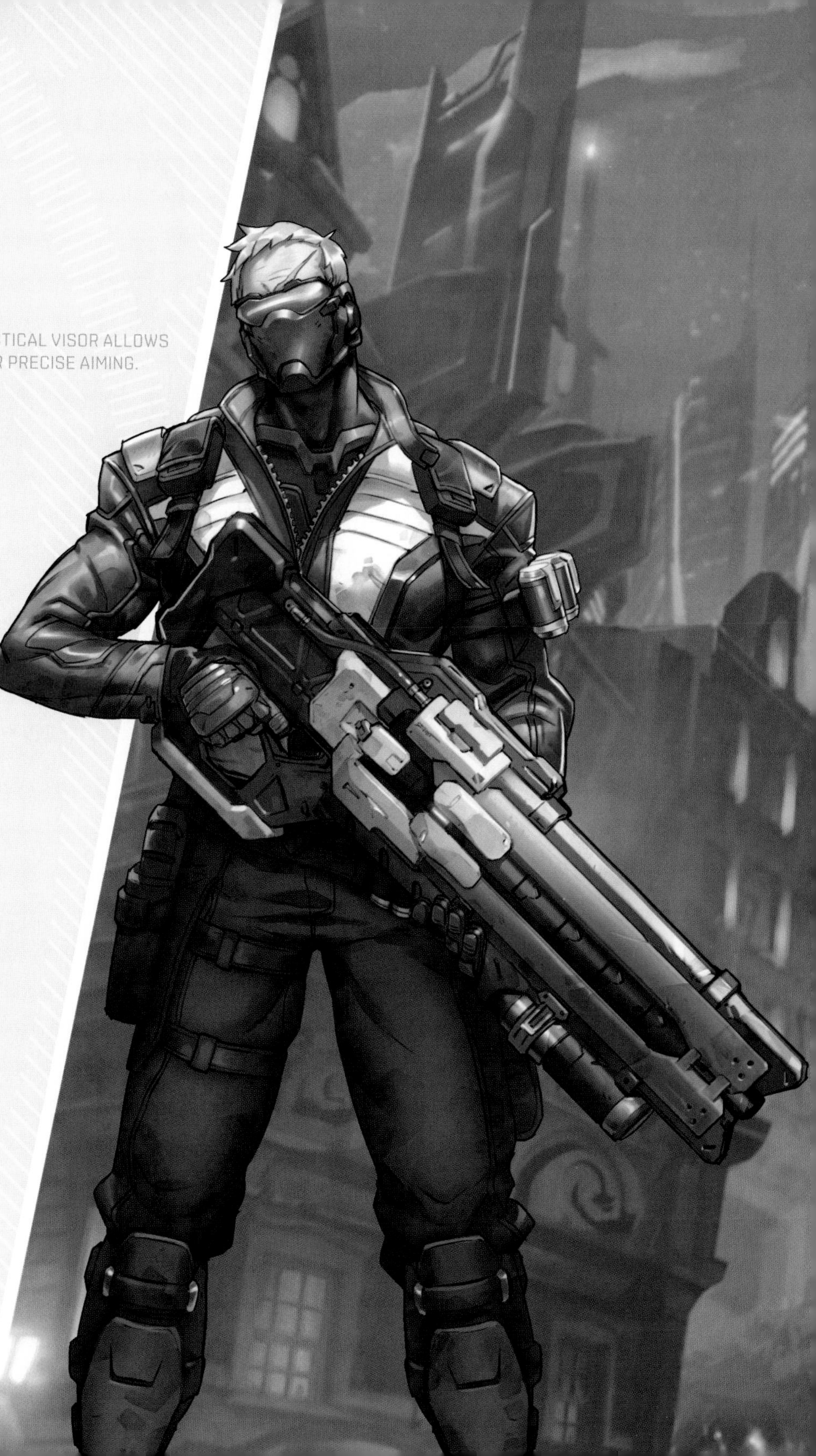

TACTICAL VISOR ALLOWS FOR PRECISE AIMING.

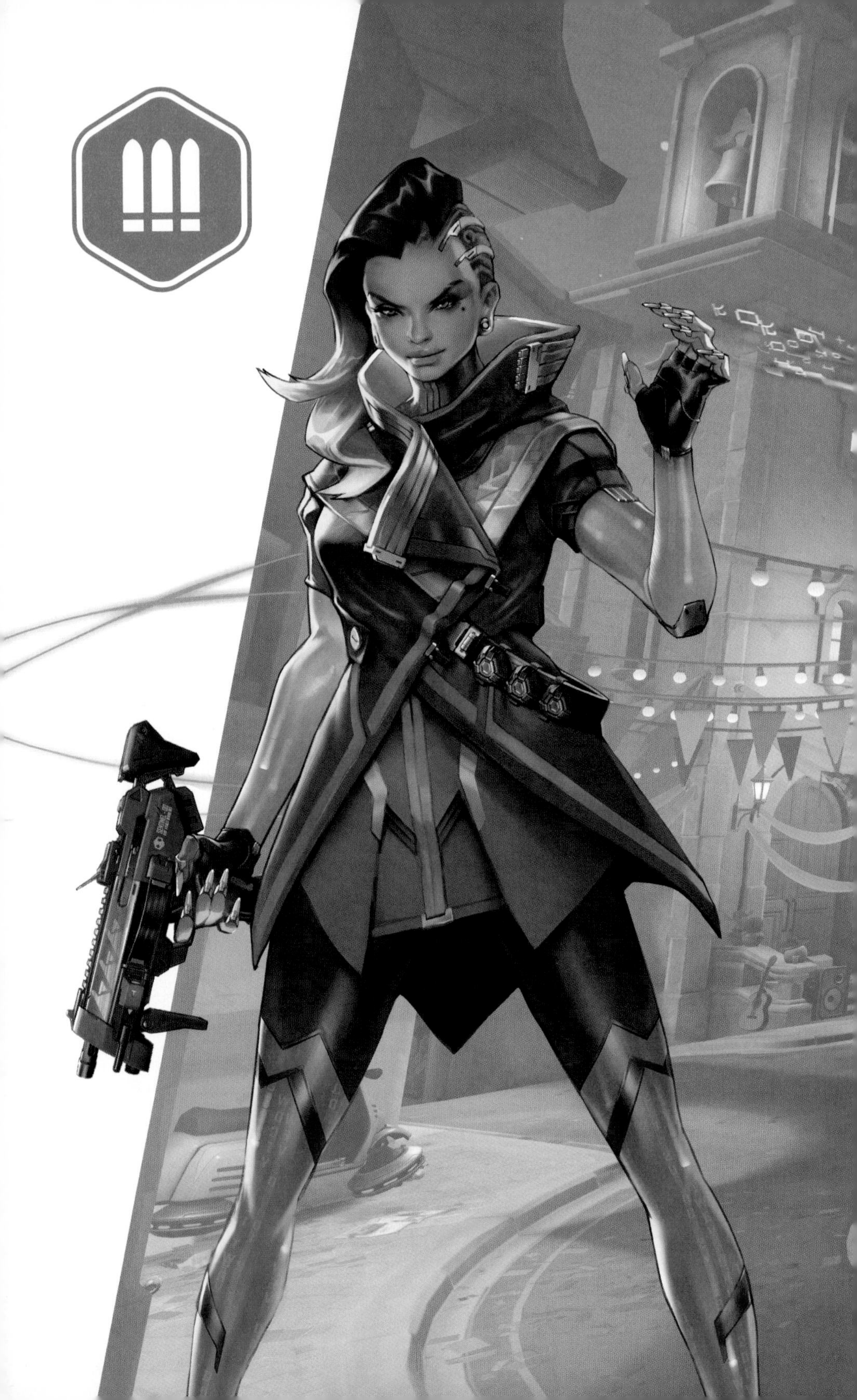

SOMBRA

NAME: **OLIVIA COLOMAR**		AGE: **30**
OCCUPATION: **HACKER**		
BASE OF OPERATIONS: **DORADO, MEXICO**		
AFFILIATION: **TALON, LOS MUERTOS** [FORMERLY]		

DAMAGE

BIOGRAPHY

Even as a young orphan on the streets of Dorado, Olivia was an unparalleled hacker. She found a home with the Los Muertos gang, and used her skills to help them in their conflict against the Mexican government. She hunted for the world's secrets until her meddling caught the attention of a dangerous global conspiracy—and she became a target. She escaped by erasing her past, modifying her body, and changing her name; now "Sombra" is uncovering the truth in secret, and working with Talon as long as it suits her.

ULTIMATE ABILITY—EMP:
Electromagnetic energy discharges from Sombra in a wide sphere, which hacks enemy abilities and destroys their barriers and shields.

MACHINE PISTOL:
This one-handed weapon fires fast and hits hard in a short-range spread.

HACK:
Sombra's enhancements let her block enemies' abilities and take control of healing items.

STEALTH:
Sombra vanishes from sight and moves quickly to surprise and disrupt her opponents.

TRANSLOCATOR:
Sombra can throw this small beacon and teleport to it from anywhere on the map.

OPPORTUNIST (PASSIVE):
Sombra can detect badly injured enemies, even through walls.

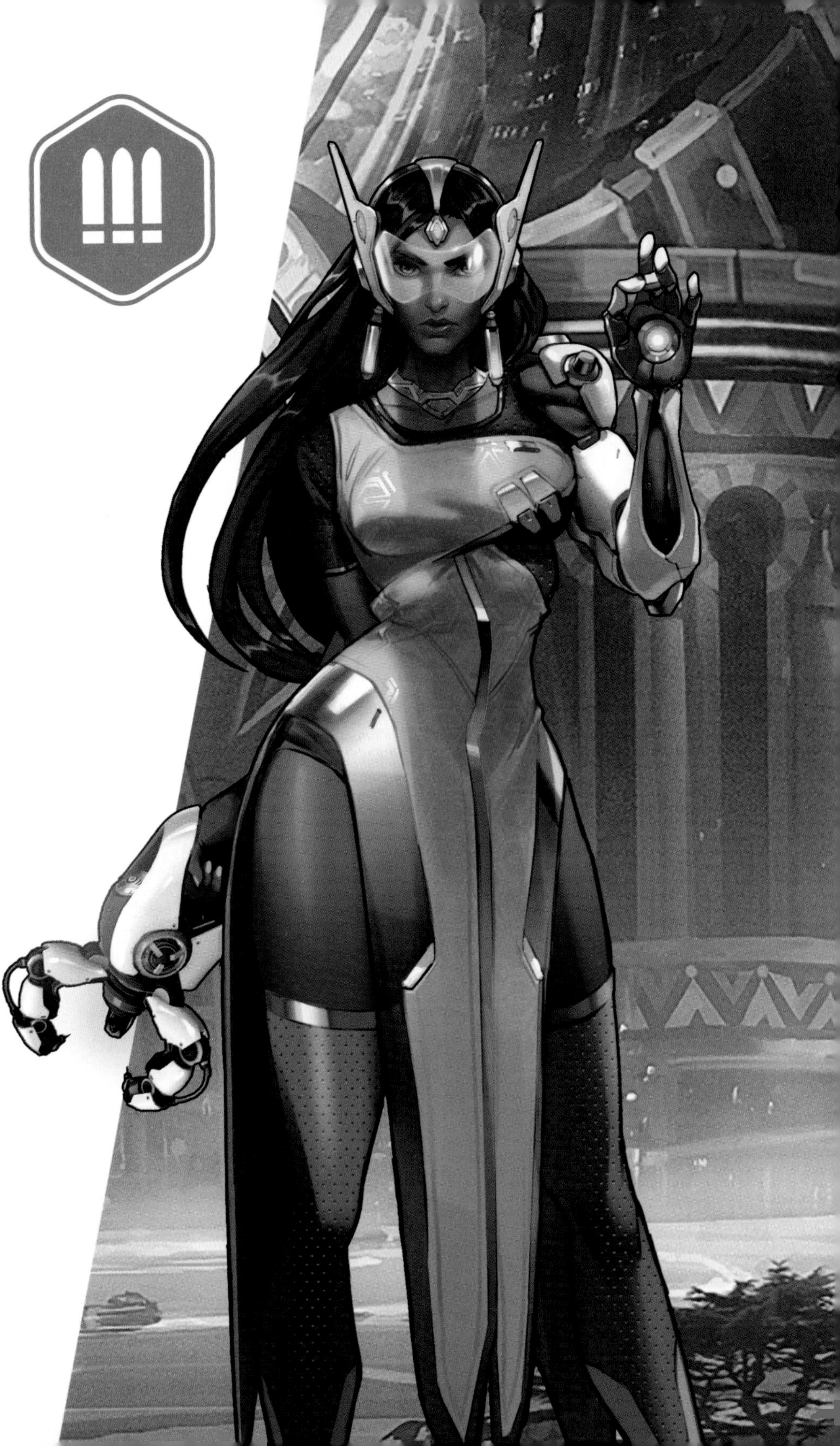

HERO PROFILE
SYMMETRA

	NAME: SATYA VASWANI	AGE: 28
	OCCUPATION: ARCHITECH	
	BASE OF OPERATIONS: UTOPAEA, INDIA	
DAMAGE	AFFILIATION: VISHKAR CORPORATION	

BIOGRAPHY

Satya Vaswani is a light-bending architech. Using technology from the Vishkar Corporation, she can instantly transform cities into the clean, orderly places the company desires. She's so good at what she does that Vishkar has dubbed her "Symmetra" and sends her out on undercover missions to uphold Vishkar's interests and spread its influence.

ULTIMATE ABILITY—PHOTON BARRIER:
Symmetra constructs a massive energy barrier to keep her team from taking damage.

PHOTON PROJECTOR:
Symmetra fires a short-range beam weapon that's damage increases over time. When she damages barriers, no ammunition is used. She can also fire explosive hard-light orbs.

SENTRY TURRET:
Symmetra can set up to three turrets that damage and slow enemies.

TELEPORTER:
To move her team into combat quickly, Symmetra can set up a teleporter.

47

In Shining Armor: Reinhardt and Torbjörn are old friends from before the fall of Overwatch—Torbjörn used to repair Reinhardt's armor!

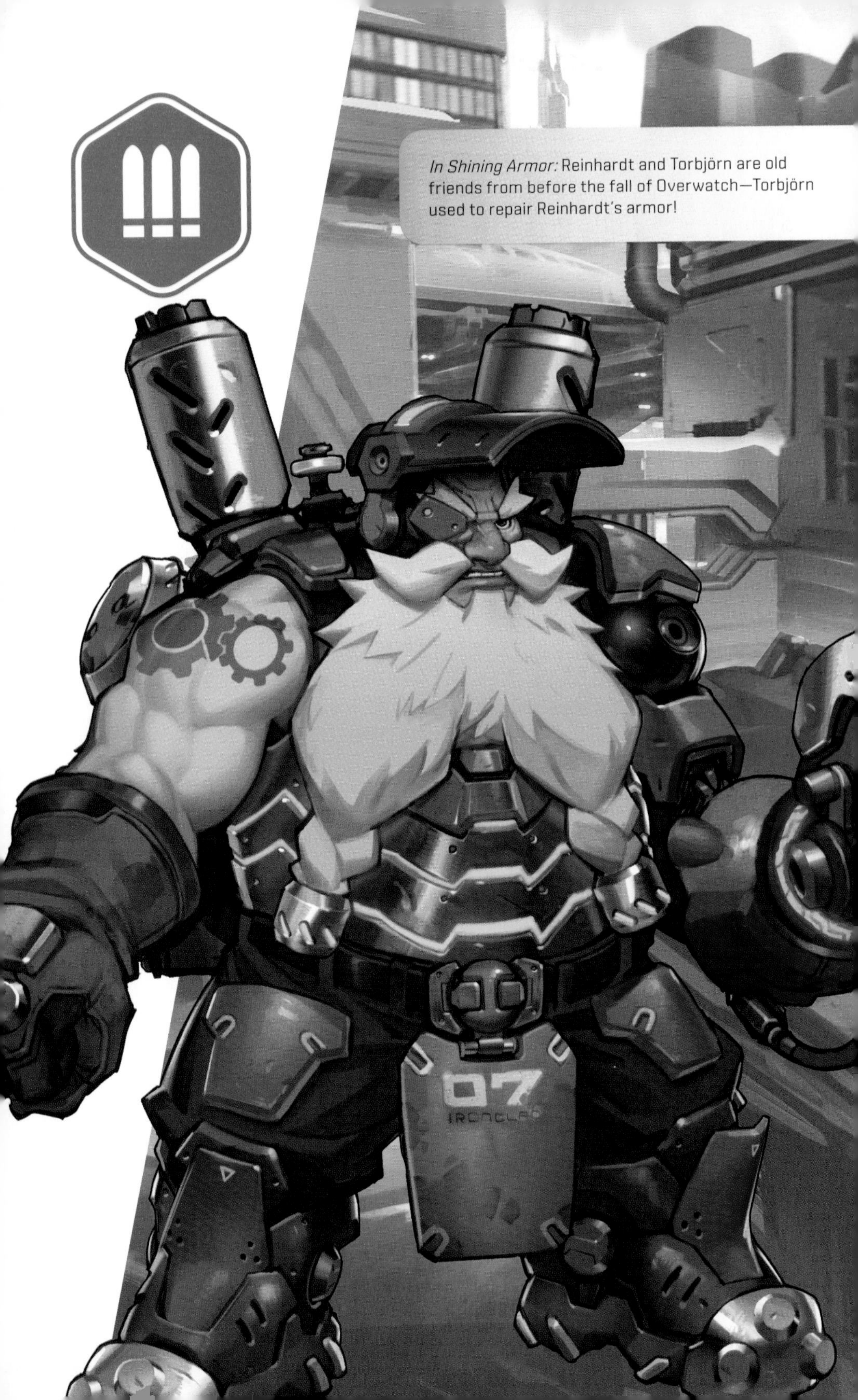
07
IRONCLAD

HERO PROFILE
TORBJÖRN

NAME: **TORBJÖRN LINDHOLM**		AGE: **57**
OCCUPATION: **WEAPONS DESIGNER**		
BASE OF OPERATIONS: **GOTHENBURG, SWEDEN**		
AFFILIATION: **OVERWATCH** (FORMERLY)		

DAMAGE

BIOGRAPHY

Torbjörn can get fiery when he's angry! But for the most part, this weapons designer has always believed that technology should help humanity, not hurt it. During the Omnic Crisis, he joined Overwatch and developed weapons to overthrow the robots. After Overwatch fell, Torbjörn's weapons were scattered around the world. He constantly searches for them, hoping they won't land in the wrong hands.

ULTIMATE ABILITY—MOLTEN CORE:
When Torbjörn overheats his personal forge, it shoots out flames and he glows like molten lava. He also gains armor and scrap, and he can build, repair, and attack faster than normal.

RIVET GUN:
This gun shoots metal rivets or bursts of molten metal.

FORGE HAMMER:
This mighty hammer can build, upgrade, and repair turrets, and it can also be swung as a weapon.

BUILD TURRET:
Torbjörn can build an enemy-tracking autocannon.

ARMOR PACK:
Torbjörn can drop armor upgrades that he or his teammates can pick up to absorb damage.

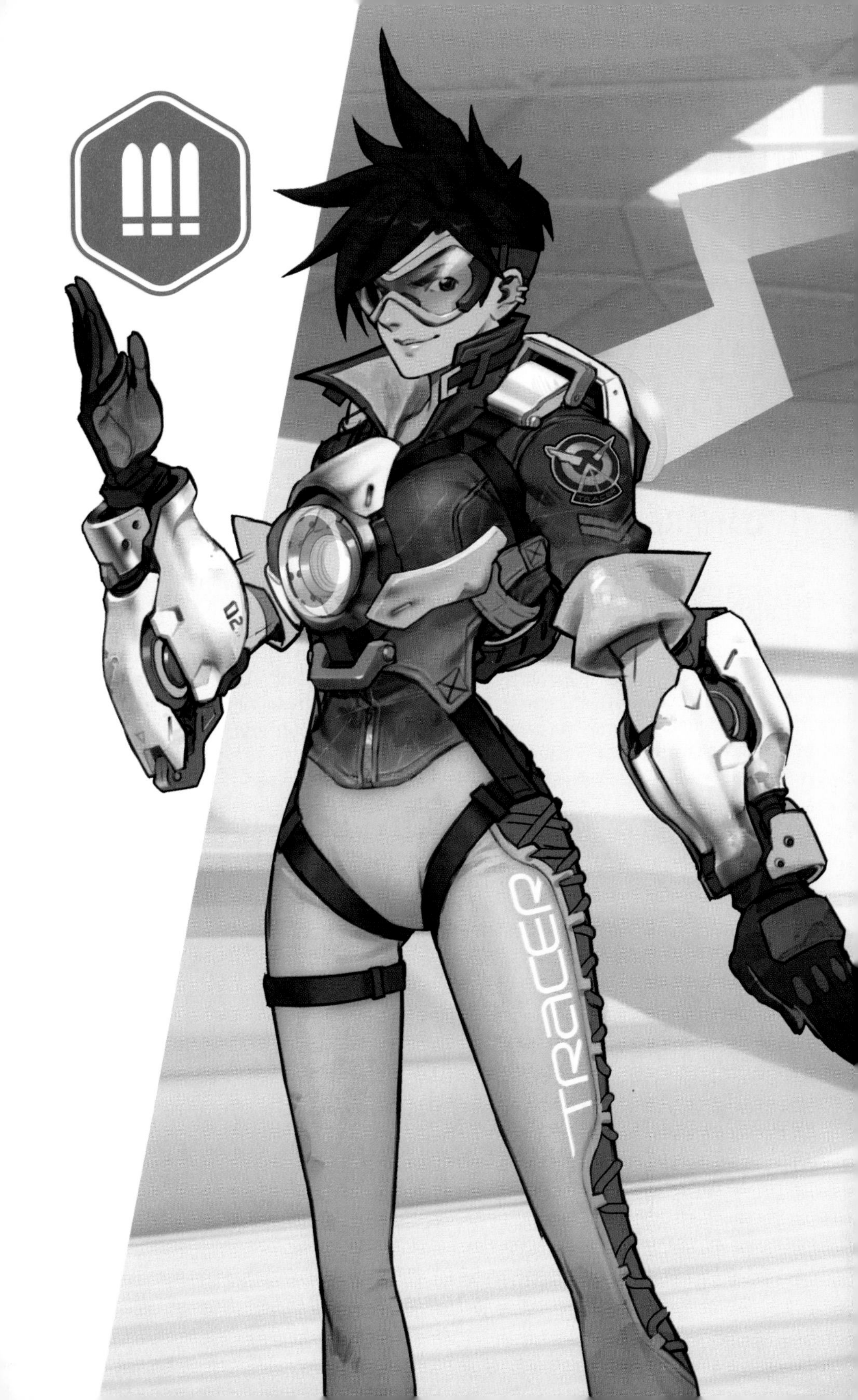
TRACER

HERO PROFILE
TRACER

	NAME: **LENA OXTON**	AGE: **26**
	OCCUPATION: **ADVENTURER**	
	BASE OF OPERATIONS: **LONDON, ENGLAND**	
DAMAGE	AFFILIATION: **OVERWATCH** [FORMERLY]	

BIOGRAPHY

A hero who can slow down and speed up her own time? That's Tracer, but she wasn't born that way. Her life changed the day she piloted an Overwatch experimental fighter and the teleportation matrix malfunctioned. The aircraft disappeared, and when Tracer turned up months later, her molecules were out of sync with time. She had become a living ghost, unable to stay in her physical form for more than a few moments.

Overwatch agent Winston found a way to help her. He developed the chronal accelerator, a device that keeps Tracer anchored in the present. But she can use the device to slow down her own time or speed it up, which gives her an advantage in combat situations.

The fall of Overwatch left Tracer with a lot of time on her hands. She spends it righting wrongs and fighting the good fight whenever she can.

>>> INCIDENT REPORT <<<

CALLSIGN:
TRACER
NAME:
LENA OXTON

TIME OF INCIDENT:
1107

CURRENT STATUS:
MISSING IN ACTION

PROFILE: LEFT

>>> INCIDENT REPORT <<<

TRACER OWES HER TIME-TRAVELING
ABILITIES TO A FREAK ACCIDENT IN
THE SLIPSTREAM, A PROTOTYPE OF
A TELEPORTING FIGHTER CRAFT.

ULTIMATE ABILITY—PULSE BOMB:

Tracer lobs a bomb that sticks to any target it hits. After a brief delay, the bomb explodes, dealing high damage to any enemies within range.

PULSE PISTOLS:

She wields a rapid-fire pistol in each hand.

BLINK:

In the time it takes to blink, Tracer can disappear and reappear a few yards away—thanks to her ability to speed up her time.

RECALL:

Out of ammo? Injured? No problem for Tracer. She can go backward in her own time and return to where she was a few seconds before—with ammo and health intact.

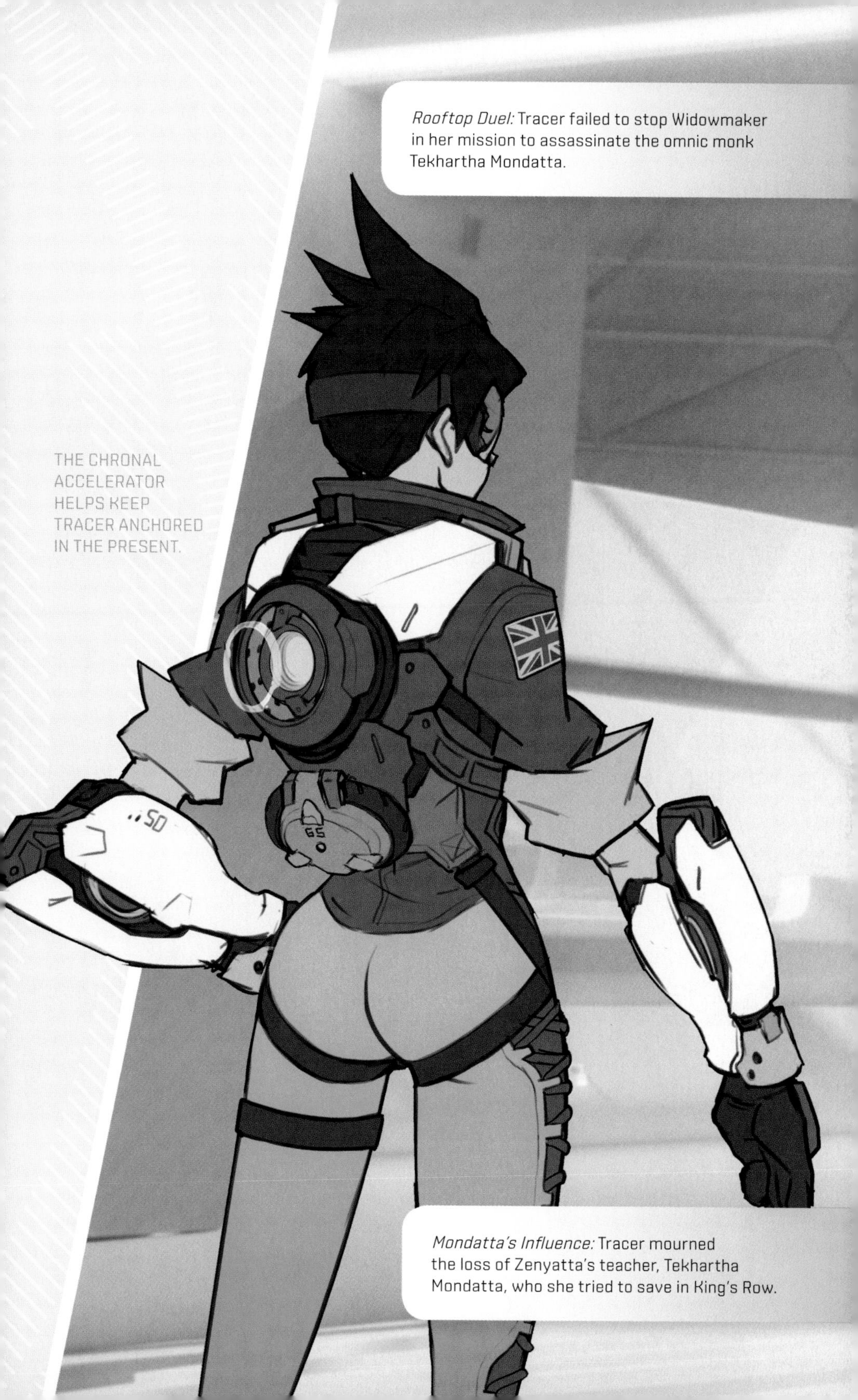

Rooftop Duel: Tracer failed to stop Widowmaker in her mission to assassinate the omnic monk Tekhartha Mondatta.

THE CHRONAL ACCELERATOR HELPS KEEP TRACER ANCHORED IN THE PRESENT.

Mondatta's Influence: Tracer mourned the loss of Zenyatta's teacher, Tekhartha Mondatta, who she tried to save in King's Row.

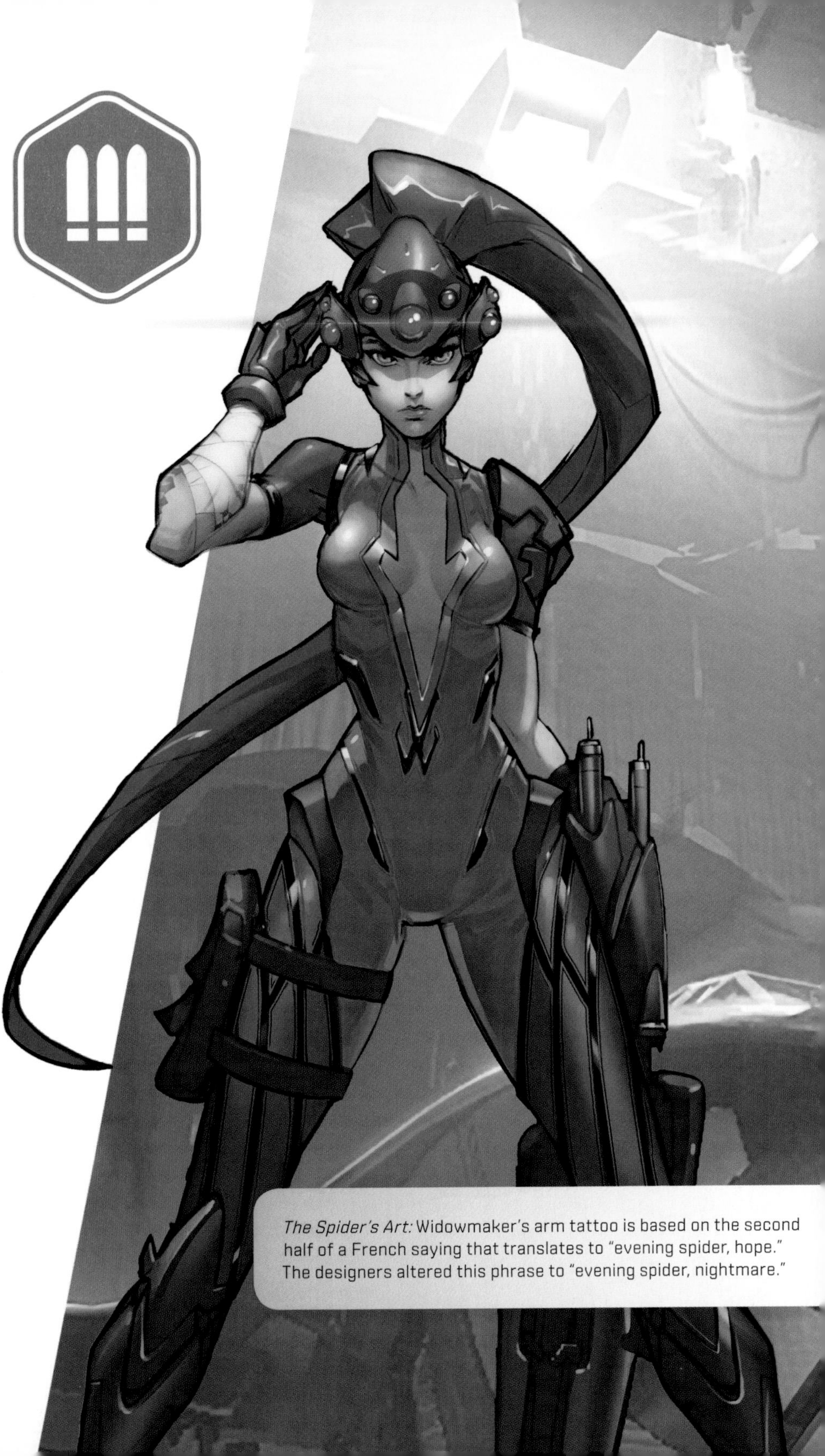

The Spider's Art: Widowmaker's arm tattoo is based on the second half of a French saying that translates to "evening spider, hope." The designers altered this phrase to "evening spider, nightmare."

WIDOWMAKER

	NAME: **AMÉLIE LACROIX**		AGE: **33**
	OCCUPATION: **ASSASSIN**		
	BASE OF OPERATIONS: **ANNECY, FRANCE**		
DAMAGE	AFFILIATION: **TALON**		

BIOGRAPHY

Once a normal woman named Amélie Lacroix, Widowmaker was turned into a cold assassin by the Talon organization. Her husband, Gérard, was an Overwatch official, so Talon used her to take him down. Talon turned her into a cruel and capable assassin. Now she swings across rooftops and takes out targets from hundreds of meters away—targets like Tekhartha Mondatta and her attempted assassination on Katya Volskaya. She may seem harsh and unemotional, but she's also literally cold—her heart was altered to beat slowly, so her skin always looks blue.

ULTIMATE ABILITY—INFRA-SIGHT:
Widowmaker wears a visor that allows her to see the heat signatures of her enemies through walls and objects.

WIDOW'S KISS:
Widowmaker's rifle can convert between a short-range assault weapon and a sniper rifle.

GRAPPLING HOOK:
This tool allows her to quickly get from one location to another.

VENOM MINE:
This motion-activated mine releases poison gas when triggered.

TANK HEROES

Tank heroes are massive characters whose purpose is to protect team members by taking damage for them. Here are some Tank hero highlights:

- Their high health pool and strong armor mean they can take damage for longer periods than other characters, and are hard to take down.
- They can jump into a heated battle and disrupt the enemy without being taken out.
- These powerhouses are also great for leading the charge into battle.

They might not be the fastest heroes around, but when you've got a Tank on your team, there's a good chance you'll get the job done!

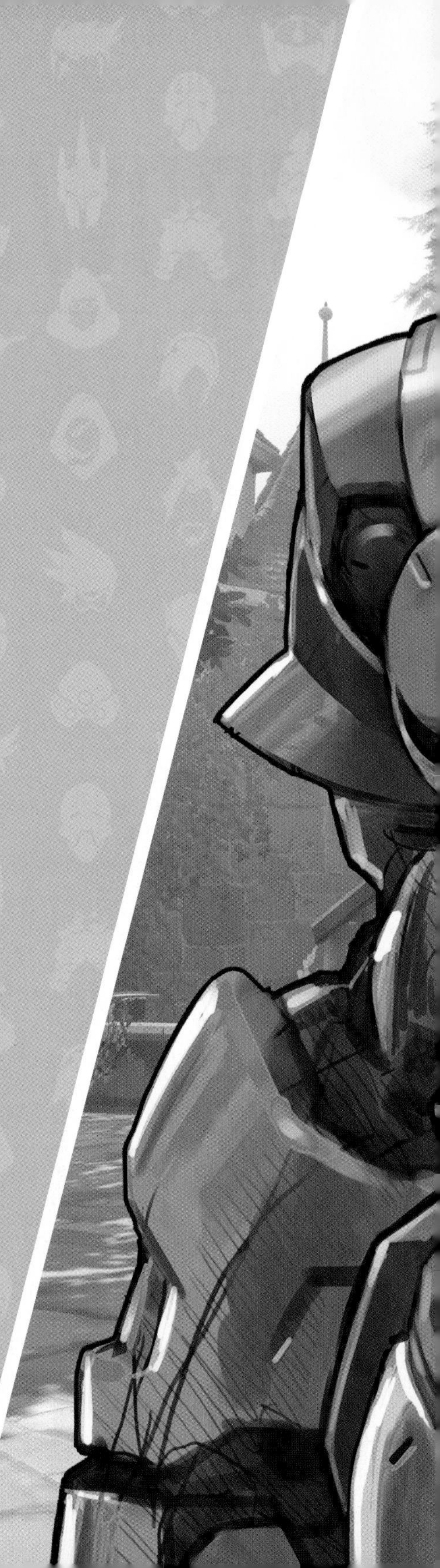

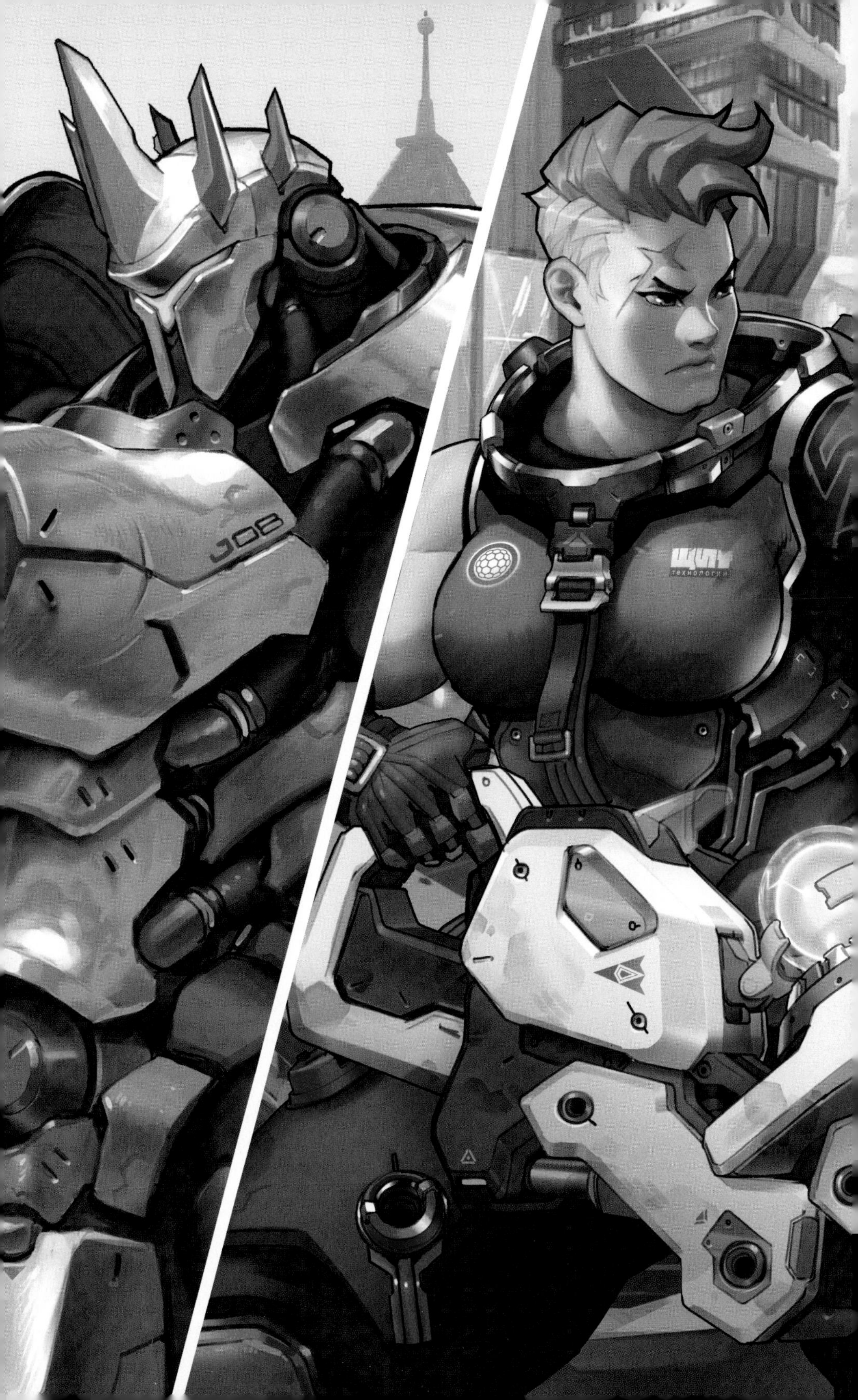
JOB
технологии

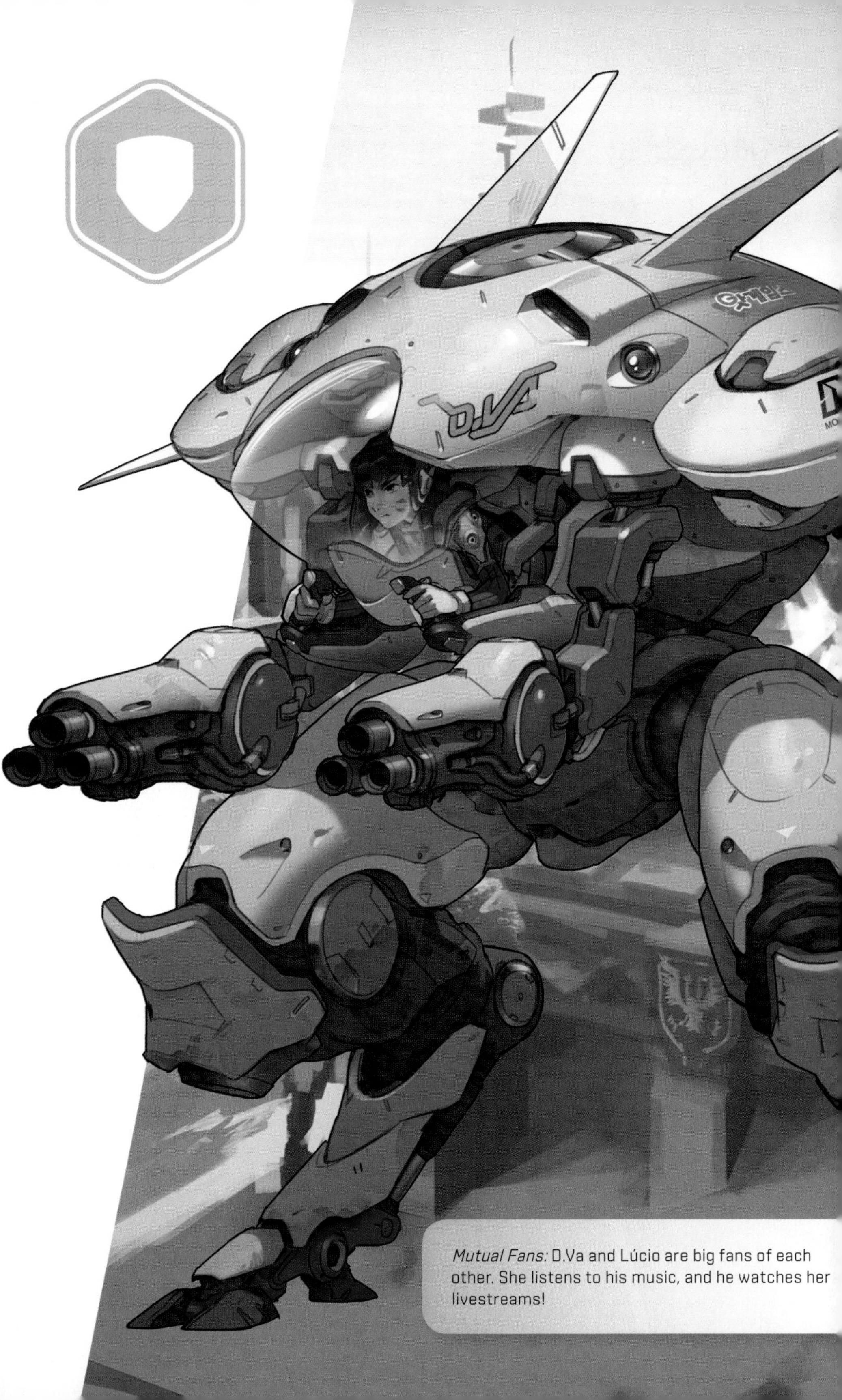
D.VA

Mutual Fans: D.Va and Lúcio are big fans of each other. She listens to his music, and he watches her livestreams!

D.VA

	NAME: **HANA SONG**		AGE: **19**
	OCCUPATION: **PRO GAMER** (FORMERLY), **MECH PILOT**		
	BASE OF OPERATIONS: **BUSAN, SOUTH KOREA**		
TANK	AFFILIATION: **MOBILE EXO-FORCE OF THE KOREAN ARMY**		

BIOGRAPHY

What's more fun than being a professional gamer, getting paid to blast digital robots for a living? How about piloting a giant mech in the military and blasting robots in real life? That's what D.Va does!

D.Va's destiny began years ago, when a colossal omnic rose from the depths of the East China Sea and attacked South Korea. The government responded with a mechanized robot program called MEKA. It recruited professional gamers to pilot the giant mechs.

At the time, Hana Song was the reigning world gaming champion known as D.Va. She was famous for being a fierce competitor who showed no mercy to her opponents—just what was needed to fight the monster omnic in the sea.

These days, D.Va charges fearlessly into battle with the rest of her MEKA unit. She streams combat operations to her adoring fans, who cheer every move this hero makes.

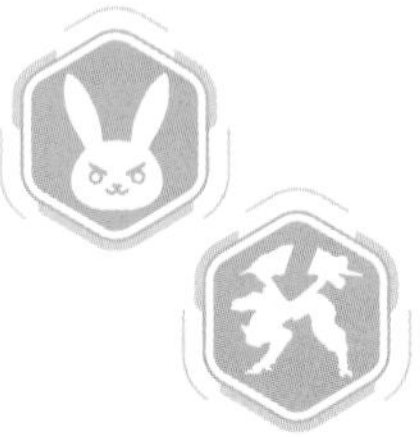

ULTIMATE ABILITY— SELF-DESTRUCT/CALL MECH:

This is a two-part ability. First, D.Va can eject from her mech and set it to explode, causing damage to nearby opponents. Then she can call down a fresh mech and return to the fight.

FUSION CANNONS:

D.Va's mech is equipped with two short-range cannons that can fire continuously without having to reload. When she uses them, they slow down her movement.

BOOSTERS:

D.Va's mech can launch into the air, changing direction or barreling through enemies to knock them back.

DEFENSE MATRIX:

When projectiles are hurtling toward D.Va, she can shoot them out of the air.

LIGHT GUN:

When she's outside her mech, D.Va can still fight, using this midrange automatic blaster.

MICRO MISSILES:

A swarm of small missiles fire from D.Va's mech.

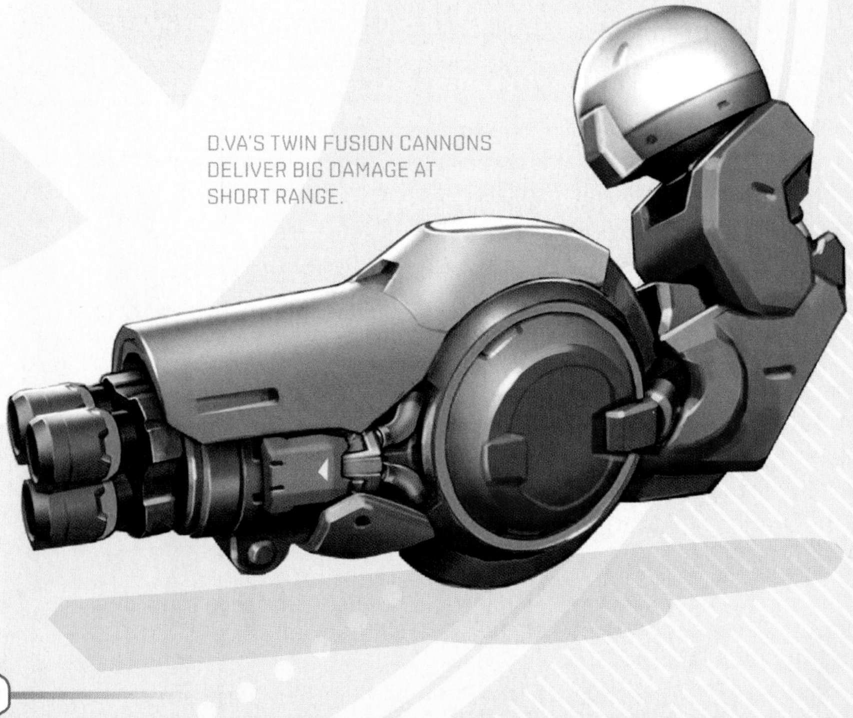

D.VA'S TWIN FUSION CANNONS DELIVER BIG DAMAGE AT SHORT RANGE.

A MECH FIGHTING SUIT IS LIKE A WALKING TANK.

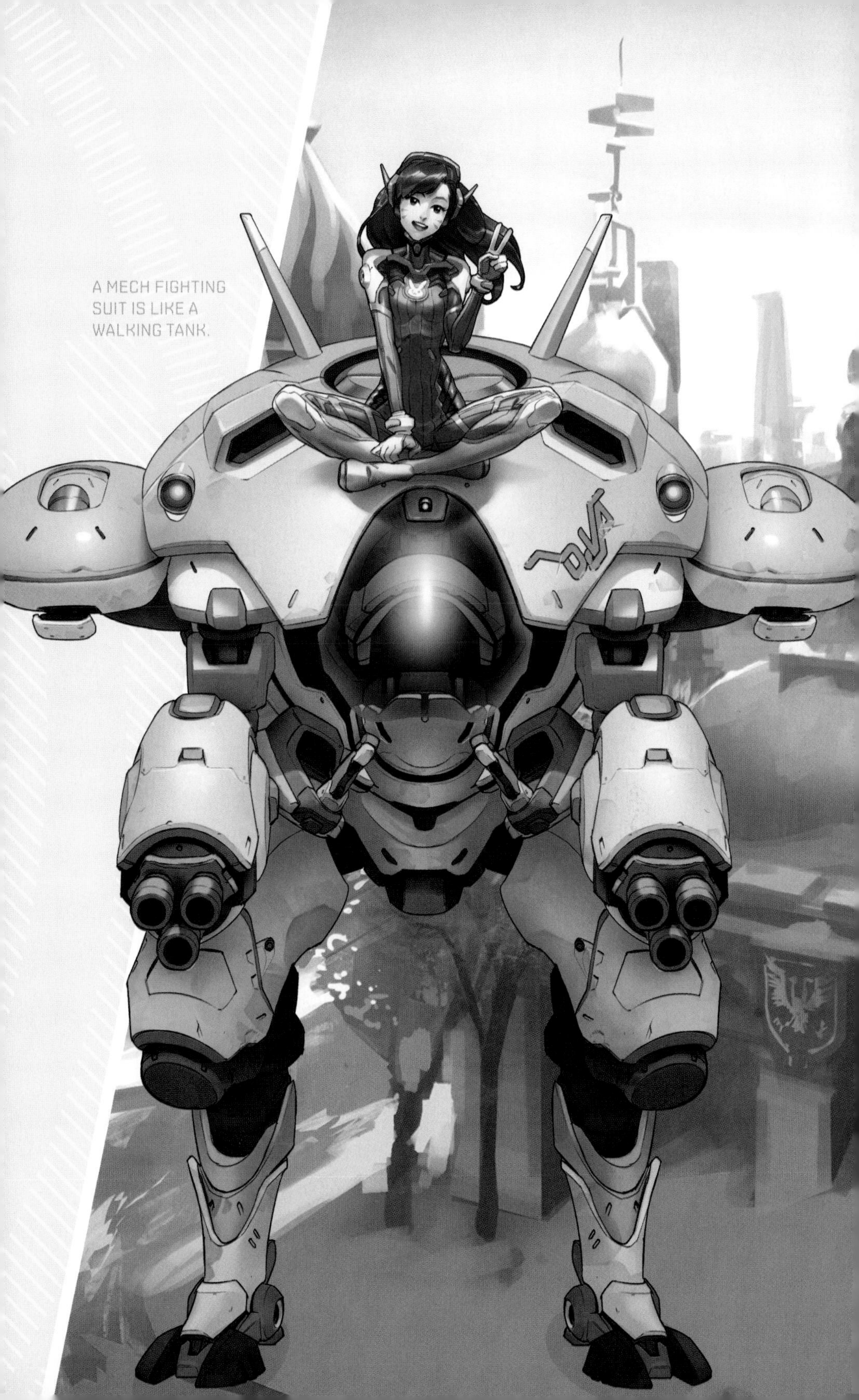

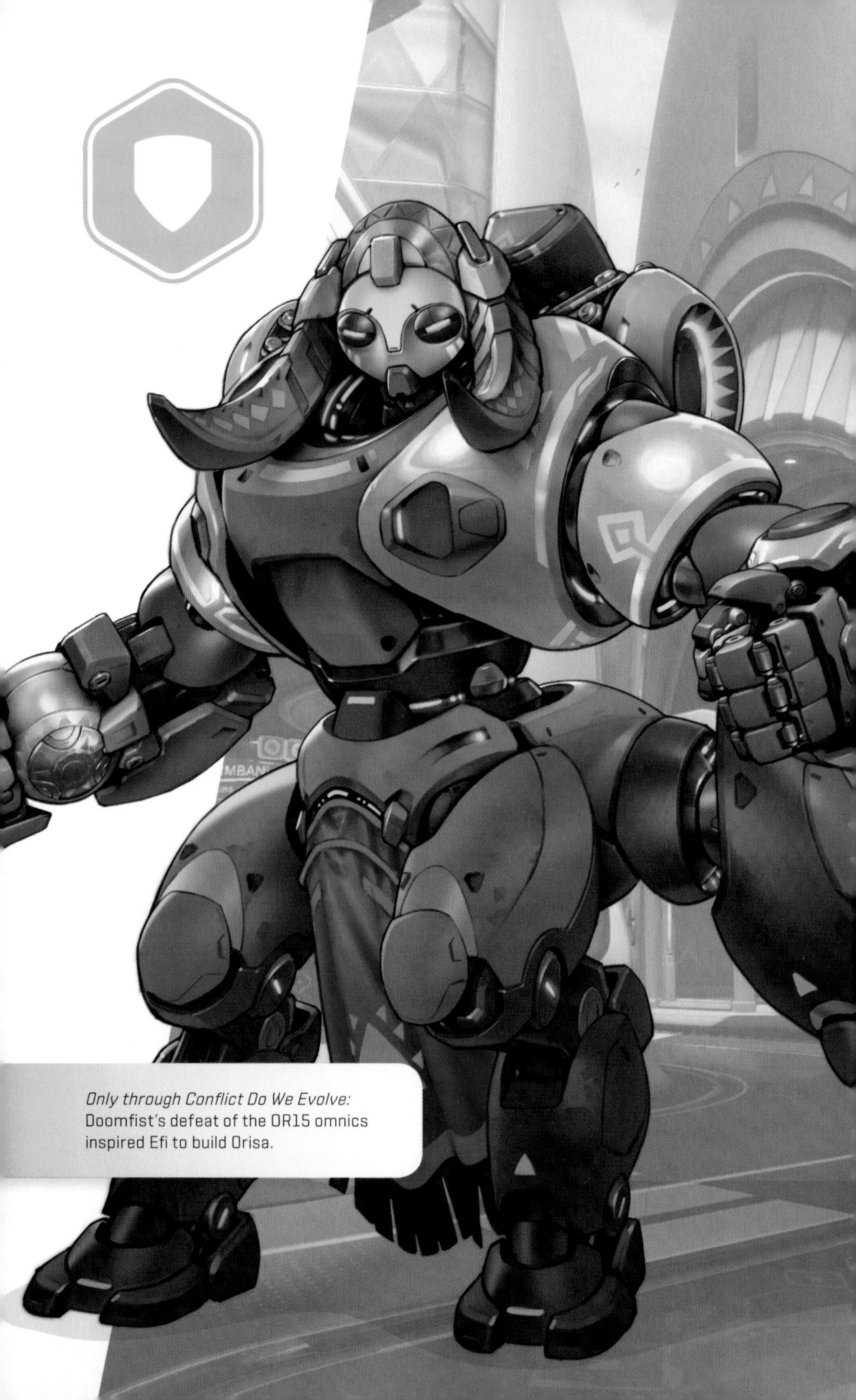

Only through Conflict Do We Evolve: Doomfist's defeat of the OR15 omnics inspired Efi to build Orisa.

HERO PROFILE
ORISA

	NAME: **ORISA**	AGE: **1 MONTH**
	OCCUPATION: **GUARDIAN ROBOT**	
	BASE OF OPERATIONS: **NUMBANI**	
TANK	AFFILIATION: **NONE**	

BIOGRAPHY

Orisa was built by eleven-year-old robotics genius Efi Oladele to guard the city of Numbani. The original OR15 models were discontinued after a brutal defeat by Doomfist, but Efi bought their leftover parts and added a brand-new personality core. Orisa's still learning the optimal protocols for being a hero—and Efi sometimes has to help her fix her mistakes—but she's always working hard to protect her city.

ULTIMATE ABILITY—SUPERCHARGER:
Orisa deploys a device that gives nearby allies a huge power boost.

FUSION DRIVER:
This long-range cannon has lots of ammo, but slows Orisa down when firing.

PROTECTIVE BARRIER:
Orisa projects a wide shield on the battlefield to protect her allies.

FORTIFY:
Orisa resists damage and her movement is unaffected by enemies' abilities.

HALT!:
Orisa shoots out a bright green graviton charge which, when detonated, slows enemies and pulls them toward its explosion.

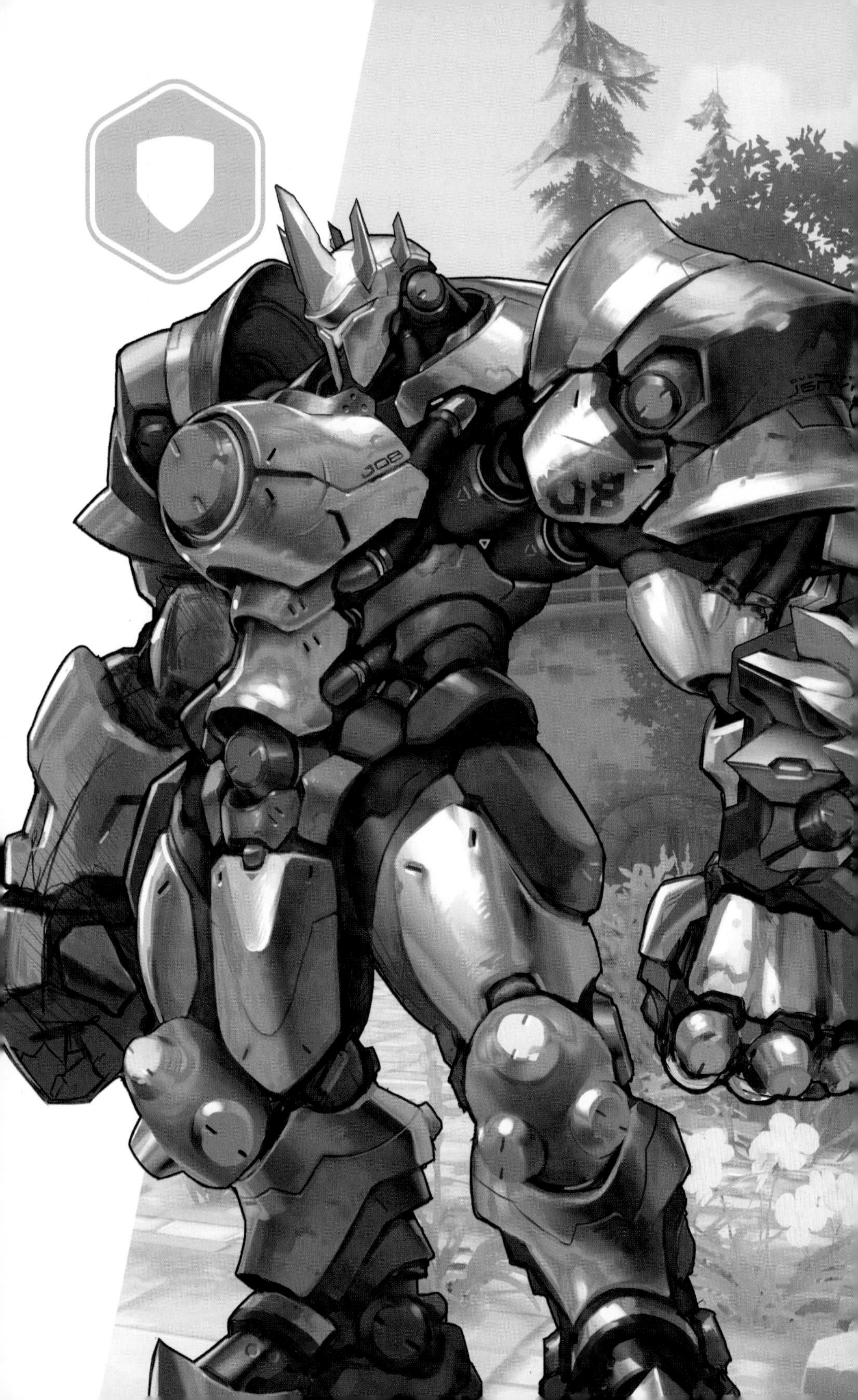

HERO PROFILE
REINHARDT

		NAME: **REINHARDT WILHELM**		AGE: **61**
		OCCUPATION: **ADVENTURER**		
		BASE OF OPERATIONS: **STUTTGART, GERMANY**		
TANK		AFFILIATION: **OVERWATCH** (FORMERLY)		

BIOGRAPHY

Like a knight in shining armor, Reinhardt fights for justice and to protect the innocent. But his Crusader armor does more than shine—it's designed to give him superhuman strength and abilities.

Before Reinhardt was an agent, he was a German soldier. His mentor, Balderich von Adler, was asked to join Overwatch. But after Balderich's death in the Battle of Eichenwalde, Reinhardt accepted the call instead. After the Omnic Crisis ended, this hero worked hard to keep peace in a war-torn world. He believed that Overwatch could be a force for good. Then when he reached his late fifties, he was forced to retire.

The sidelined soldier was forced to watch as Overwatch was accused of corruption and finally disbanded. Disgusted, Reinhardt couldn't stand by any longer. He donned his Crusader armor again and fought for justice without them—until he received Winston's recall.

THIS MASSIVE ROCKET HAMMER IS SO HEAVY THAT IT NEEDS ROCKETS TO GIVE IT MOMENTUM.

The Family Business: Torbjörn's daughter, Brigitte, is Reinhardt's squire, who repairs his armor and travels the world with him. She built herself a suit of armor and now fights alongside her mentor.

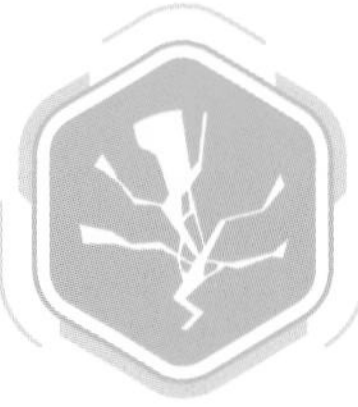

ULTIMATE ABILITY—EARTHSHATTER:

Reinhardt forcefully slams his hammer into the ground, knocking down and damaging all the enemies in front of him.

ROCKET HAMMER:

This weapon deals punishing damage in a wide arc with every swing.

BARRIER FIELD:

When Reinhardt projects this energy barrier in front of him, he can't attack. But he can protect himself and his companions from substantial damage while it is up.

CHARGE:

When Reinhardt charges forward with rocket power, he can grab an enemy and then slam into a wall. Reinhardt's armor will protect him, but his foe will take extreme damage.

FIRE STRIKE:

Reinhardt's hammer can sling a flaming projectile that will damage any enemy it touches.

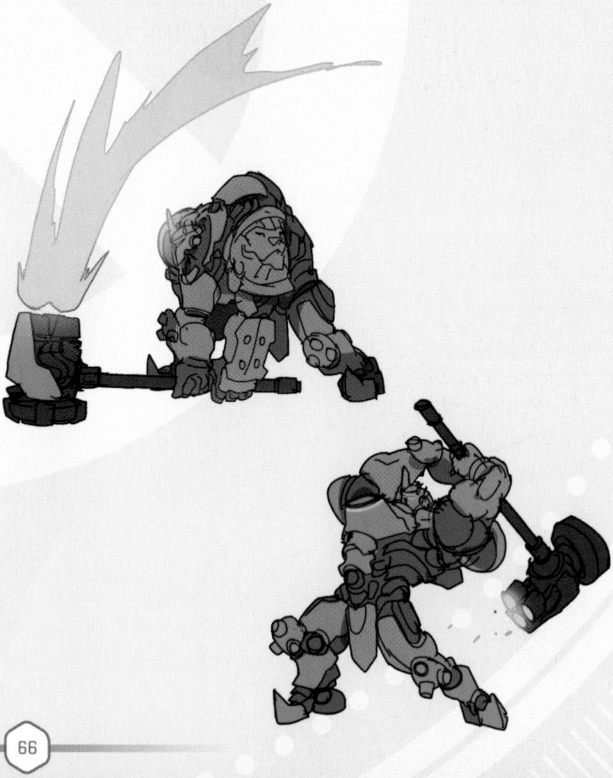

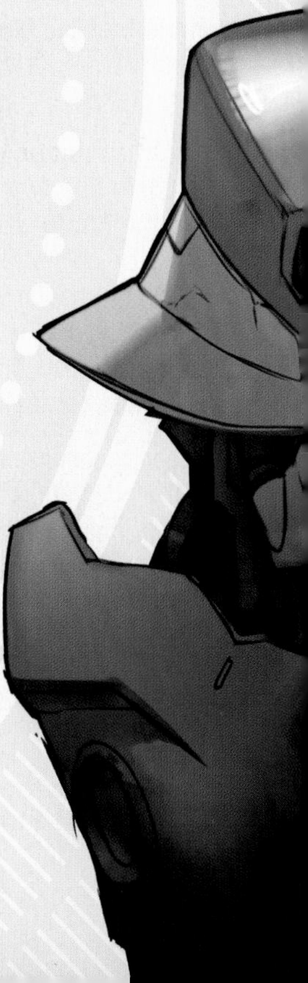

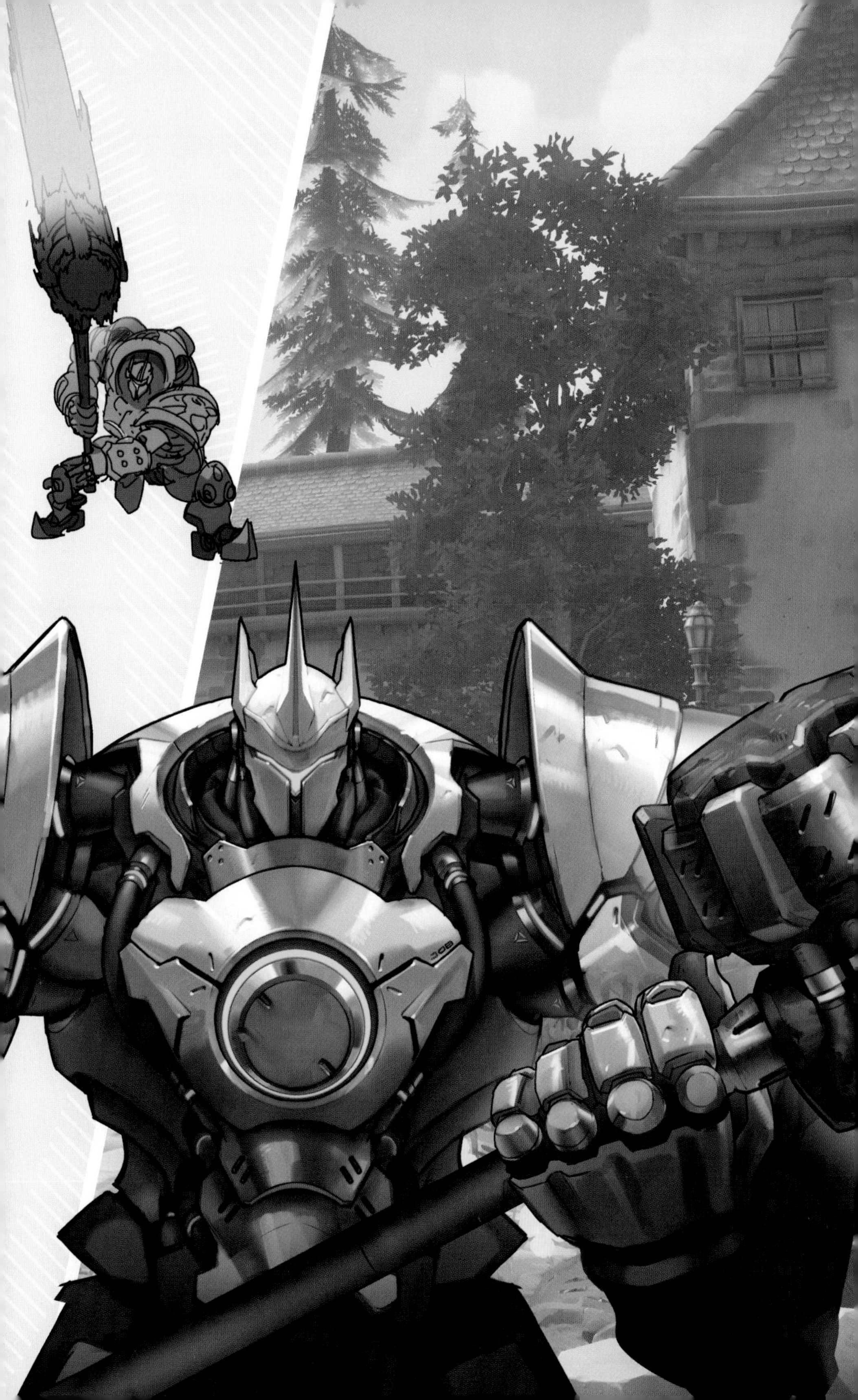

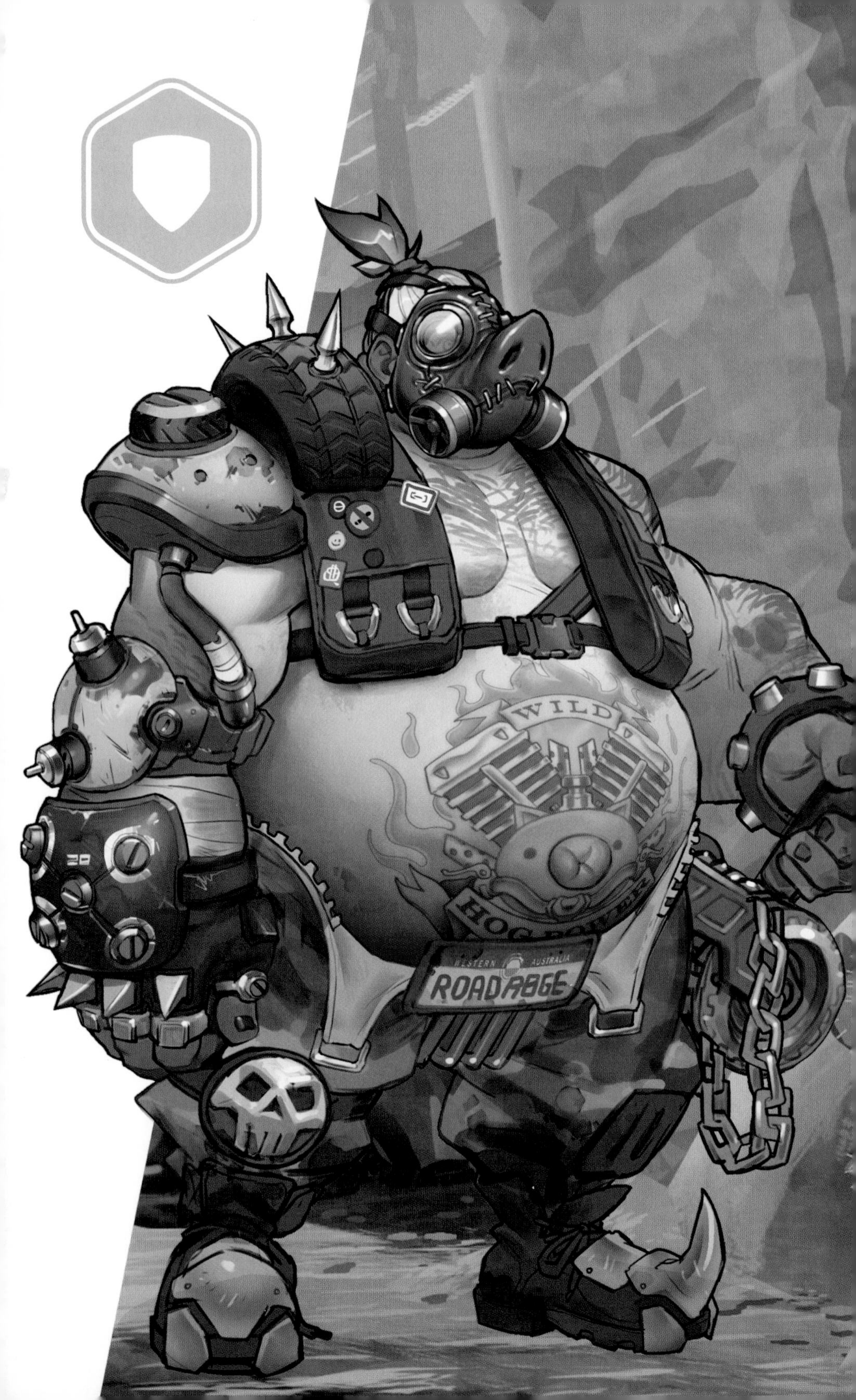
WILD
WESTERN AUSTRALIA
ROADRAGE

HERO PROFILE

ROADHOG

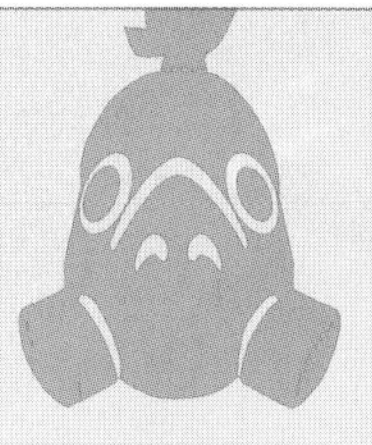

TANK

NAME: **MAKO RUTLEDGE**	AGE: **48**
OCCUPATION: **ENFORCER** (FORMERLY), **BODYGUARD**	
BASE OF OPERATIONS: **JUNKERTOWN, AUSTRALIA** (FORMERLY)	
AFFILIATION: **JUNKERS** (FORMERLY)	

BIOGRAPHY

When the Australian government gave away Mako Rutledge's home to omnics after the Omnic Crisis, Mako and other displaced residents fought back. A huge battle caused a massive explosion at the Australian omnium that left the Outback a radioactive wasteland.

Mako became Roadhog and focused on survival . . . until he met Junkrat in Junkertown, a city built from the omnium's ruins. The queen of Junkertown kicked them out for causing too much trouble. Now they're on a global crime spree—making explosive messes, stealing lots of gold . . . and planning their revenge on the queen.

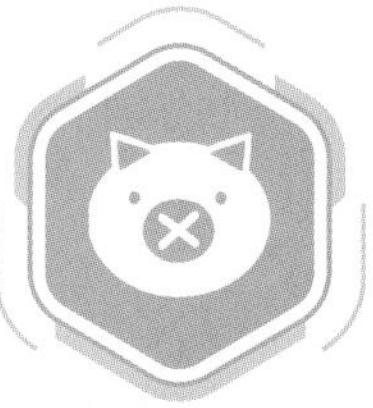

ULTIMATE ABILITY—WHOLE HOG:

Roadhog can crank out a stream of shrapnel from his Scrap Gun.

SCRAP GUN:

This weapon can repurpose any scrap metal into ammunition.

TAKE A BREATHER:

When he's hurt, he can restore a chunk of his health.

CHAIN HOOK:

Opponents caught by Roadhog's chain get yanked into close range—which is not a good place to be!

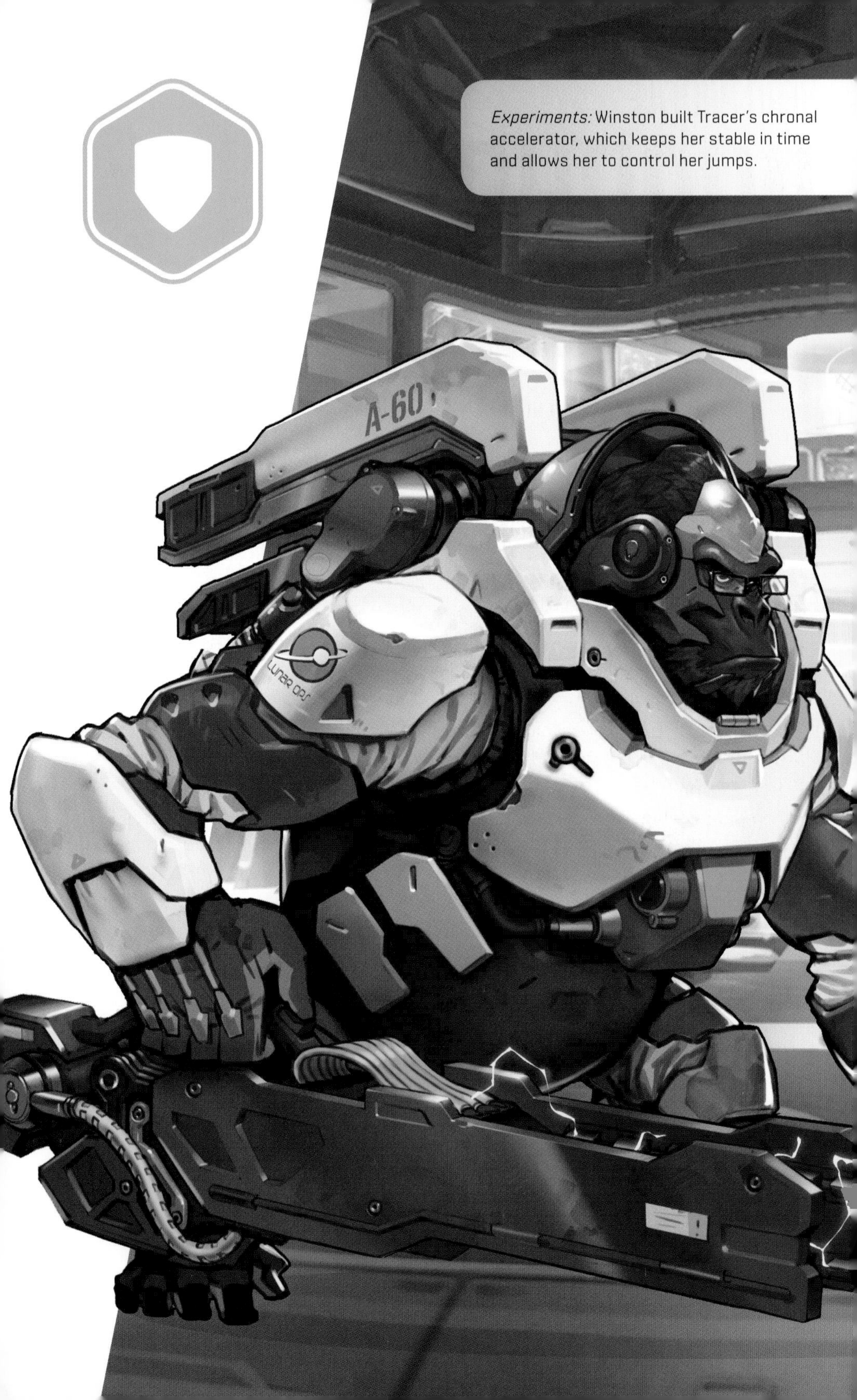

Experiments: Winston built Tracer's chronal accelerator, which keeps her stable in time and allows her to control her jumps.

HERO PROFILE

WINSTON

TANK	NAME: WINSTON	AGE: 29
	OCCUPATION: SCIENTIST, ADVENTURER	
	BASE OF OPERATIONS: WATCHPOINT: GIBRALTAR	
	AFFILIATION: OVERWATCH (FORMERLY)	

BIOGRAPHY

Winston may look like a big, powerful gorilla, but he is more human—and has a bigger heart—than some of the world's other heroes.

This gorilla's first memories are of life on a moon base, the Horizon Lunar Colony. He and other genetically enhanced gorillas were there to test the effects of living on the moon for a long time. But he developed much more quickly than the others, and he was taken under the wing of Dr. Harold Winston, who taught him science.

Tragedy struck when the other gorillas rebelled, killing all the humans on the moon. This gorilla took the name Winston after his beloved human caretaker, and then he built a makeshift rocket ship, fled to Earth, and became an Overwatch agent.

Even when Overwatch fell, Winston never lost faith in humanity. There is no place in this world for him now, and he lives in seclusion. But when Winston is called in to fight for what's right, he is fully committed to the cause. He is massively strong and will destroy anything in his path when his animal nature takes over.

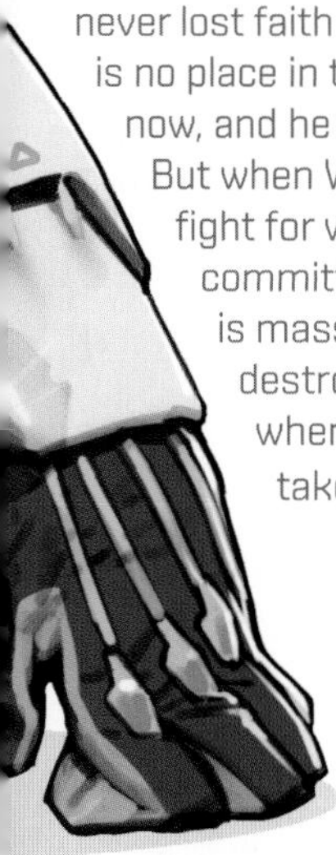

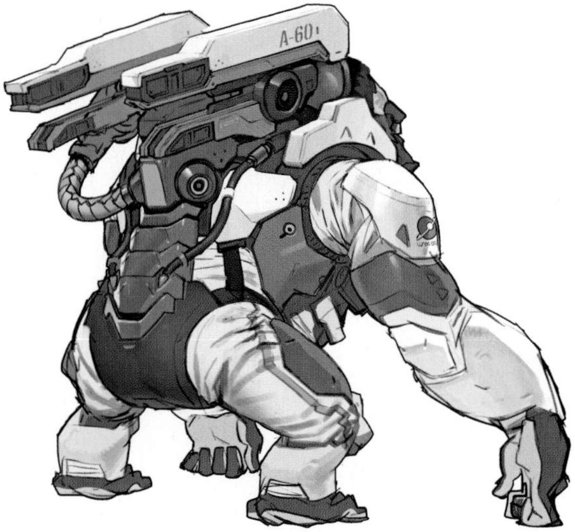
A-60

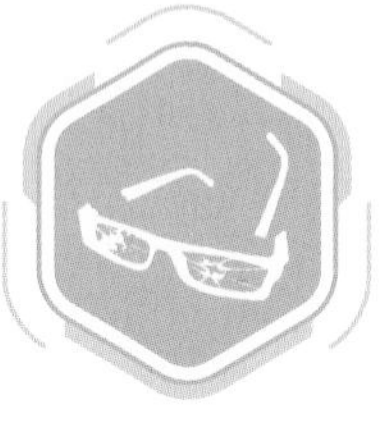

ULTIMATE ABILITY—PRIMAL RAGE:

When Winston embraces his animal nature, he becomes an almost unstoppable force. This ability boosts his health, strengthens his melee attack, and allows him to use his Jump Pack ability more frequently. While raging, he can't use any other abilities except for melee and Jump Pack—but he is nearly impossible to take down.

TESLA CANNON:

This weapon fires a continuous barrage of electric energy at short range.

JUMP PACK:

Winston's energy pack allows him to lunge through the air, dealing significant damage to anything he makes contact with.

BARRIER PROJECTOR:

This device projects a bubble-shaped field that protects Winston and his allies from damage until it's destroyed. Allies protected by the barrier can return fire from within it.

YOUNG WINSTON

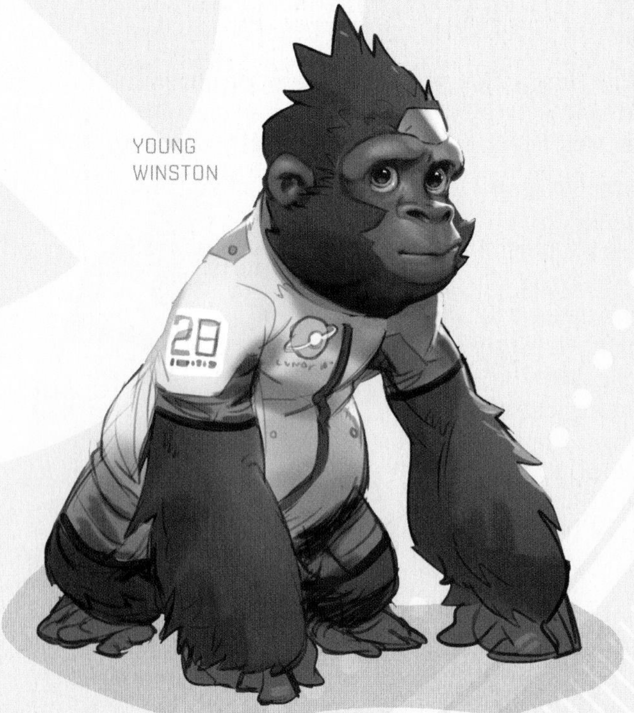

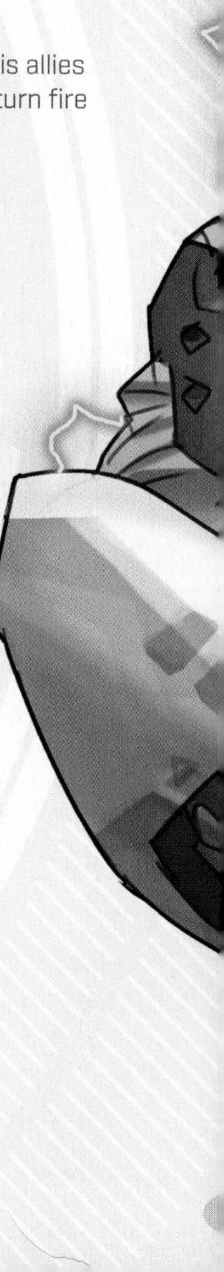

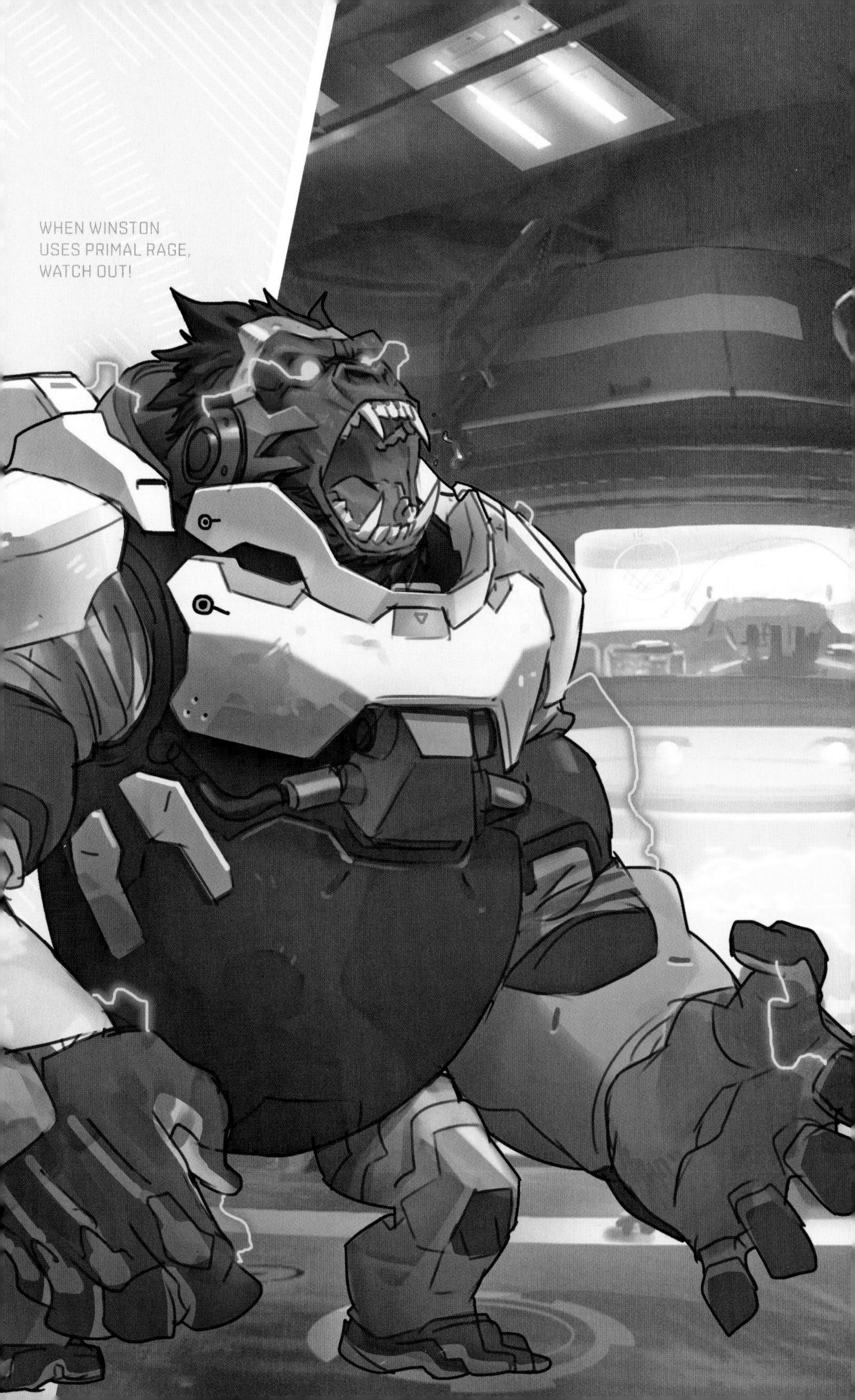

WHEN WINSTON USES PRIMAL RAGE, WATCH OUT!

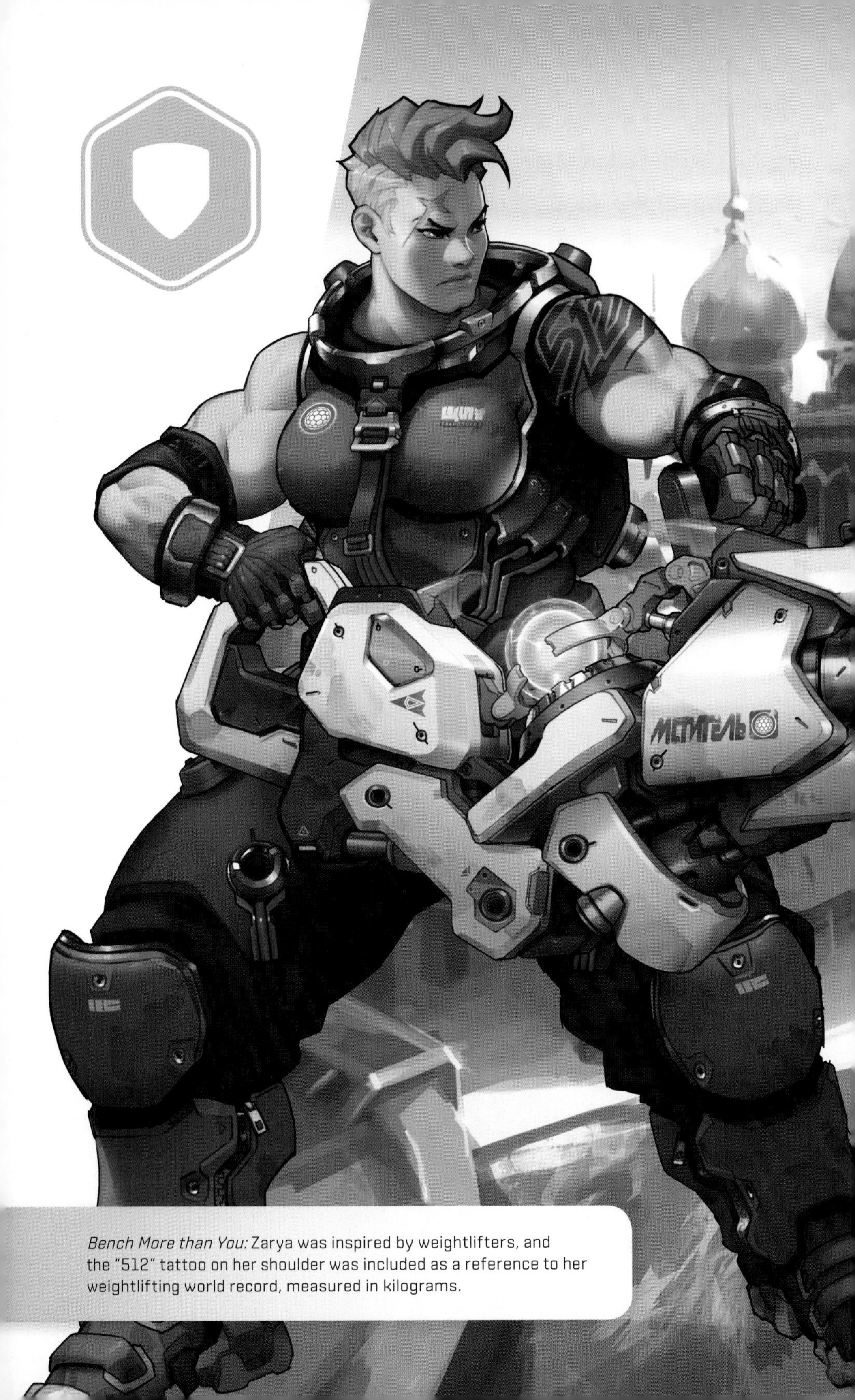

Bench More than You: Zarya was inspired by weightlifters, and the "512" tattoo on her shoulder was included as a reference to her weightlifting world record, measured in kilograms.

HERO PROFILE
ZARYA

	NAME: **ALEKSANDRA ZARYANOVA**	AGE: **28**
	OCCUPATION: **SOLDIER**	
	BASE OF OPERATIONS: **KRASNOYARSK FRONT, RUSSIA**	
TANK	AFFILIATION: **RUSSIAN DEFENSE FORCES**	

BIOGRAPHY

Need some muscle for your team? Someone who will do anything to protect her friends and family? Then call on Zarya.

When she was a little girl in Siberia, Zarya saw her village devastated by the war against the omnics. Her people defeated the robots and their omnium—a massive robot-producing factory—but at a high cost. Seeing the destruction around her, Zarya vowed that she would gain the strength to help her people recover.

She grew up to be a champion weightlifter and bodybuilder. But before she could enter the world championships, the omnium became active again and her village was attacked. She quickly returned home and joined the local defense forces, sacrificing fame and fortune to help her people.

Zarya's massive build allows her to wield mighty weapons and fight off attackers. But her true strength comes from the love and loyalty she has for those she cares about.

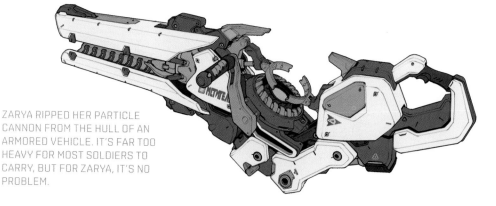

ZARYA RIPPED HER PARTICLE CANNON FROM THE HULL OF AN ARMORED VEHICLE. IT'S FAR TOO HEAVY FOR MOST SOLDIERS TO CARRY, BUT FOR ZARYA, IT'S NO PROBLEM.

ZARYA CAN STILL FIRE HER WEAPON WHEN SHE'S PROTECTED BY THE PARTICLE BARRIER.

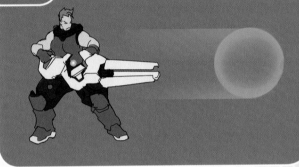

ULTIMATE ABILITY—GRAVITON SURGE:
Zarya launches a gravity bomb that draws her enemies toward it. While they're trapped, they are dealt serious damage.

PARTICLE CANNON:
Bring on the boom! Zarya's Particle Cannon can unleash a short-range beam of destructive energy or produce a blast to strike multiple opponents.

PARTICLE BARRIER:
The Particle Cannon can emit a protective shield for Zarya. Not only does it prevent her from receiving damage, but it redirects the energy to widen the beam of the Particle Cannon and increase the damage it can dish out.

PROJECTED BARRIER:
Zarya can give one of her teammates a protective shield, which will also boost the power of her Particle Cannon.

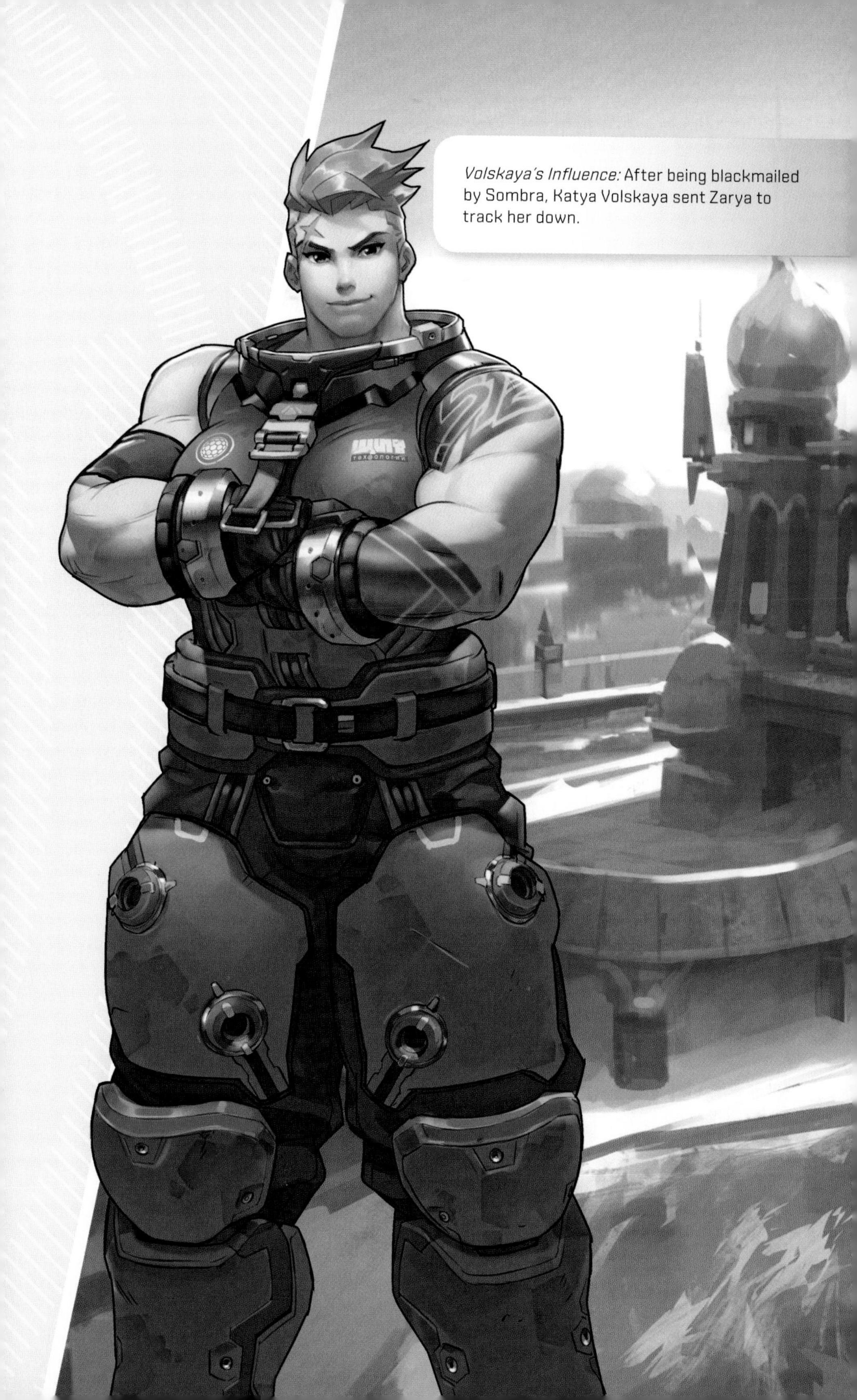

Volskaya's Influence: After being blackmailed by Sombra, Katya Volskaya sent Zarya to track her down.

SUPPORT HEROES

No mission can succeed without the aid of a support hero.

Often originating from the sciences, support heroes boast useful abilities that can give their team an advantage, like shielding or extra speed. When thrown into battle, support heroes can quickly turn the tide.

» They can heal team members and replenish shielding.

» They can give a "debuff," or a negative effect, to an enemy to make them weaker or slower.

» They can dish out "buffs," or positive effects, to their team members to keep them strong in the fight.

Support heroes hold the entire team together. Keep them close, and they'll keep you safe!

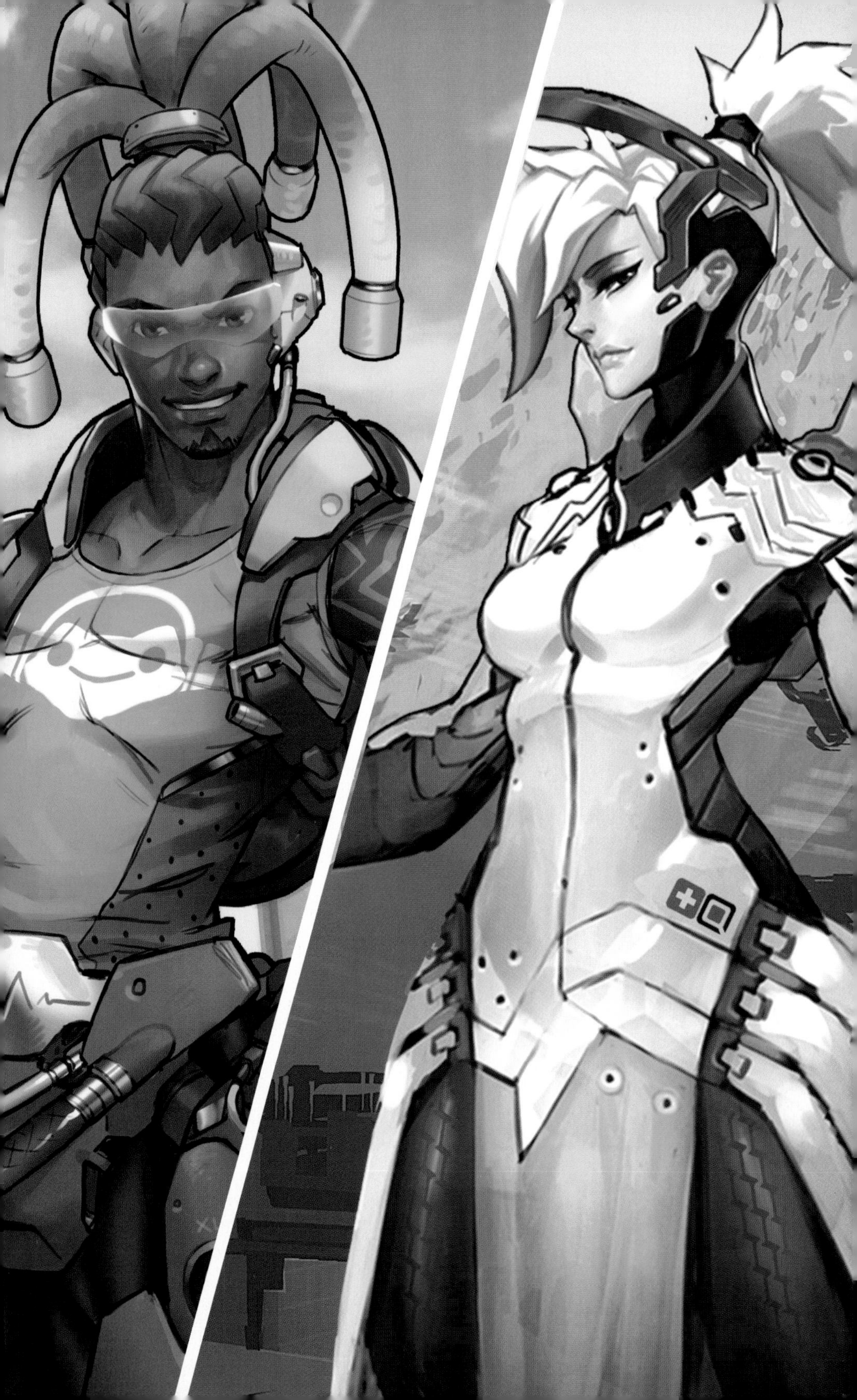

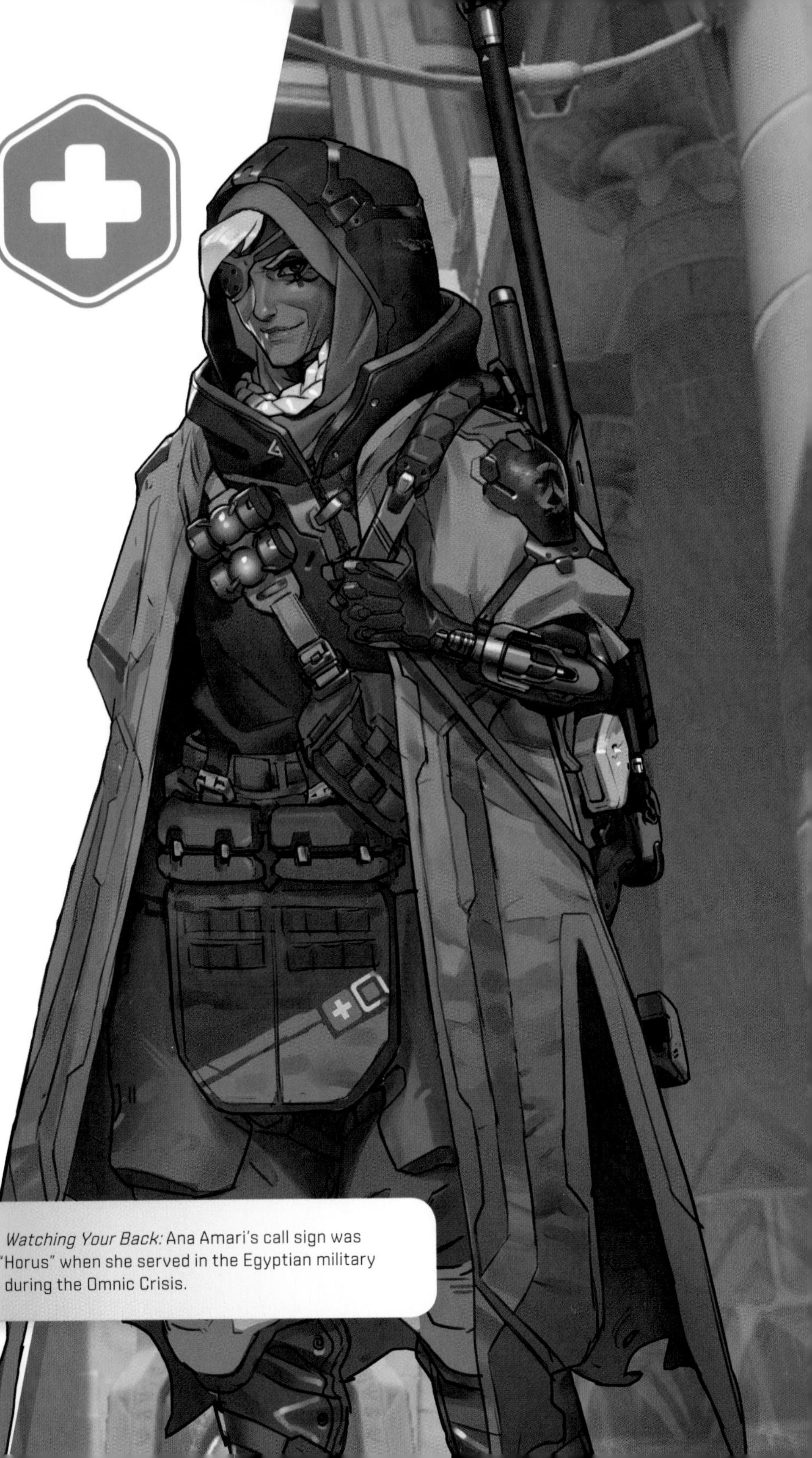

Watching Your Back: Ana Amari's call sign was "Horus" when she served in the Egyptian military during the Omnic Crisis.

HERO PROFILE
ANA

	NAME: **ANA AMARI**	AGE: **60**
	OCCUPATION: **BOUNTY HUNTER**	
	BASE OF OPERATIONS: **CAIRO, EGYPT**	
SUPPORT	AFFILIATION: **OVERWATCH** [FORMERLY]	

BIOGRAPHY

Ana Amari was once considered the world's most skilled sniper. She was a natural pick for the Overwatch strike team that ended the Omnic Crisis, and she was later second-in-command. She stayed on active duty well into her fifties, when she was thought to have been killed by Widowmaker. In truth, Ana survived . . . though her right eye didn't. She reconsidered her involvement in the world's conflicts, but as time passed, she could no longer watch from the sidelines. Ana has rejoined the fight.

ULTIMATE ABILITY—NANO BOOST:
After Ana hits an ally with a combat boost, they temporarily move faster, deal more damage, and take less damage.

BIOTIC RIFLE:
This rifle can deal damage to her enemies and restore health to her allies.

SLEEP DART:
This dart will knock an enemy unconscious, but further damage will wake that enemy up.

BIOTIC GRENADE:
Allies in this bomb's area of effect receive increased healing, while enemies caught in the blast cannot be healed temporarily.

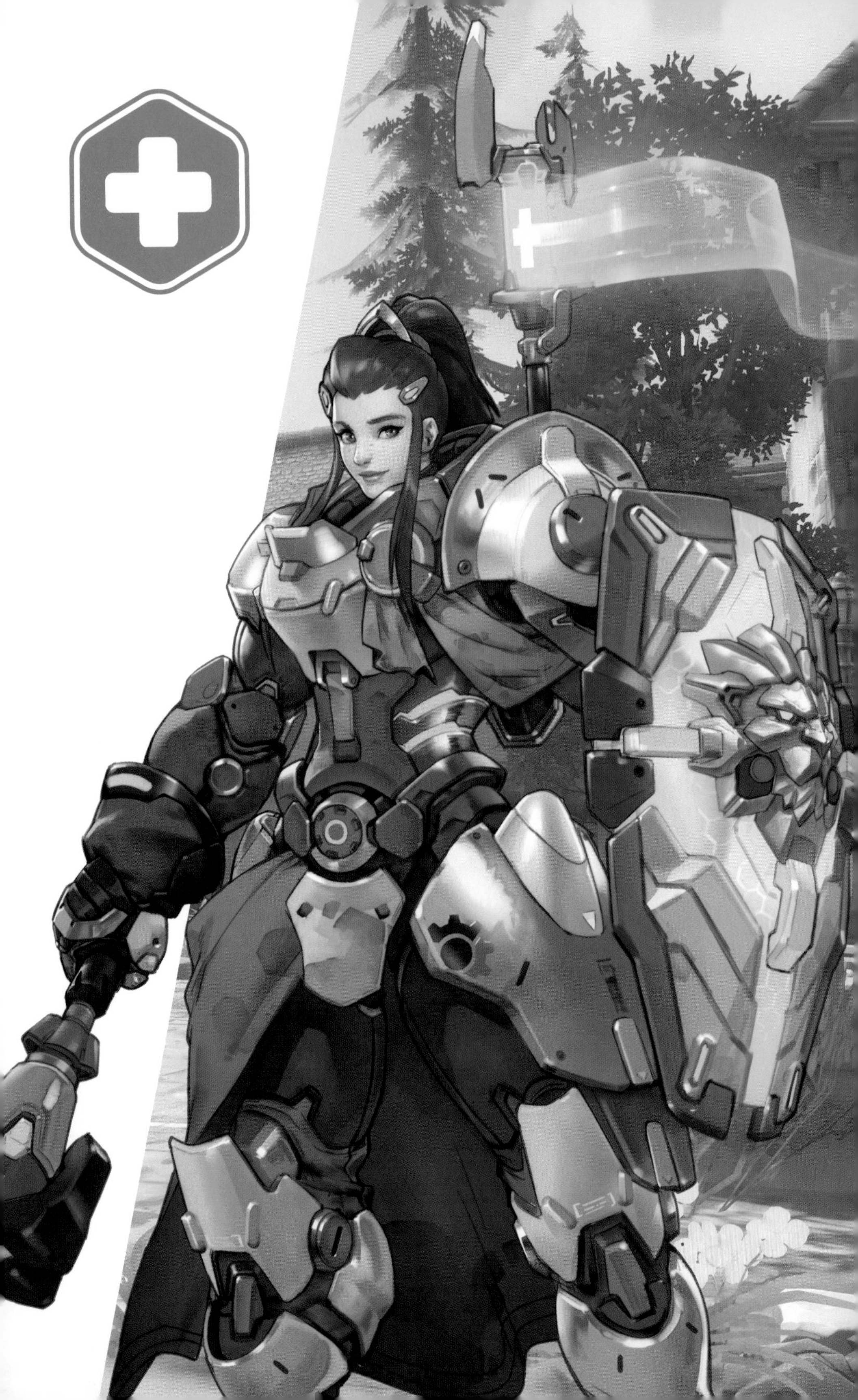

HERO PROFILE
BRIGITTE

	NAME: **BRIGITTE LINDHOLM**	AGE: **23**
	OCCUPATION: **MECHANICAL ENGINEER, ADVENTURER**	
	BASE OF OPERATIONS: **GOTHENBURG, SWEDEN** [FORMERLY]	
SUPPORT	AFFILIATION: **NONE**	

BIOGRAPHY

Brigitte learned mechanical engineering in the workshop of her father, the famous Torbjörn Lindholm. Unlike her father, who specialized in weaponry, she was more interested in building things that protected people, like shields and armor. When her godfather, Reinhardt, announced his plan to travel the world as a knight-errant, Brigitte eagerly volunteered to be his squire. For a while, she repaired his armor and supported him behind the scenes—but now she's decided to join the fight against evil, and put her designs to the test helping those in need!

All in the Family: Brigitte has a gear tattoo on her shoulder that matches her father's.

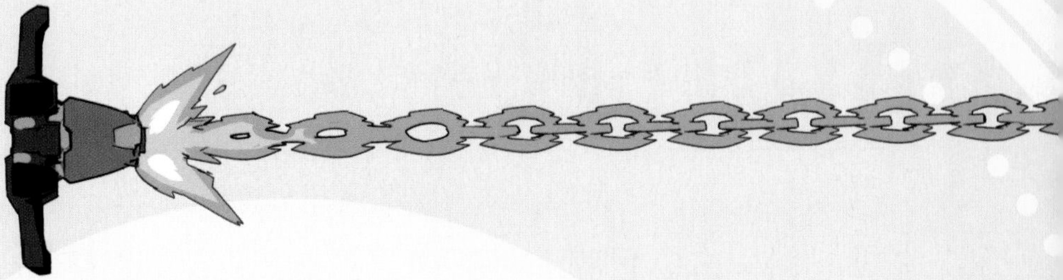

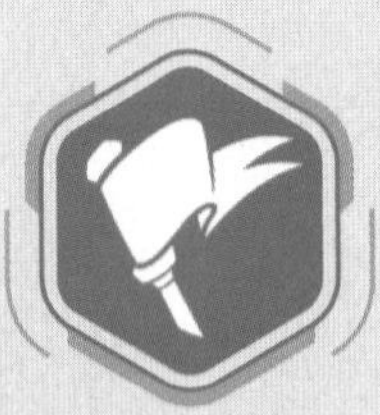

ULTIMATE ABILITY—RALLY:

Brigitte protects all nearby allies with extra armor and moves faster for a short period of time.

ROCKET FLAIL:

Brigitte's weapon extends on a long chain and bashes all enemies in its range.

REPAIR PACK:

These devices heal allies and build extra armor to protect them from future damage.

WHIP SHOT:

The rocket flail flies straight ahead, knocking enemies away.

BARRIER SHIELD:

Brigitte raises an energy barrier that absorbs attacks from the front.

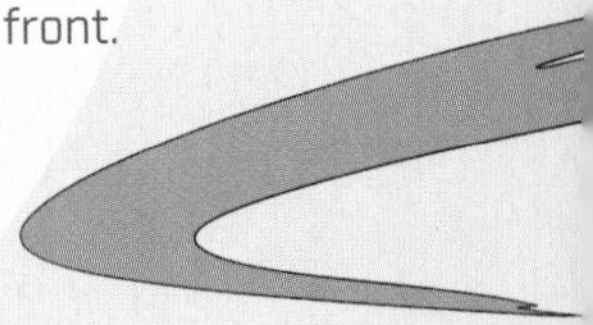

SHIELD BASH:

A quick, shield-first dash that can stun attacking enemies.

INSPIRE (PASSIVE):

As long as Brigitte is doing damage to enemies, she will heal friendly heroes nearby.

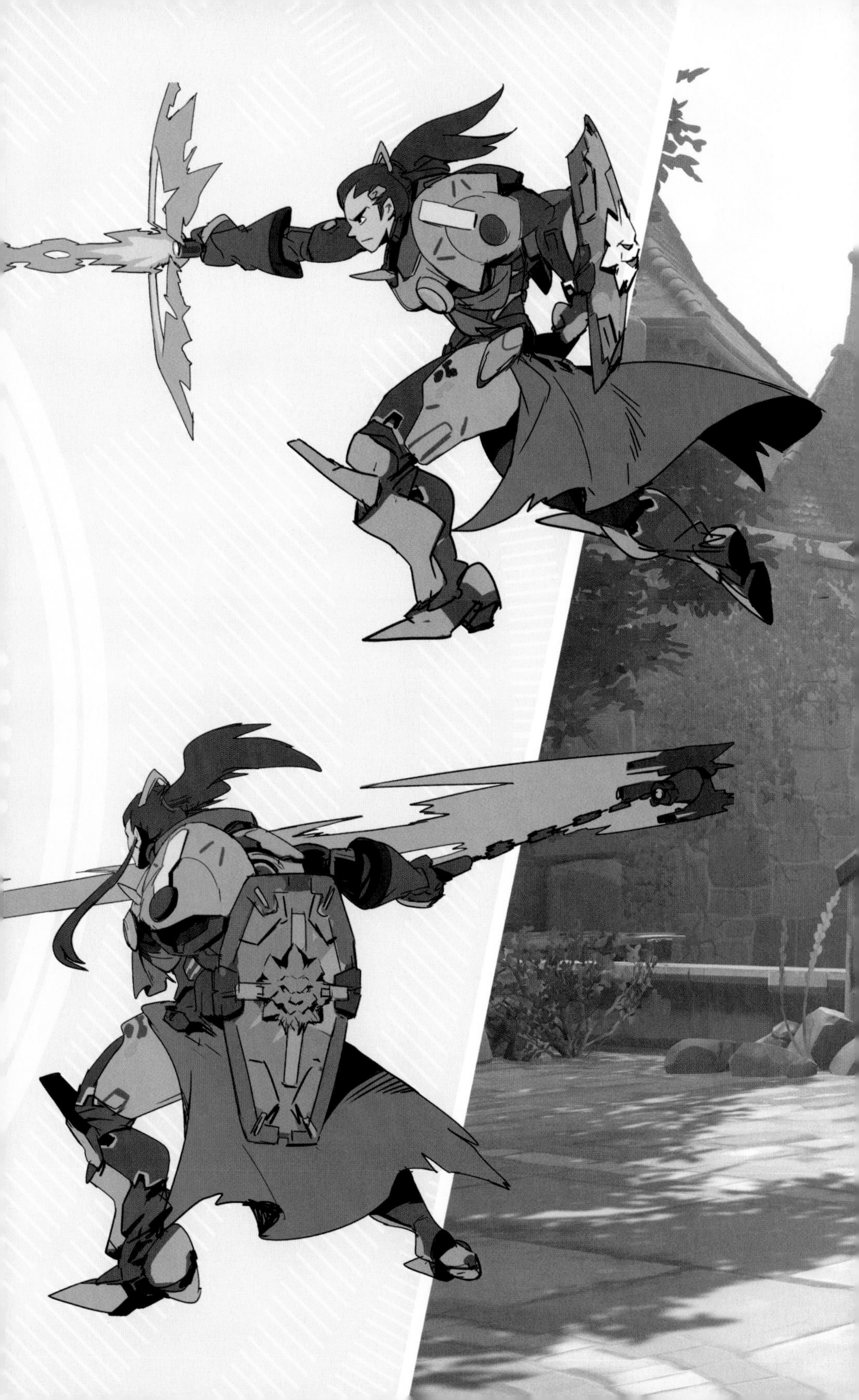

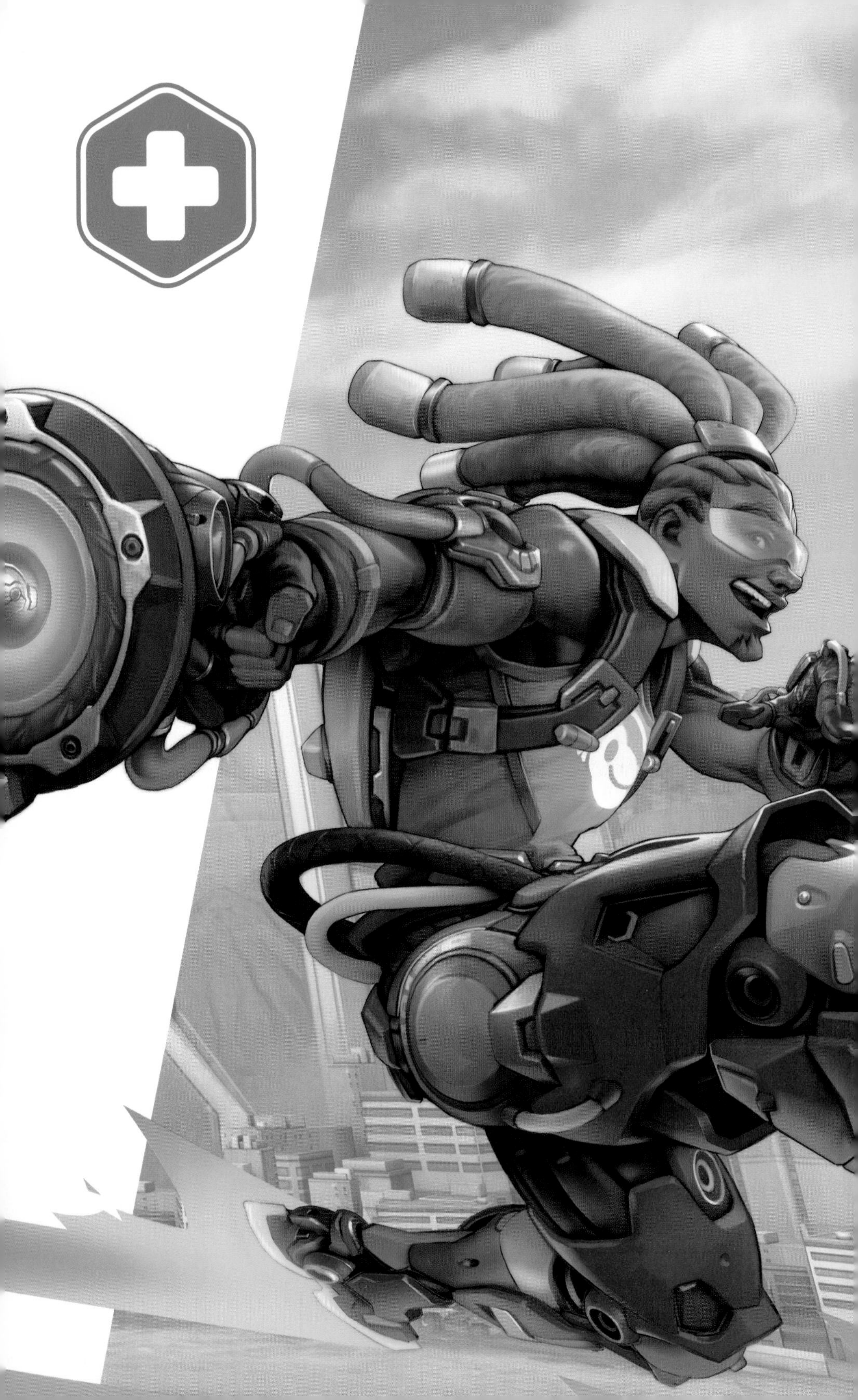

HERO PROFILE
LÚCIO

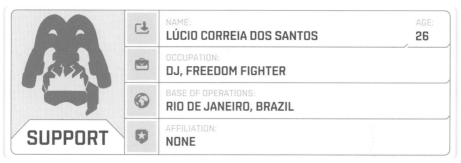

	NAME: **LÚCIO CORREIA DOS SANTOS**	AGE: **26**
	OCCUPATION: **DJ, FREEDOM FIGHTER**	
	BASE OF OPERATIONS: **RIO DE JANEIRO, BRAZIL**	
SUPPORT	AFFILIATION: **NONE**	

BIOGRAPHY

Spinning wild beats, long dreads bouncing on his shoulders, Lúcio makes a splash whenever he appears. This musical artist energizes large crowds when he performs, but he's more than just a DJ—he's a hero to the people.

Lúcio grew up in Rio de Janeiro, Brazil, and quickly discovered he had a gift for music. He became legendary for performing in underground shows, and it looked like the party would never end—until the Vishkar Corporation came to Rio.

Vishkar started imposing strict rules on the residents, enforcing curfews and cracking down on what the company called "lawless" behavior. Lúcio fought back. He repurposed Vishkar sonic technology and used it to start a revolution. The residents of Rio de Janeiro drove Vishkar out of their neighborhoods.

Lúcio became an overnight superstar, and he set out on a world tour. "My heart beats for Brazil," he told Atlas News. "I get inspired by the people here. Their struggles. Their triumphs. I want to share that energy—the energy of their lives—with the rest of the world."

Hard Light: Lúcio fights against the Vishkar Corporation, the same company that employs Symmetra.

THE SONIC AMPLIFIER CAN BE USED OFFENSIVELY OR DEFENSIVELY.

ULTIMATE ABILITY—SOUND BARRIER:

When Lúcio activates his Sonic Amplifier, protective waves flow out, providing him and his teammates with temporary personal shields.

SONIC AMPLIFIER:

What's that sound? It's the sound of Lúcio's enemies falling when he hits them with sonic projectiles or powerful sound blasts.

CROSSFADE:

Lúcio and his teammates are constantly charged with energy from his music. He can switch between two songs: one that boosts speed, and another that restores health.

AMP IT UP:

When Lúcio turns up the volume on his songs, it increases their effects.

Audio Medic: Lúcio's frog tattoo is the giant monkey frog: a bright green amphibian from the Amazon basin that's used in traditional healing ceremonies.

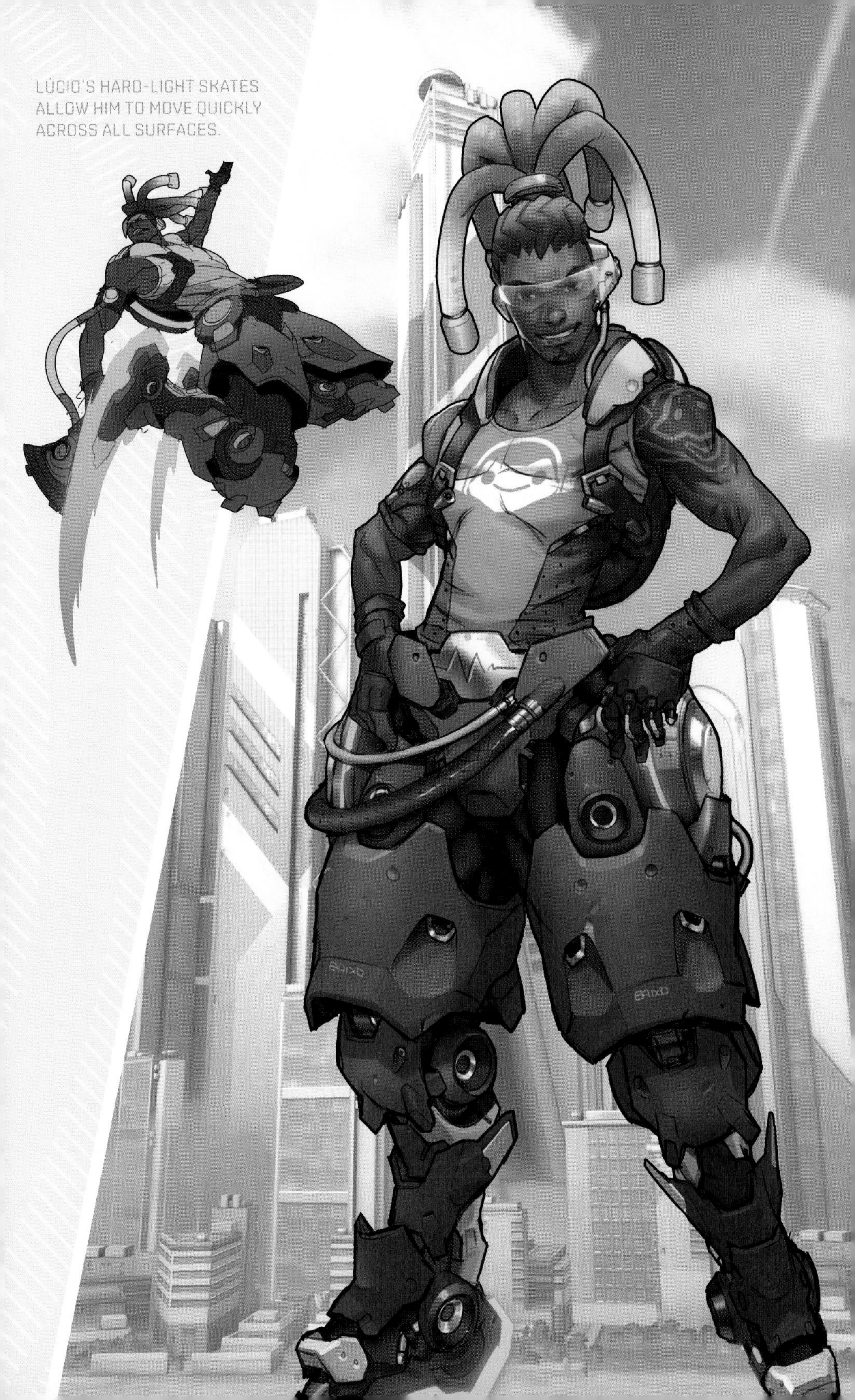
BAIXO
BAIXO

LÚCIO'S HARD-LIGHT SKATES ALLOW HIM TO MOVE QUICKLY ACROSS ALL SURFACES.

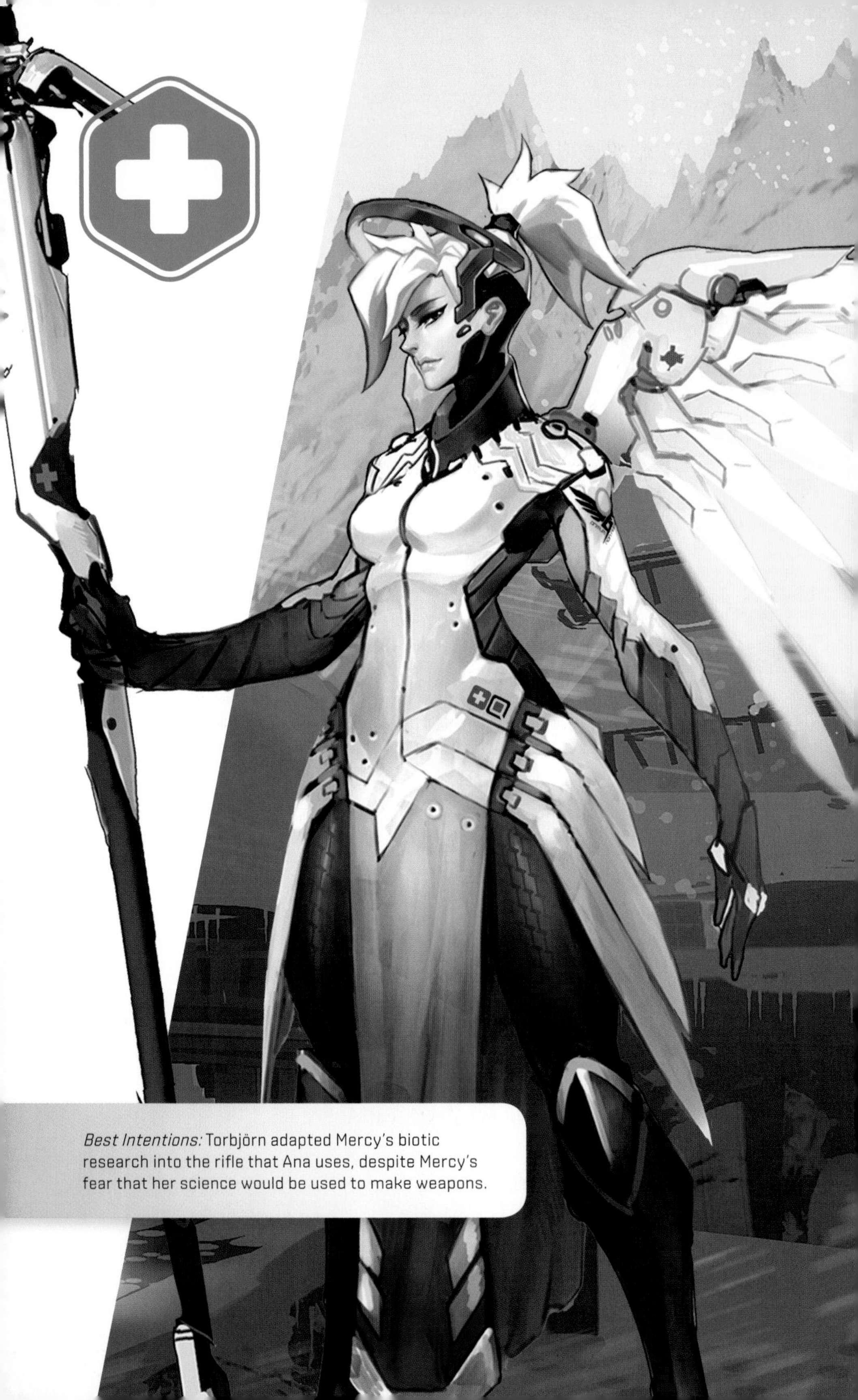

Best Intentions: Torbjörn adapted Mercy's biotic research into the rifle that Ana uses, despite Mercy's fear that her science would be used to make weapons.

HERO PROFILE

MERCY

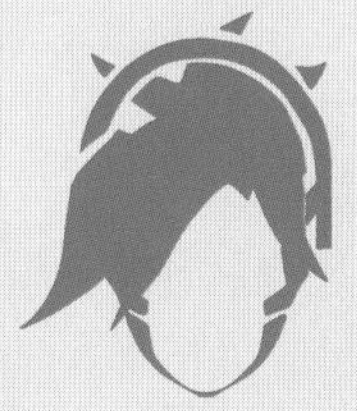

SUPPORT	NAME: **ANGELA ZIEGLER** — AGE: **37**
	OCCUPATION: **FIELD MEDIC, FIRST RESPONDER**
	BASE OF OPERATIONS: **ZÜRICH, SWITZERLAND**
	AFFILIATION: **OVERWATCH** (FORMERLY)

BIOGRAPHY

You can't make an appointment with this doctor, but if you're hurt, she'll come to your aid in a flash. A brilliant surgeon, Dr. Angela Ziegler was head of medical research for Overwatch. Since the fall of Overwatch, she has traveled the world, aiding innocent victims of war. Wearing the Valkyrie swift-response suit, she can quickly fly to help someone hurt on the battlefield. To many, Mercy is an angel on Earth.

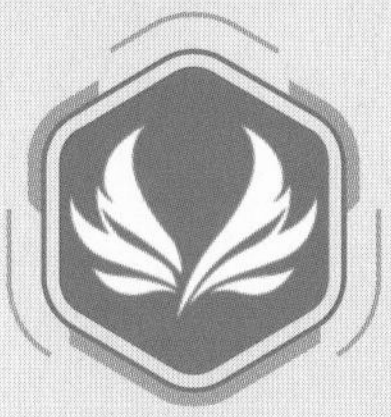

ULTIMATE ABILITY—VALKYRIE:

Mercy can fly around the map, and her speed and healing abilities become supercharged for a short period of time.

CADUCEUS STAFF:

When a beam from this staff touches one of Mercy's teammates, she can restore their health or increase the damage they deal.

CADUCEUS BLASTER:

Mercy has a sidearm to use for emergency personal defense.

GUARDIAN ANGEL:

Mercy can quickly fly to friends who need help.

ANGELIC DESCENT:

Her Valkyrie suit allows her to fall slowly from great heights.

RESURRECT:

Mercy can revive one of her teammates, getting them back into the fight quickly.

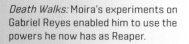

Death Walks: Moira's experiments on Gabriel Reyes enabled him to use the powers he now has as Reaper.

HERO PROFILE
MOIRA

	NAME: **MOIRA O'DEORAIN**		AGE: **48**
	OCCUPATION: **GENETICIST**		
	BASE OF OPERATIONS: **DUBLIN, IRELAND; OASIS, IRAQ**		
SUPPORT	AFFILIATION: **TALON, BLACKWATCH** [FORMERLY]		

BIOGRAPHY

Moira is a talented geneticist who was pushed out of the scientific community when she published a controversial method for altering DNA. Overwatch's covert ops division, Blackwatch, quietly welcomed her as a developer of new weapons and technologies until it fell under scrutiny and Overwatch was disbanded. Now she works with the scientists in Oasis, but the secretive Talon organization has been aiding her experiments for their own purposes. Moira is always looking for her next big breakthrough, no matter what it takes.

ULTIMATE ABILITY—COALESCENCE:
A powerful, long-range beam of biotic energy flows from both of Moira's hands, healing allies and hurting enemies—even through barriers.

BIOTIC GRASP:
Moira's right hand drains enemies' health and saps biotic energy for her left hand to release as a healing spray.

BIOTIC ORB:
Moira can create a yellow bouncing sphere that heals nearby allies, or a purple one that deals damage.

FADE:
Moira disappears and teleports a short distance to escape from enemies or surprise them from behind.

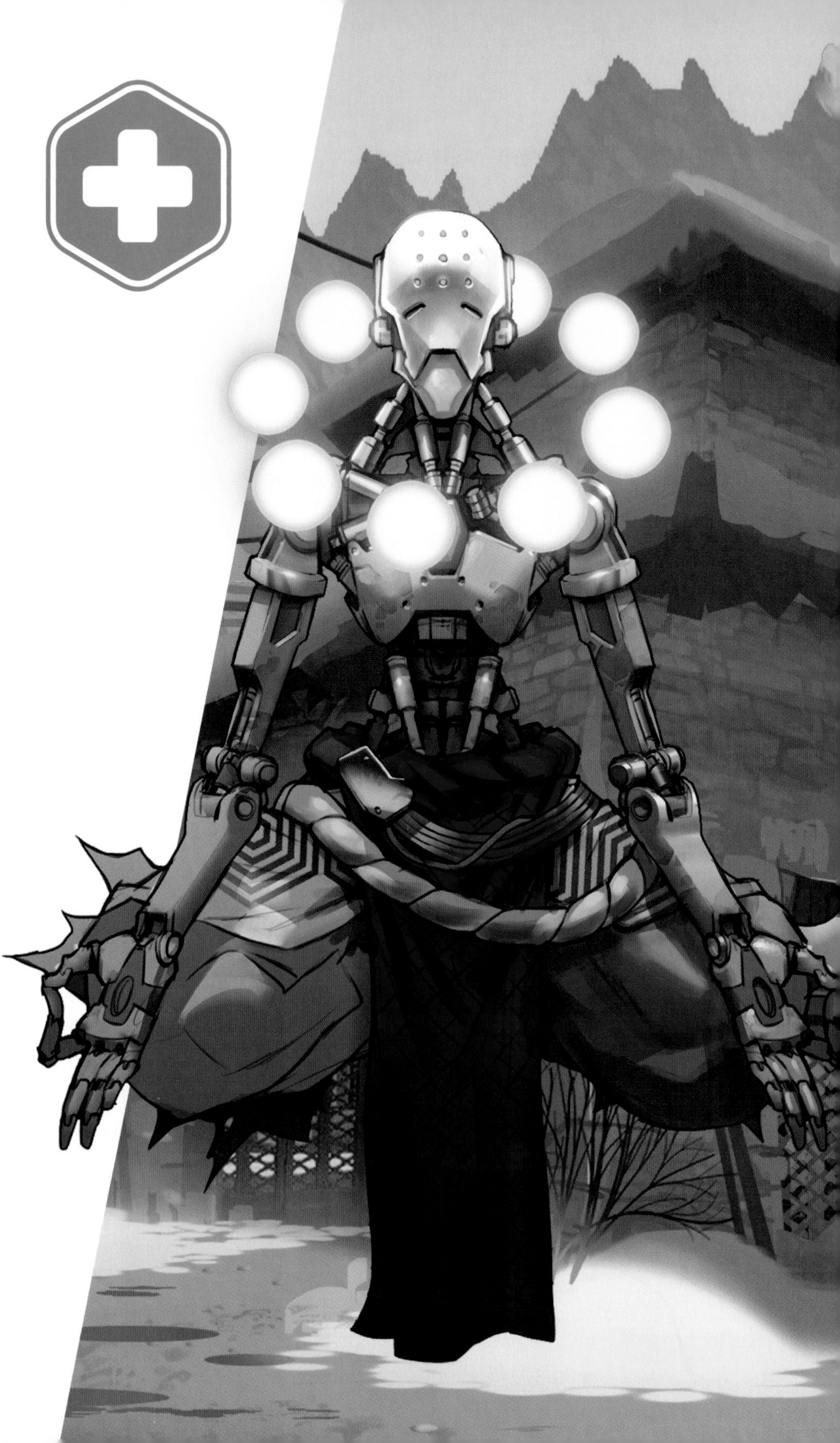

HERO PROFILE
ZENYATTA

	NAME:	AGE:
	TEKHARTHA ZENYATTA	**20**
	OCCUPATION: **WANDERING GURU, ADVENTURER**	
	BASE OF OPERATIONS: **SHAMBALI MONASTERY, NEPAL** [FORMERLY]	
SUPPORT	AFFILIATION: **THE SHAMBALI** [FORMERLY]	

BIOGRAPHY

Do robots have souls? That's the question that a group of outcast robots asked themselves after the Omnic Crisis. They fled to the mountains of the Himalayas and meditated for years. In the end, they agreed that omnic robots possessed souls, just like humans.

These robot monks became world famous and led a movement trying to bring robots and humans together through their teachings. Zenyatta is one robot monk who decided to come down from the mountains to spread this message far and wide.

This robot monk believes the best way to repair the relationship between humans and omnics is for the two species to connect with each other. He travels the world, helping those he meets to find inner peace. And while he himself is peaceful, he will use force to defend himself—and others—when necessary.

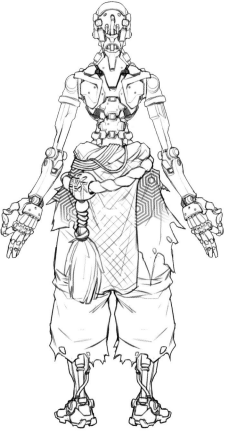

ZENYATTA'S ORBS ARE CARVED AT THE SHAMBALI MONASTERY. THEY CAN BE USED IN PEACEFUL OR DESTRUCTIVE WAYS.

ULTIMATE ABILITY—TRANSCENDENCE:

Zenyatta enters an altered state for a short period of time. While transcendent, he can't use any of his other abilities or weapons. But he can fully restore his own health, along with the health of nearby allies.

ORB OF DESTRUCTION:

When attacked, Zenyatta will fight back. He can project one of these exploding orbs or shoot them repeatedly, rapid-fire.

ORB OF HARMONY:

If one of his allies needs healing, Zenyatta casts this orb over his friend's shoulder to slowly restore them. He can only aid one teammate at a time with this orb.

ORB OF DISCORD:

When this orb attaches to one of Zenyatta's opponents, it will increase the amount of damage that opponent takes.

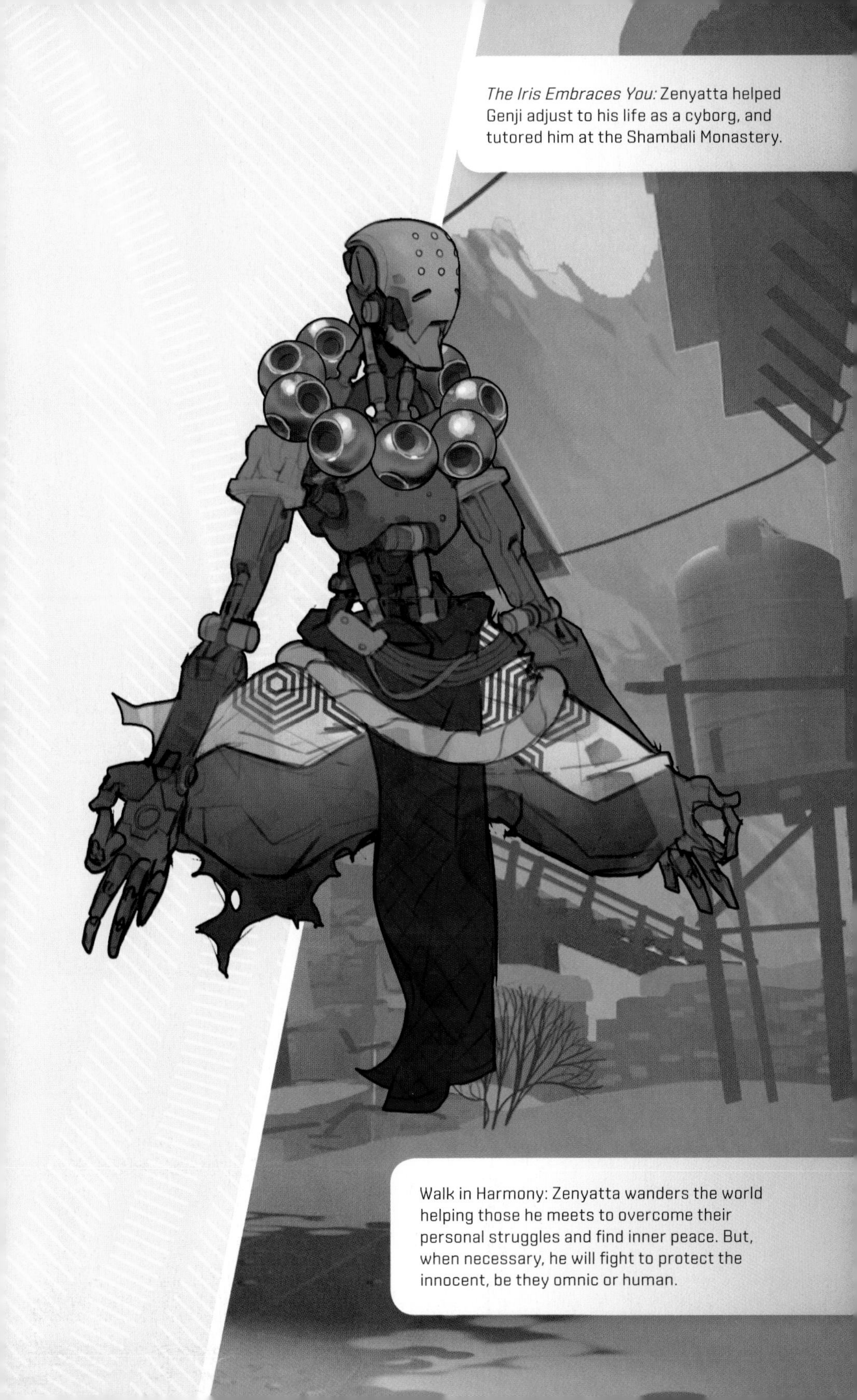

The Iris Embraces You: Zenyatta helped Genji adjust to his life as a cyborg, and tutored him at the Shambali Monastery.

Walk in Harmony: Zenyatta wanders the world helping those he meets to overcome their personal struggles and find inner peace. But, when necessary, he will fight to protect the innocent, be they omnic or human.

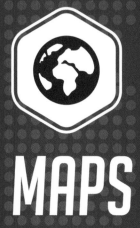

MAPS

What is the world like in the aftermath of the Omnic Crisis? Much of the world has been reshaped by new technology and tough battles. New dangers can appear anywhere, so heroes have to be ready for anything.

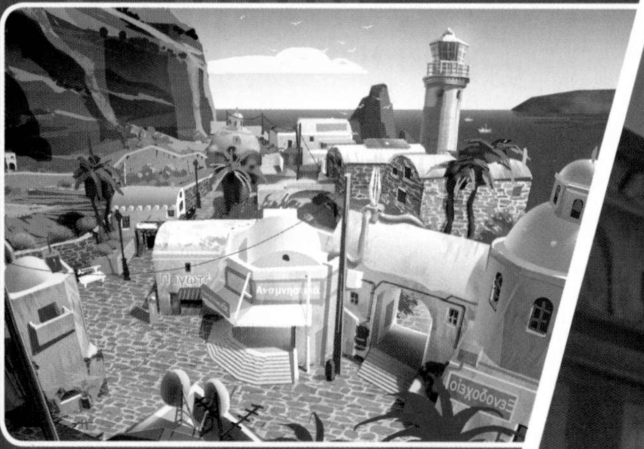

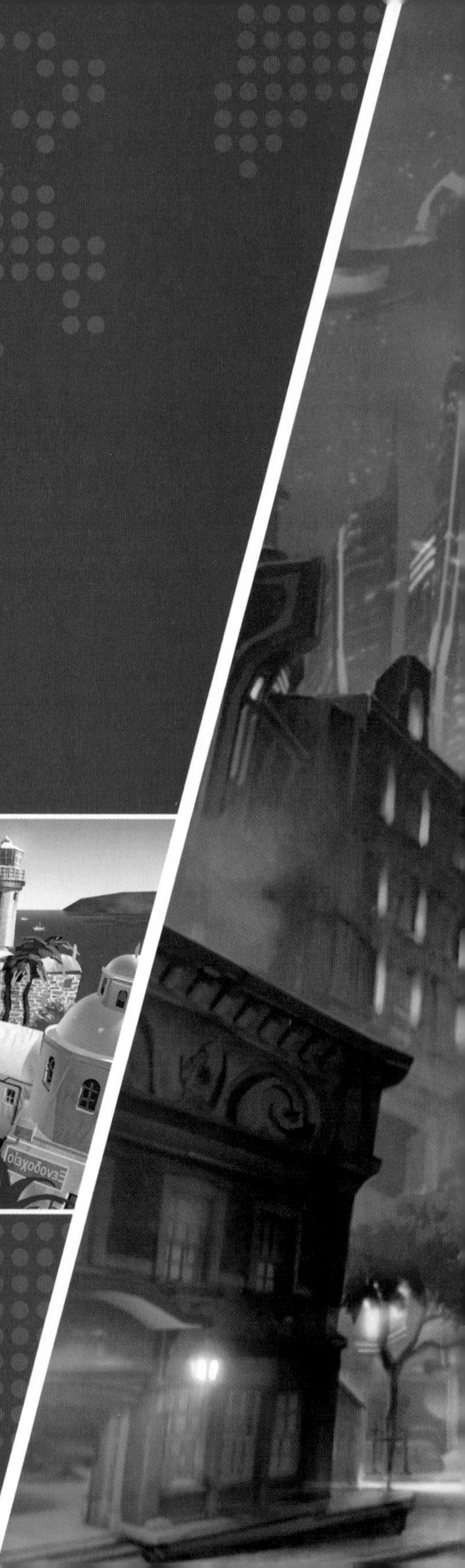

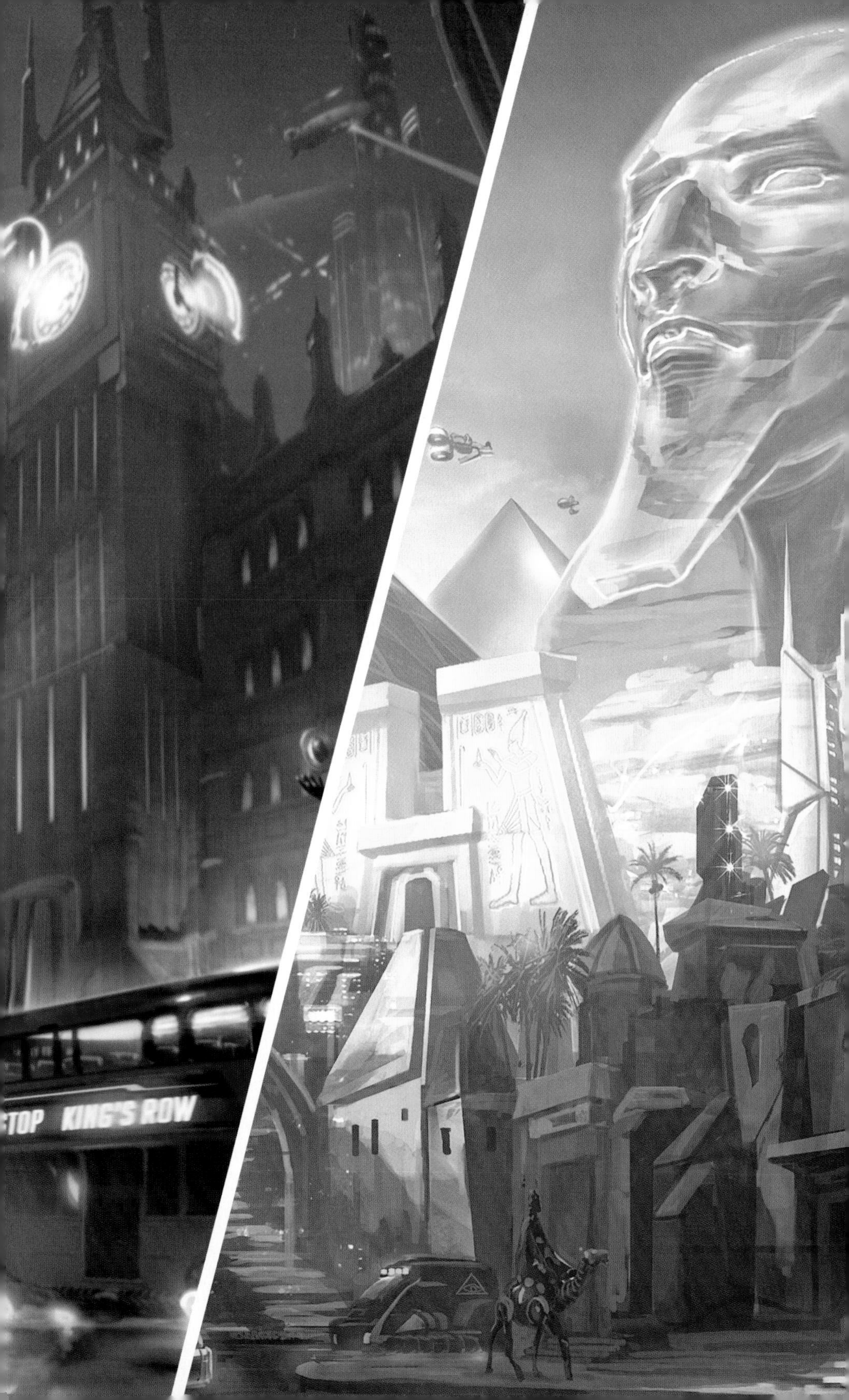
TOP KING'S ROW

AYUTTHAYA

	OBJECTIVE DETAILS: **CAPTURE THE FLAG**
	COUNTRY: **THAILAND**
	FLAG:

SECLUDED BEAUTY

Heroes travel to this temple from all over the world for games of capture the flag. Take a breather from the Lunar New Year celebrations to admire the ornate statues and calming fountains, or jump right in and keep your eyes on the prize. Some abilities are against the rules once you grab the flag, though—be careful not to drop it!

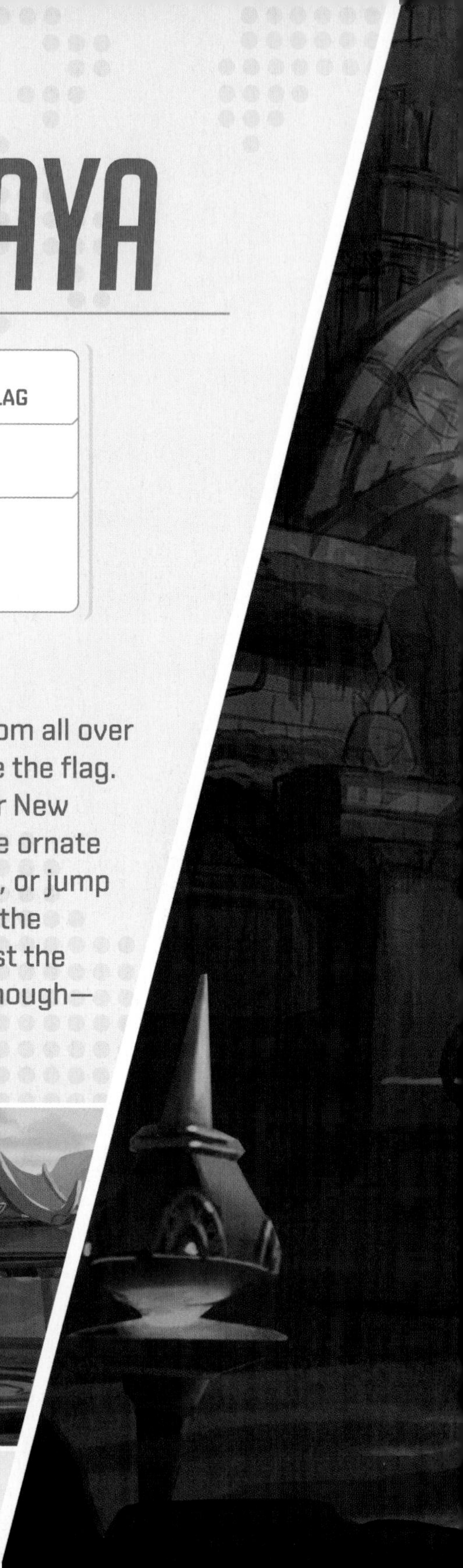

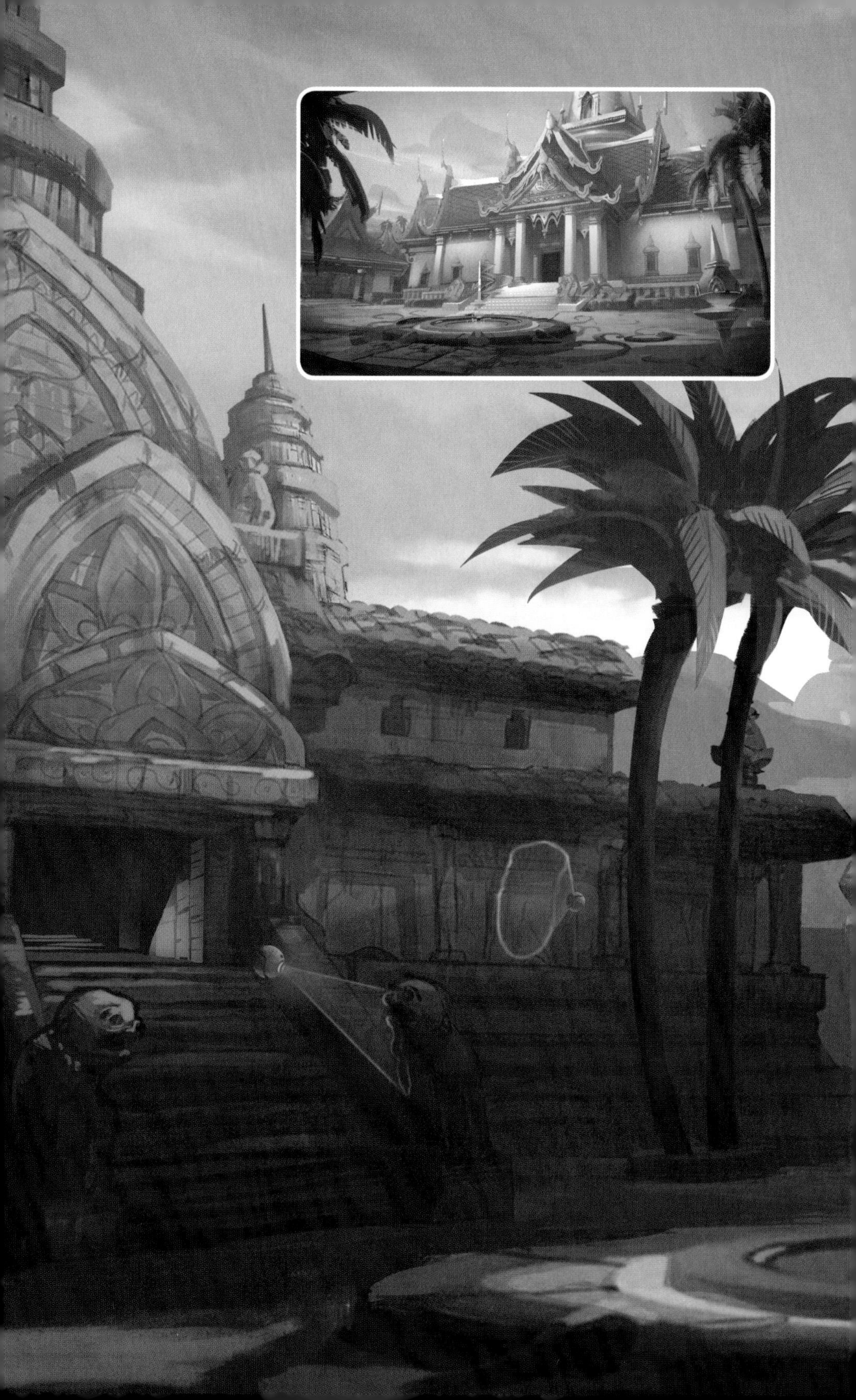

MAP

HANAMURA

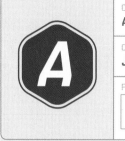

A	OBJECTIVE DETAILS: **ASSAULT**
	COUNTRY: **JAPAN**
	FLAG:

DRAGON BATTLEGROUND

The trees in this peaceful Japanese village burst into bloom every spring, blanketing the town in pink blossoms. But Hanamura has a dangerous past. It was once home to the powerful Shimada family, a ninja clan that transformed into a criminal organization. Now there is danger lurking inside the former Shimada compound, hidden in the shadows . . .

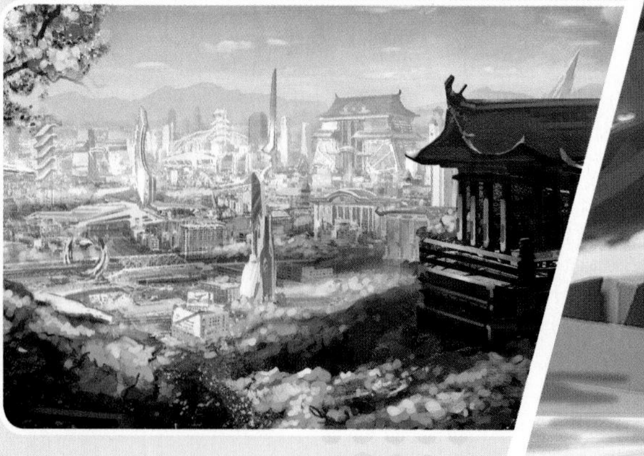

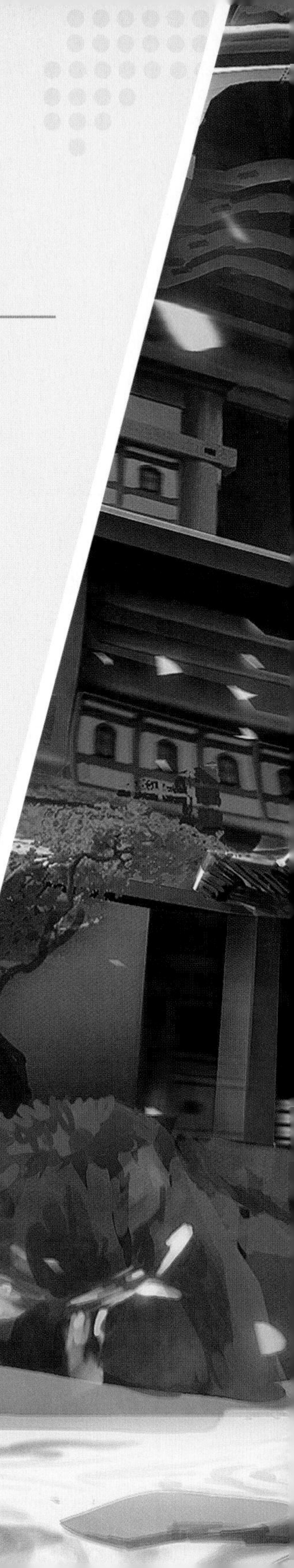

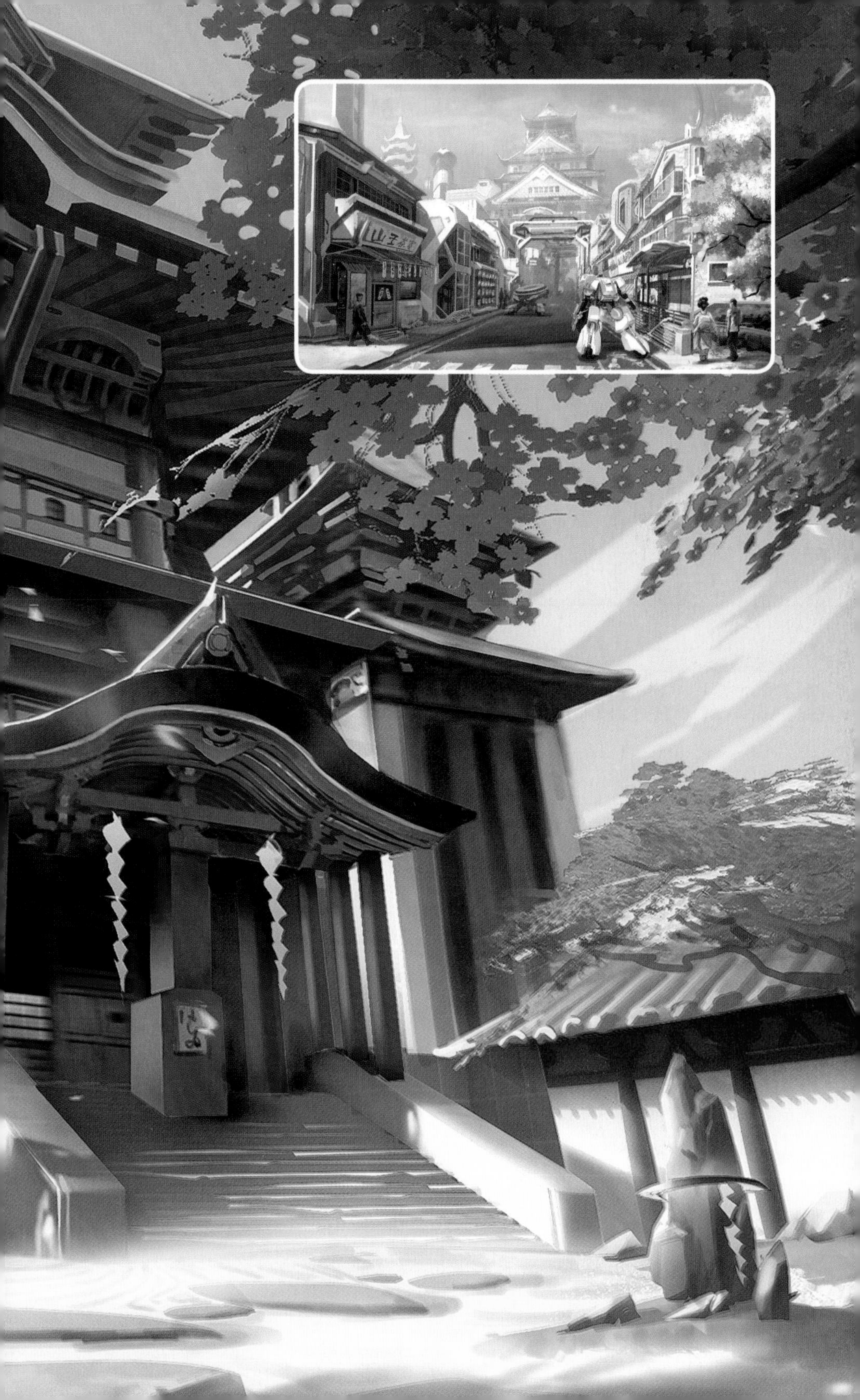

MAP

HORIZON LUNAR COLONY

OBJECTIVE DETAILS:
ASSAULT

COUNTRY:
EARTH'S MOON

FLAG:

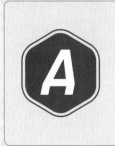

ONE GIANT LEAP

The Horizon Lunar Colony was developed as a first long-term step into space: humans and genetically engineered gorillas lived together to examine the effects of prolonged habitation in space and the repercussions on both life forms. Winston escaped when the gorillas rebelled against their human partners, and since then, all contact with the base has been lost. But with the life support systems still running, many wonder: What's happening up there, so far away from Earth?

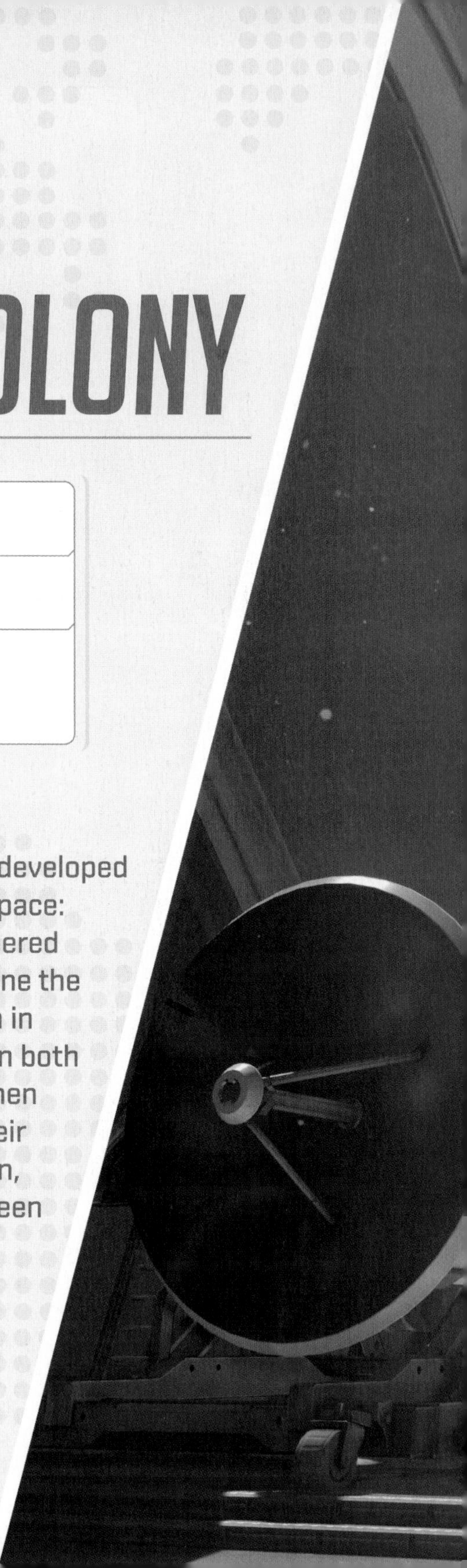

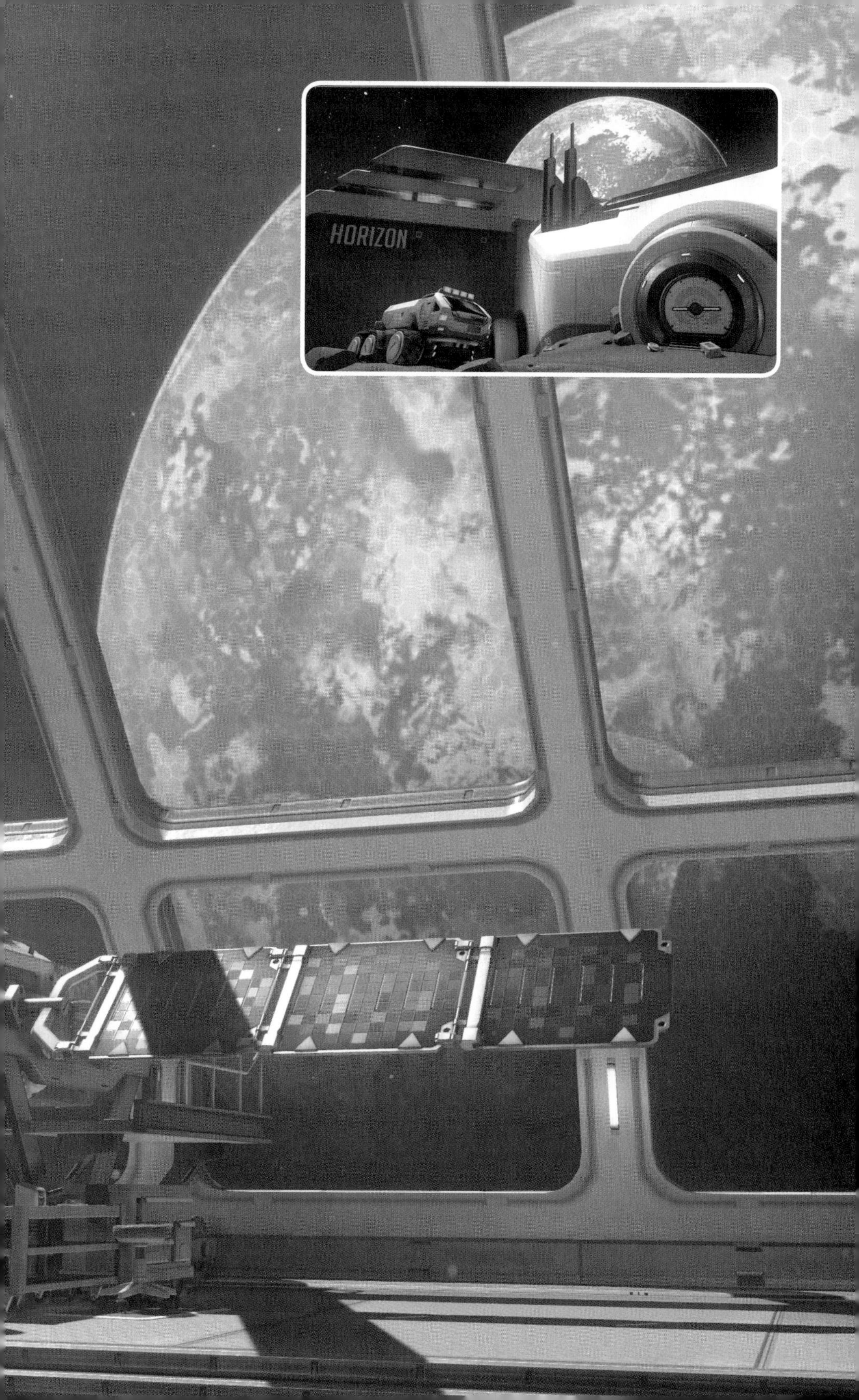
HORIZON

MAP

TEMPLE OF ANUBIS

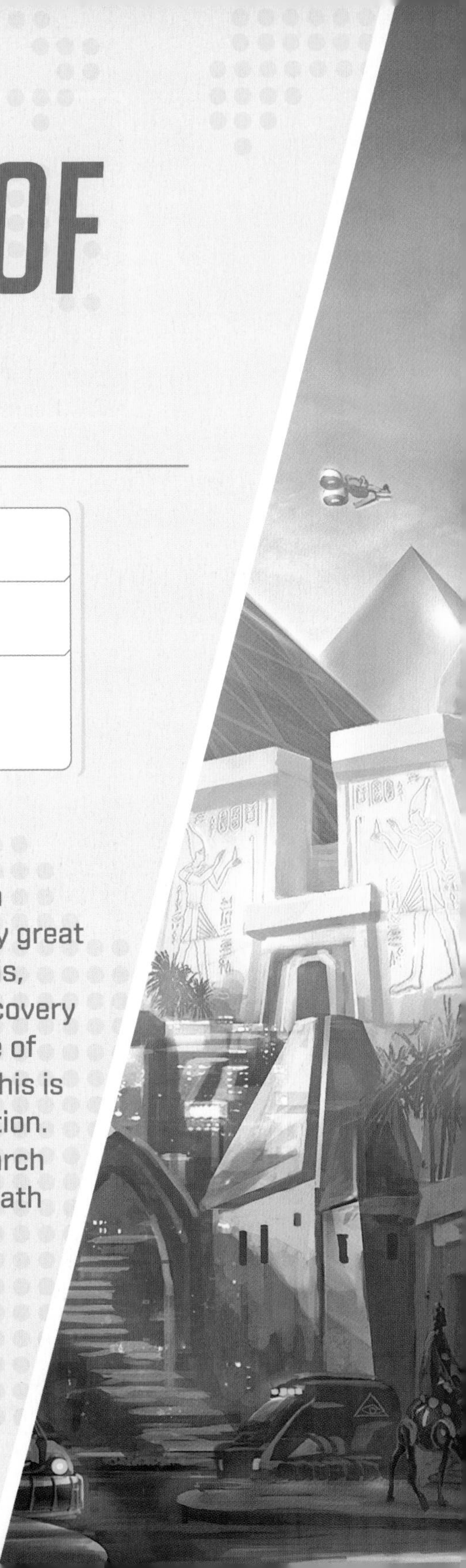

A	OBJECTIVE DETAILS: **ASSAULT**
	COUNTRY: **EGYPT**
	FLAG: 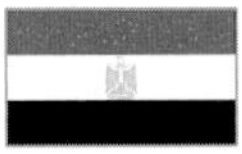

MYSTERY IN THE DESERT

You may have heard of the Giza Plateau in Egypt, home to many great pyramids. After the Omnic Crisis, explorers unearthed a new discovery in the desert sands: the Temple of Anubis. Many don't know that this is more than just a tourist attraction. It hides the entrance to a research facility that extends deep beneath the earth. Only a few agents at Helix Security International, the private firm that guards the facility, know what they're protecting.

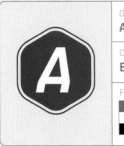

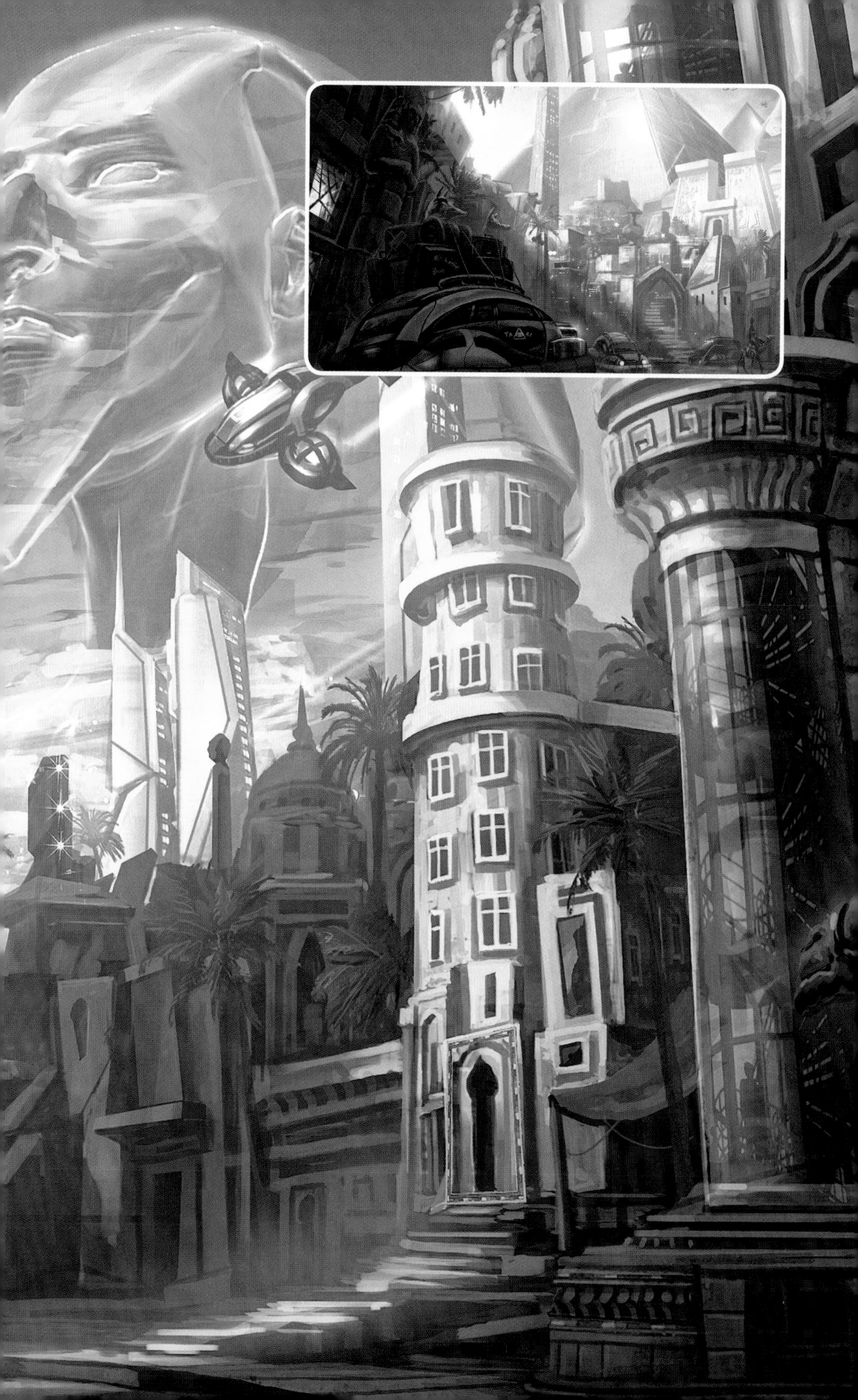

MAP

VOLSKAYA INDUSTRIES

A

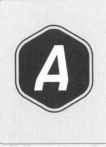

OBJECTIVE DETAILS:
ASSAULT

COUNTRY:
RUSSIA

FLAG:

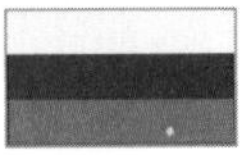

WHERE MECHS ARE BORN

After Russia was nearly destroyed by the Omnic Crisis, it took years for the country to recover—but it did, by becoming a center of cutting-edge technology. When the Siberian omnium became active again, churning out battle-ready omnics, the Russians were prepared. Volskaya Industries produces Svyatogor mechs—huge robots piloted by humans—capable of confronting new omnic threats head-on.

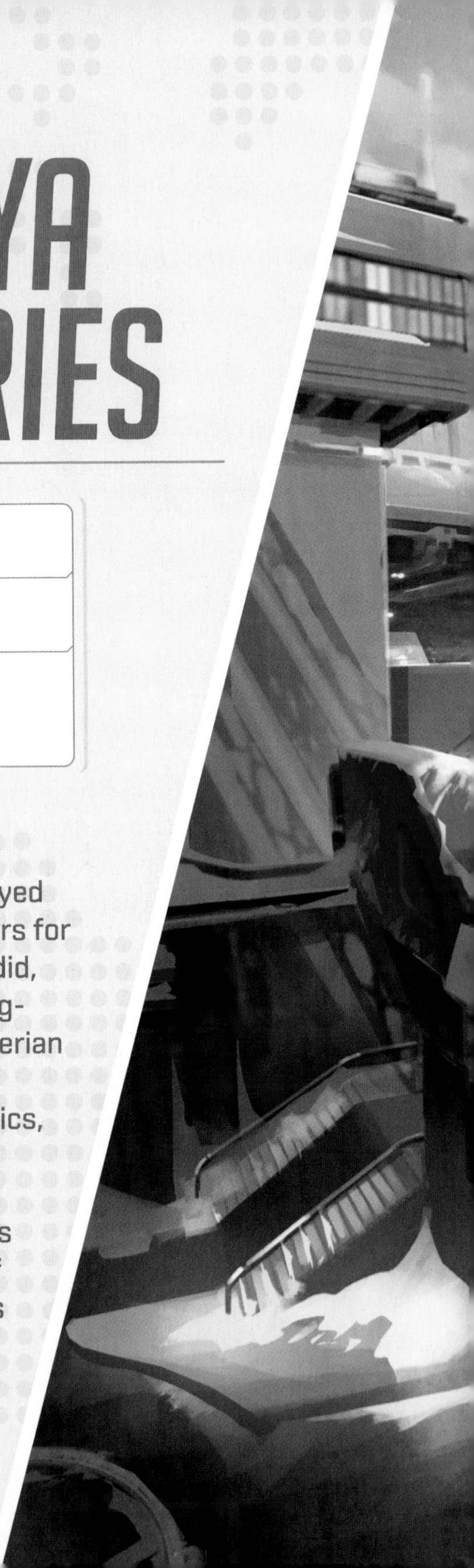

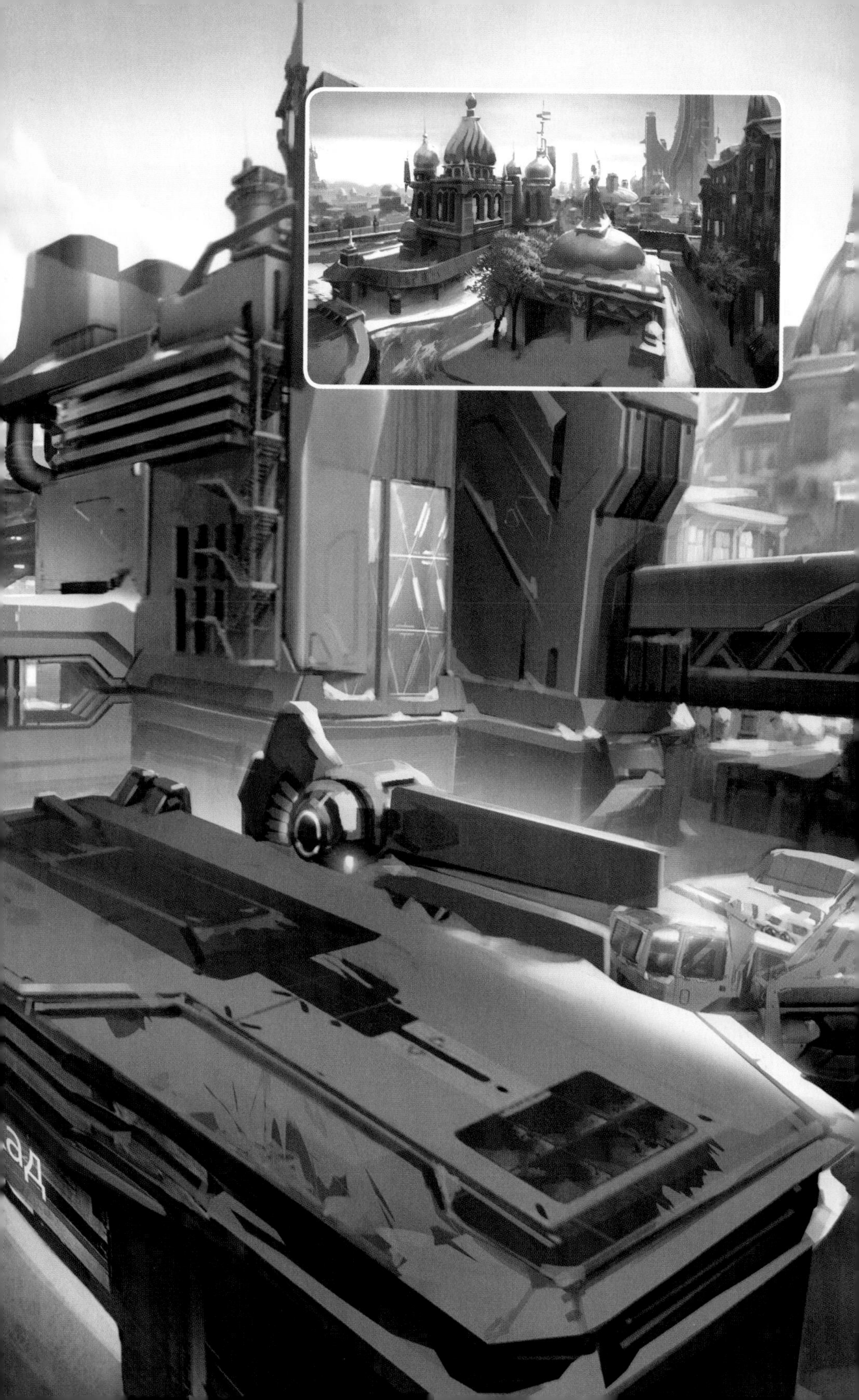

MAP

DORADO

OBJECTIVE DETAILS:	ESCORT
COUNTRY:	MEXICO
FLAG:	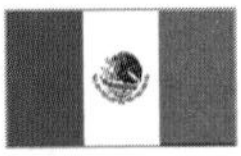

A NEW ERA DAWNS

During the Omnic Crisis, the country of Mexico was plunged into darkness due to a destroyed power grid. Each year, residents remember this dark time with the Festival de la Luz. But a new day is about to dawn in Dorado, with the opening of fusion plants providing clean, free energy to the Mexican people.

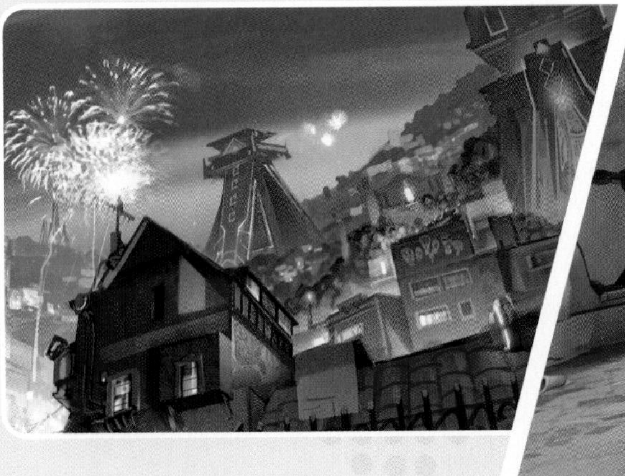

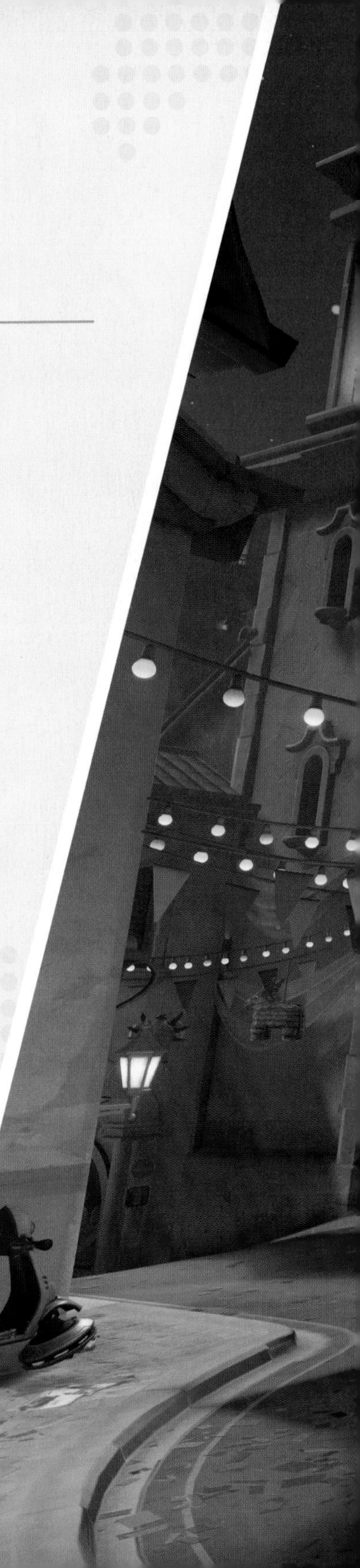

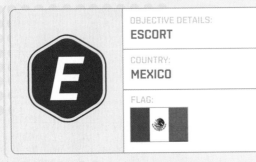

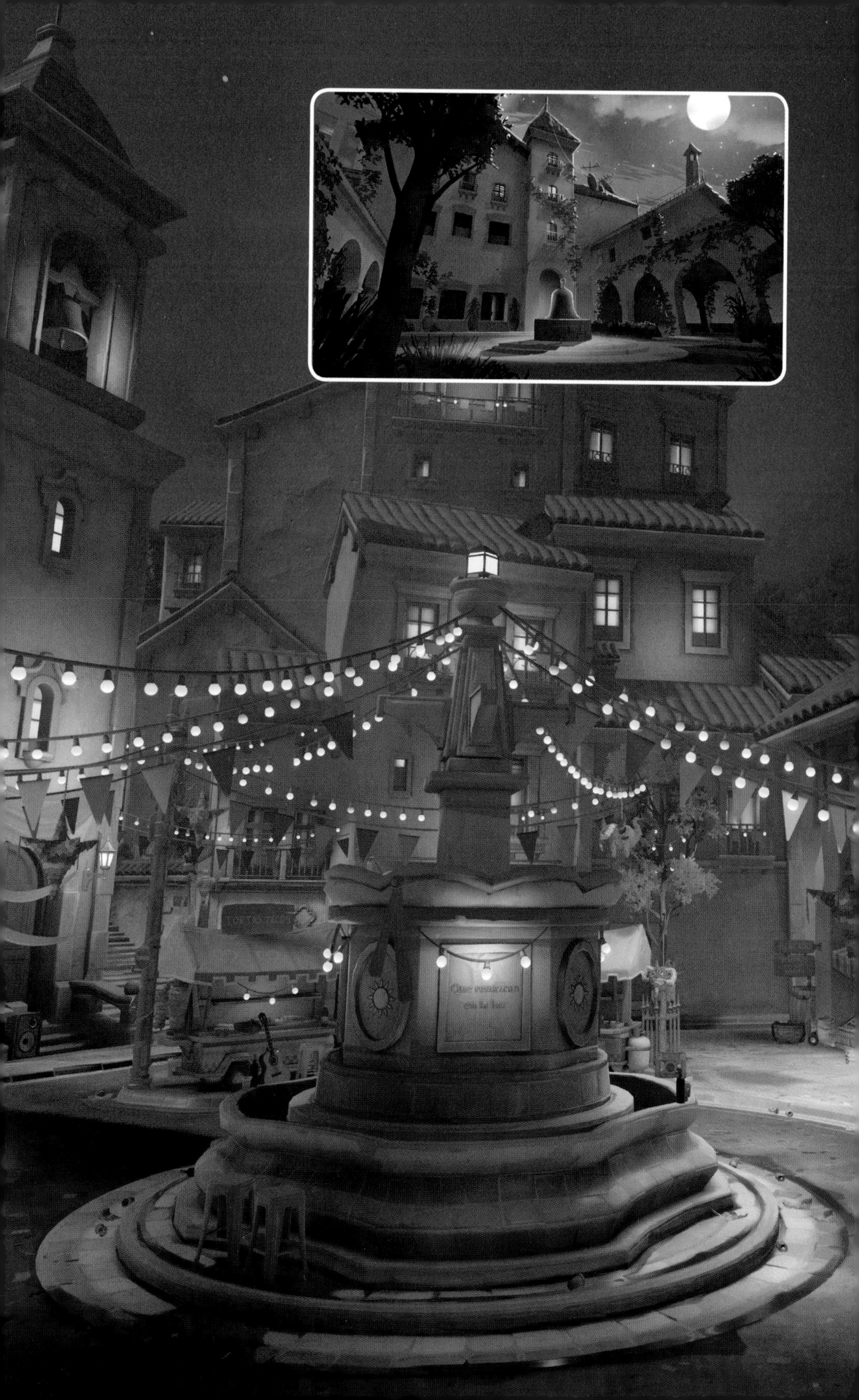

MAP

JUNKERTOWN

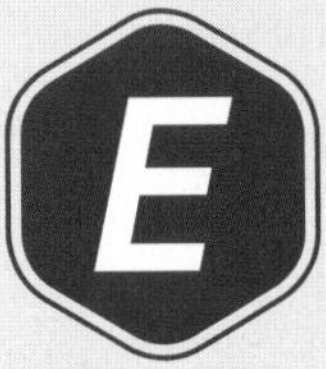

OBJECTIVE DETAILS:
ESCORT

COUNTRY:
AUSTRALIA

FLAG:

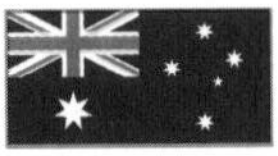

SALVAGING VICTORY

Not all Omniums are abandoned. Australia's was claimed by a group of lawless scavengers called the Junkers. Here, competitors risk everything in a massive arena called the Scrapyard—and try not to get on the bad side of the town's vicious queen. Life without rules can be exciting, but it can also get . . . explosive. Especially when Junkrat's involved!

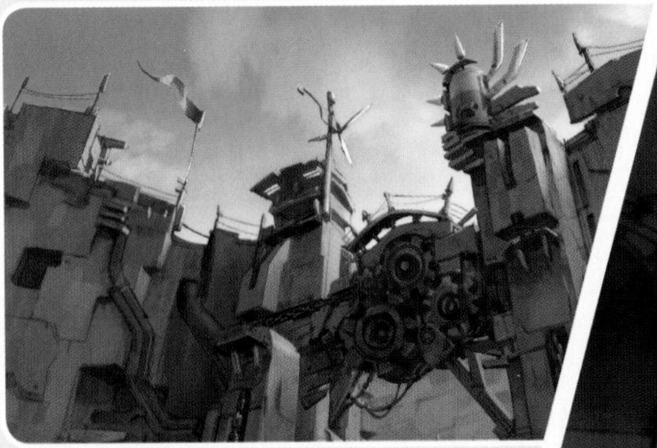

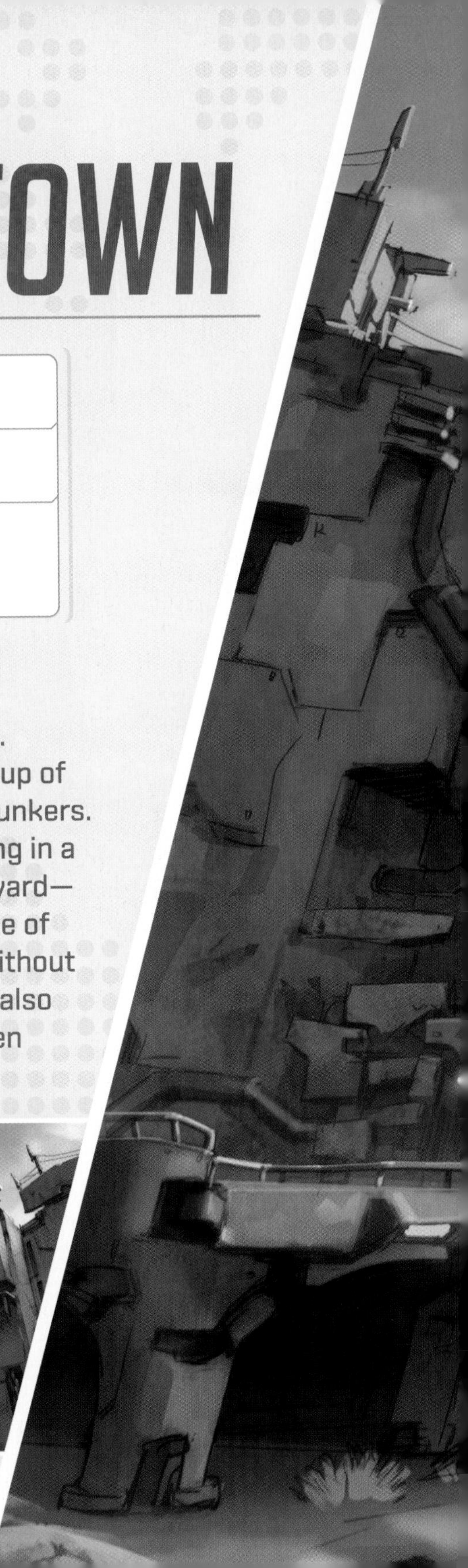

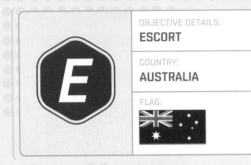

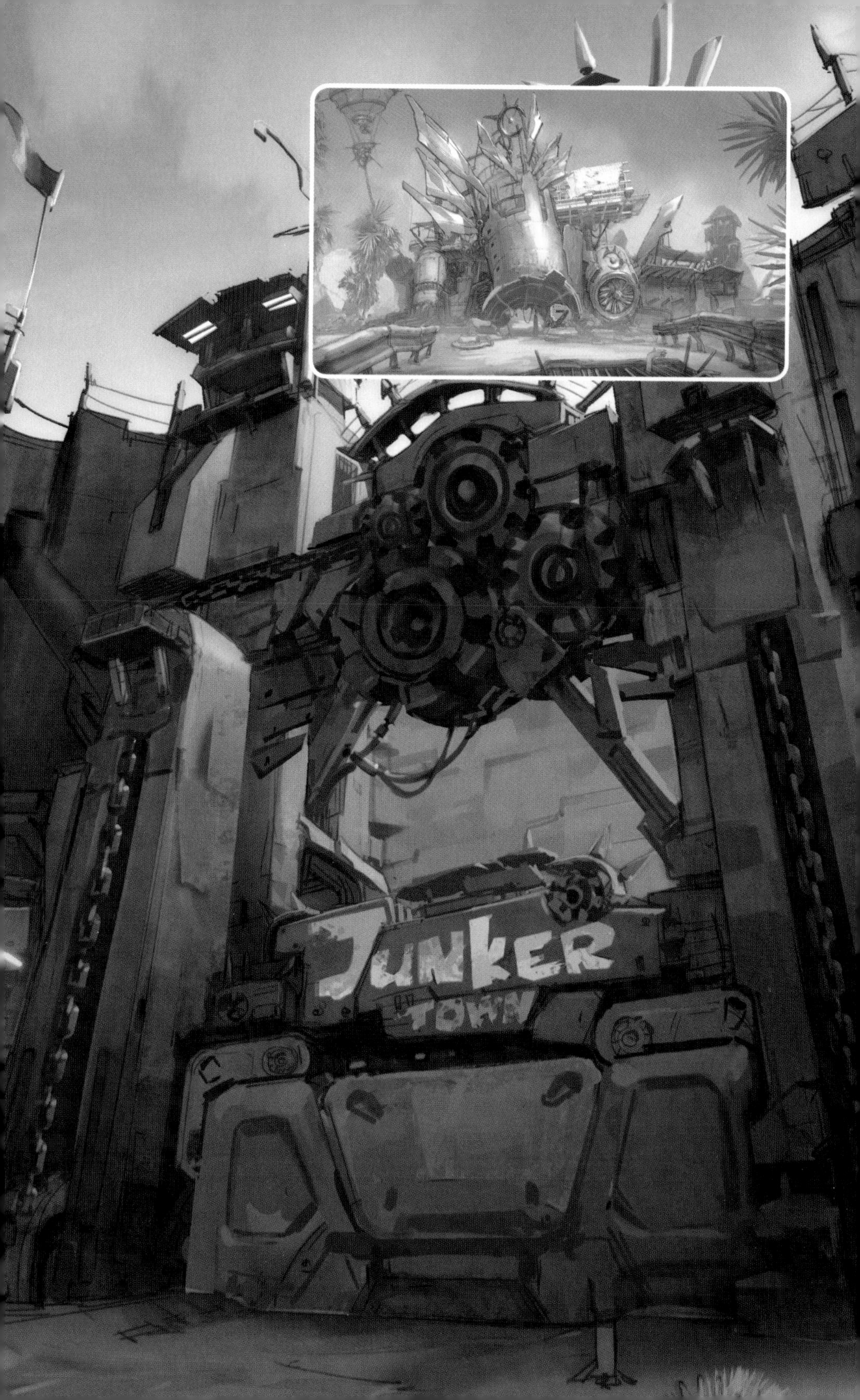
JUNKER
TOWN

RIALTO

	OBJECTIVE DETAILS:
E	**ESCORT**
	COUNTRY:
	ITALY
	FLAG:

Rialto was home to the notorious Talon agent Antonio Bartalotti's estate and the backdrop of the infamous "Venice Incident." The Italian government has taken great steps to maintain the picturesque landscape of Venice. Tourists visiting this Italian town can enjoy a gondola ride down the canals or simply take in the sights with a leisurely stroll through the winding cobblestone streets.

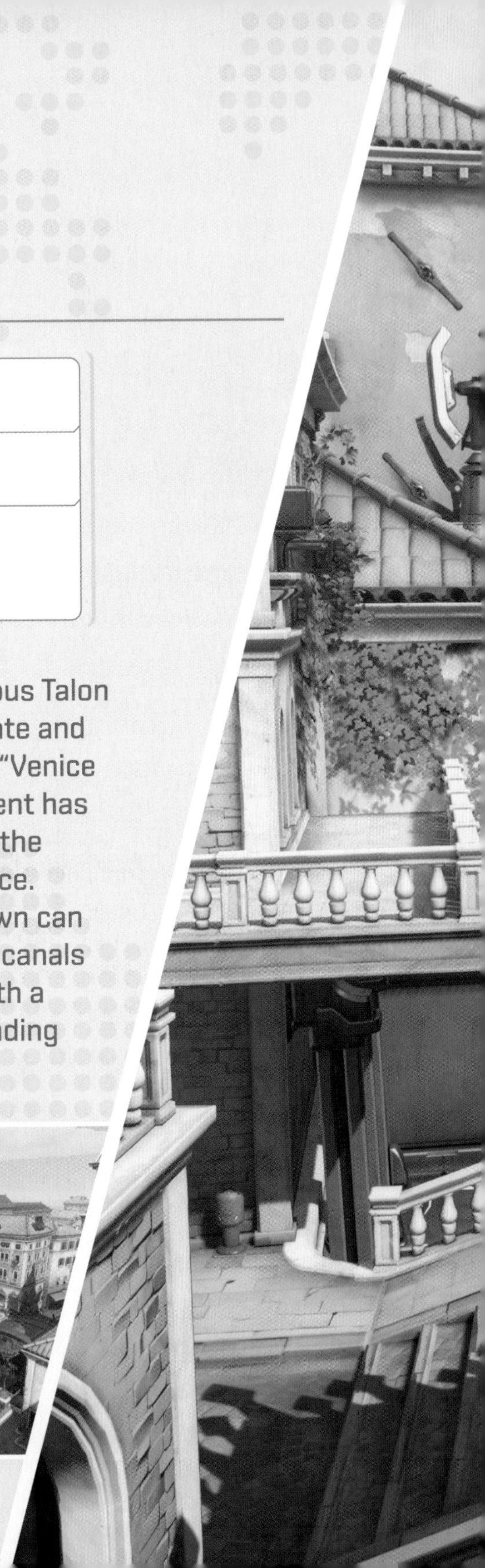

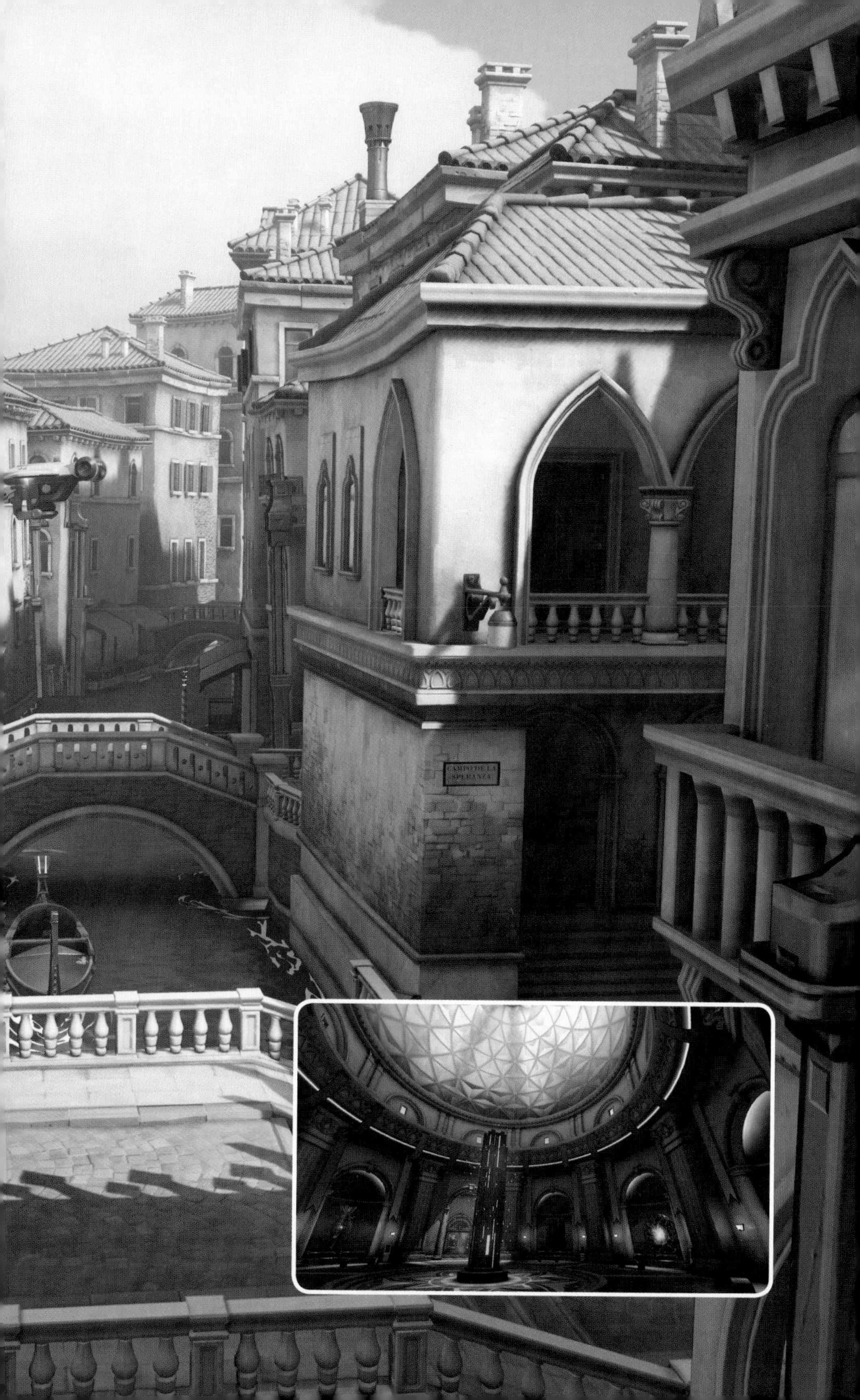

MAP

ROUTE 66

OBJECTIVE DETAILS:	ESCORT
COUNTRY:	USA
FLAG:	

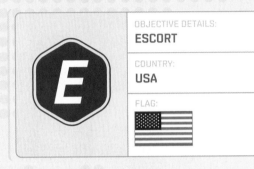

HOME TO OUTLAWS

This highway was once America's most popular road, lined with gleaming diners and roadside attractions. Today, most of the gas stations, shops, and restaurants are empty. A cross-country train runs along the route, and passengers stare out the windows at ghost towns, like Deadlock Gorge, as they pass by. But Deadlock Gorge isn't totally deserted—it is home to the notorious Deadlock Gang, and they're about to make their biggest heist yet.

SCENIC VIEW

HISTORIC
ROUTE
US
66
ROUTE

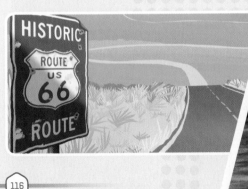

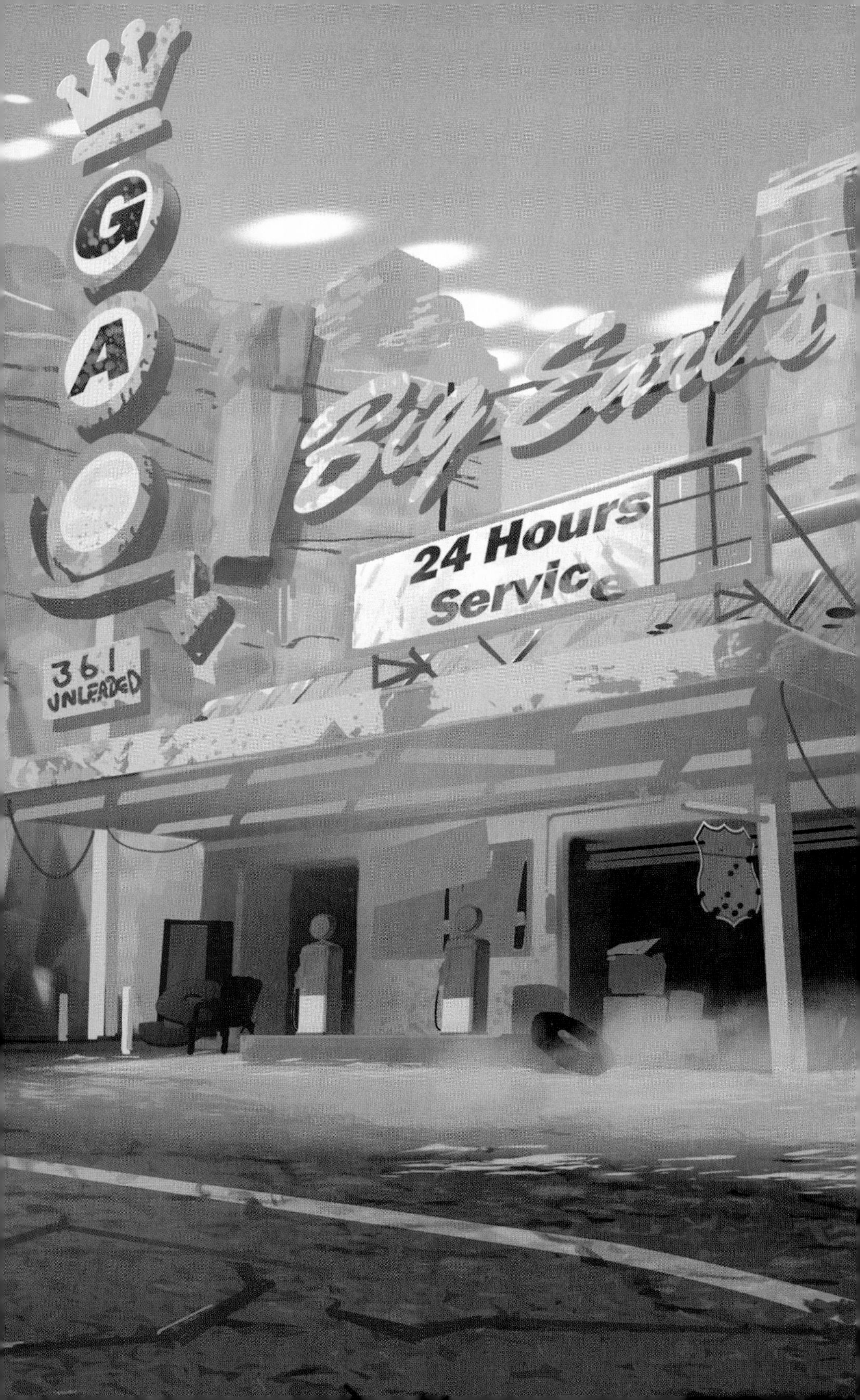

G
A
Big Earl's
24 Hours
Service
361
UNLEADED

MAP

WATCHPOINT: GIBRALTAR

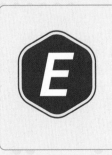

	OBJECTIVE DETAILS: **ESCORT**
E	TERRITORY: **GIBRALTAR**
	FLAG:

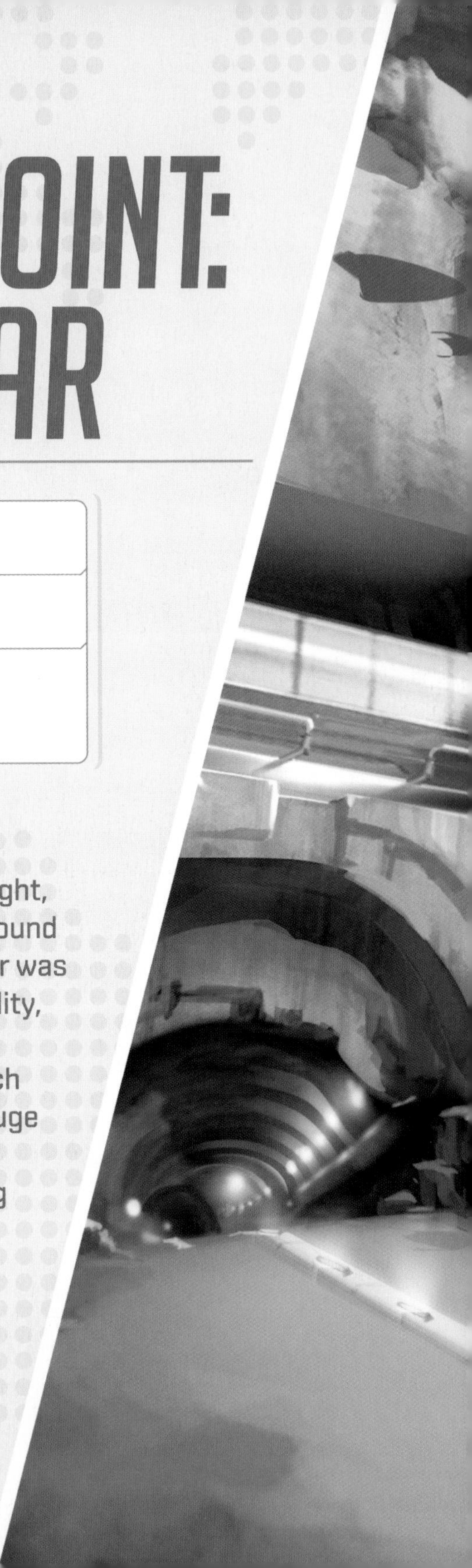

EYES TO THE SKIES

When Overwatch was at its height, it established several bases around the world. Watchpoint: Gibraltar was set up as an orbital launch facility, a spaceport designed to send spacecraft into orbit. Overwatch veteran Winston has taken refuge here. Sensing that the world needed help, he began recalling former Overwatch agents and putting them back into action.

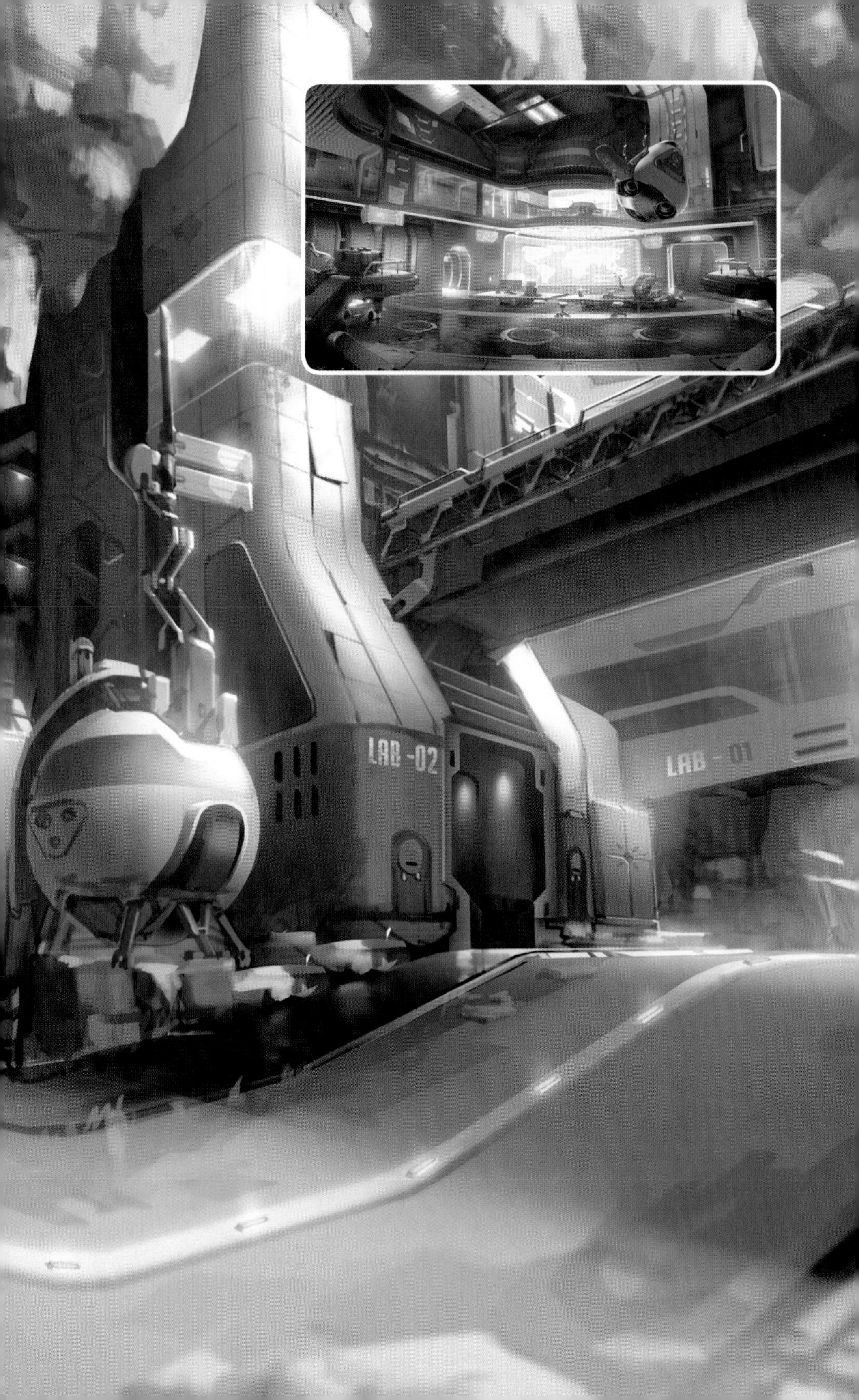
LAB -02
LAB - 01

MAP

BLIZZARD WORLD

OBJECTIVE DETAILS:
ASSAULT/ESCORT

COUNTRY:
USA

FLAG:

EPIC FUN

Explore the cathedrals of *Diablo*, the command centers of *StarCraft*, and the streets of Stormwind in *World of Warcraft* all in one place! Blizzard Entertainment has opened a theme park, attracting heroes and villains alike. Play some cards in the *Hearthstone* tavern or visit the *Heroes of the Storm* arcade while you guide the payload to the throne of the Skeleton King! The monsters aren't real here, but the fun is—so long as everyone plays nice.

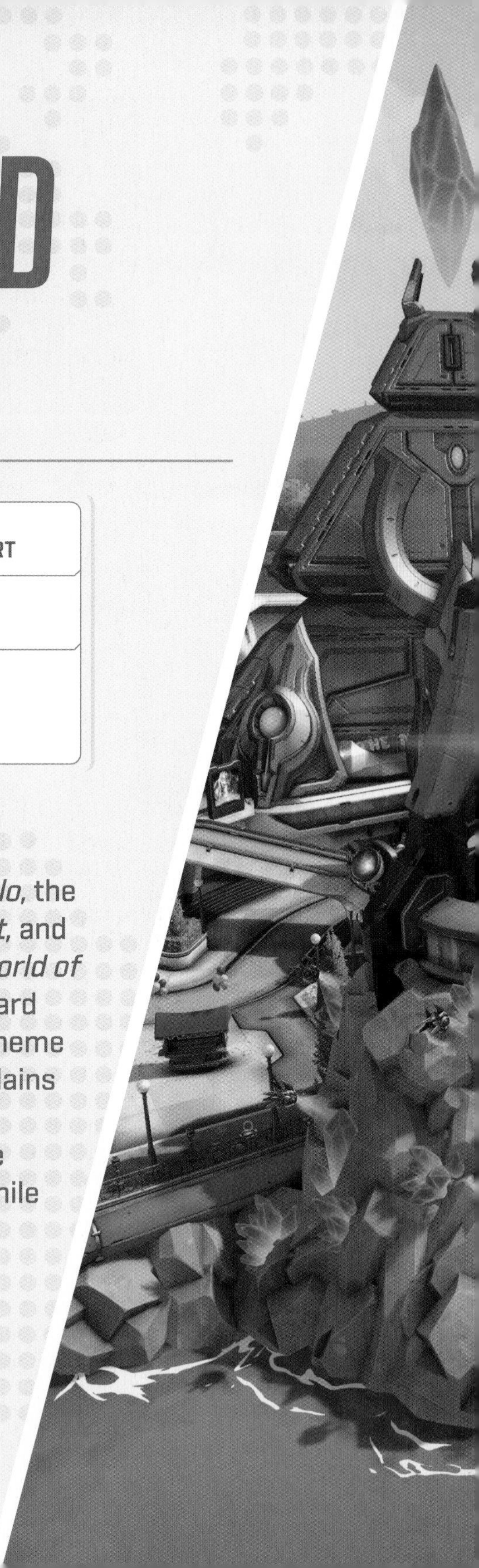

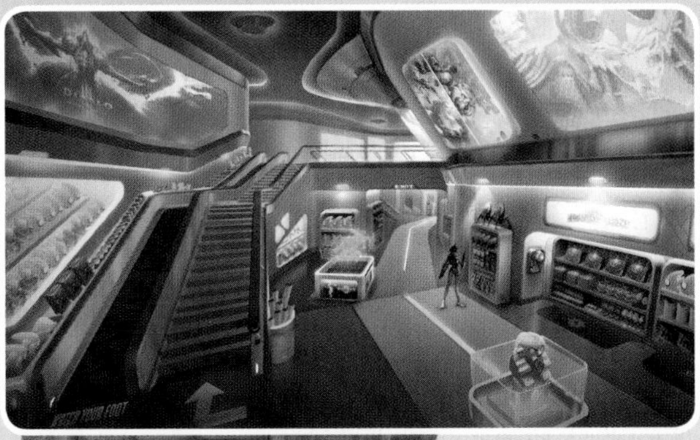

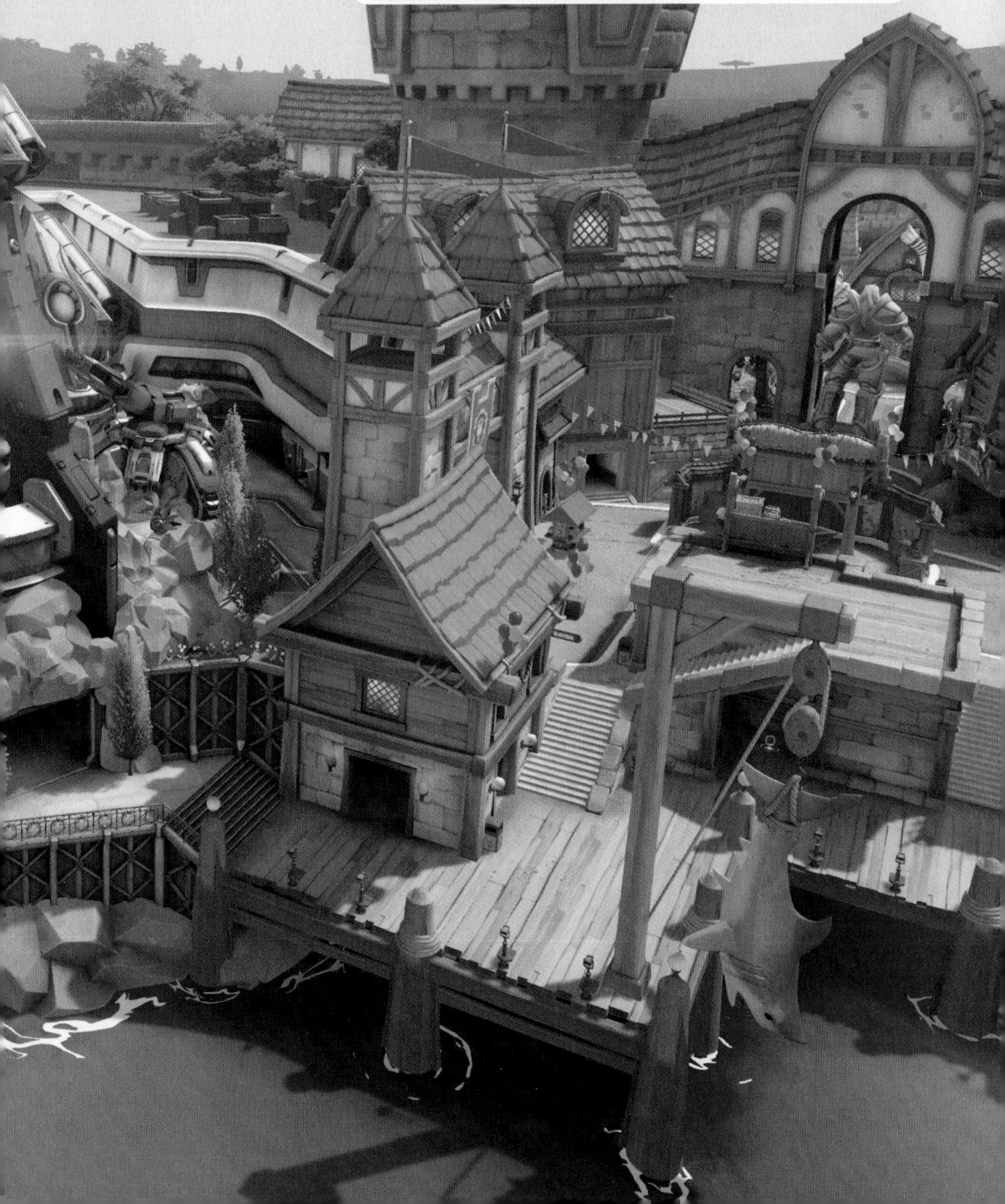

MAP

EICHENWALDE

OBJECTIVE DETAILS:
ASSAULT/ESCORT

COUNTRY:
GERMANY

FLAG:

A HEARTFELT RETURN

This castle town was abandoned after one of the most well-known battles of the Omnic Crisis. Many Crusaders lost their lives to the omnic army, but Balderich von Adler led them to a slim victory with the help of Reinhardt. Balderich's armor remains on the throne where he fell, but some believe it's time to disturb those old ghosts.

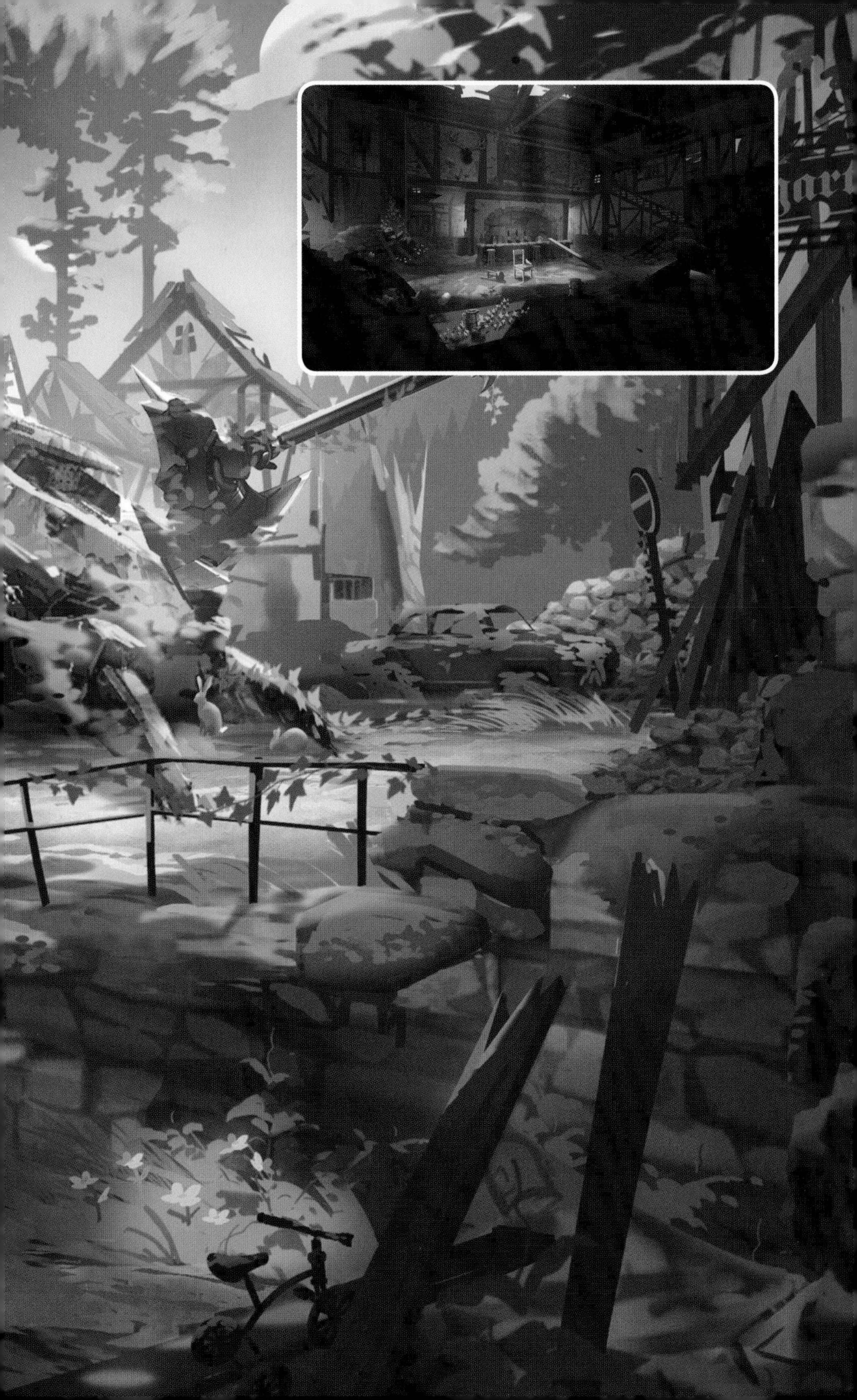

MAP
HOLLYWOOD

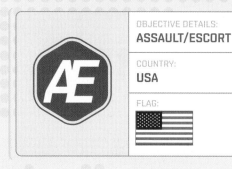

OBJECTIVE DETAILS:	ASSAULT/ESCORT
COUNTRY:	USA
FLAG:	

TROUBLE IN TINSELTOWN

Hollywood survived the Omnic Crisis with all its glitz and glamour intact. Palm trees line the streets. Movie stars, directors, and high-powered studio executives work here. These days, one of the popular directors is a robot: HAL-Fred Glitchbot, creator of *They Came from Beyond the Moon* and *Six-Gun Killer*. But while Glitchbot has his fans, he has been targeted by the anti-omnic movement thanks to his outspoken opinions. Will this robot's real-life story end in tragedy or triumph?

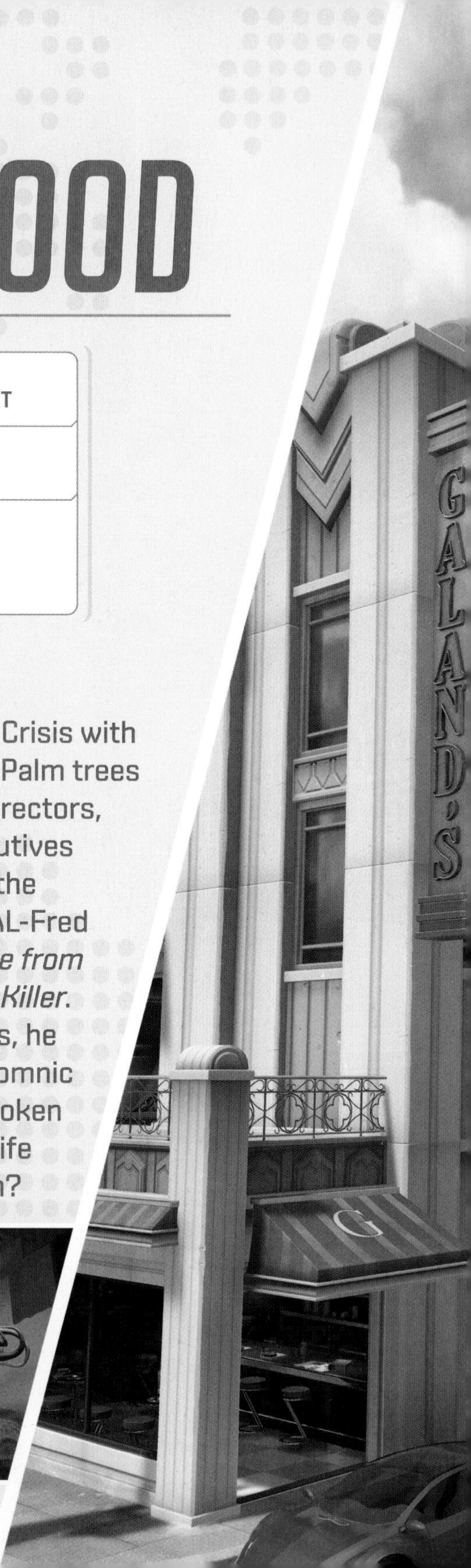
GALAND'S
G

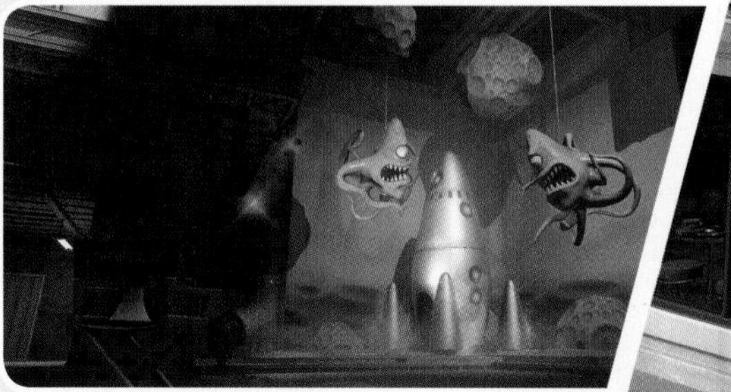

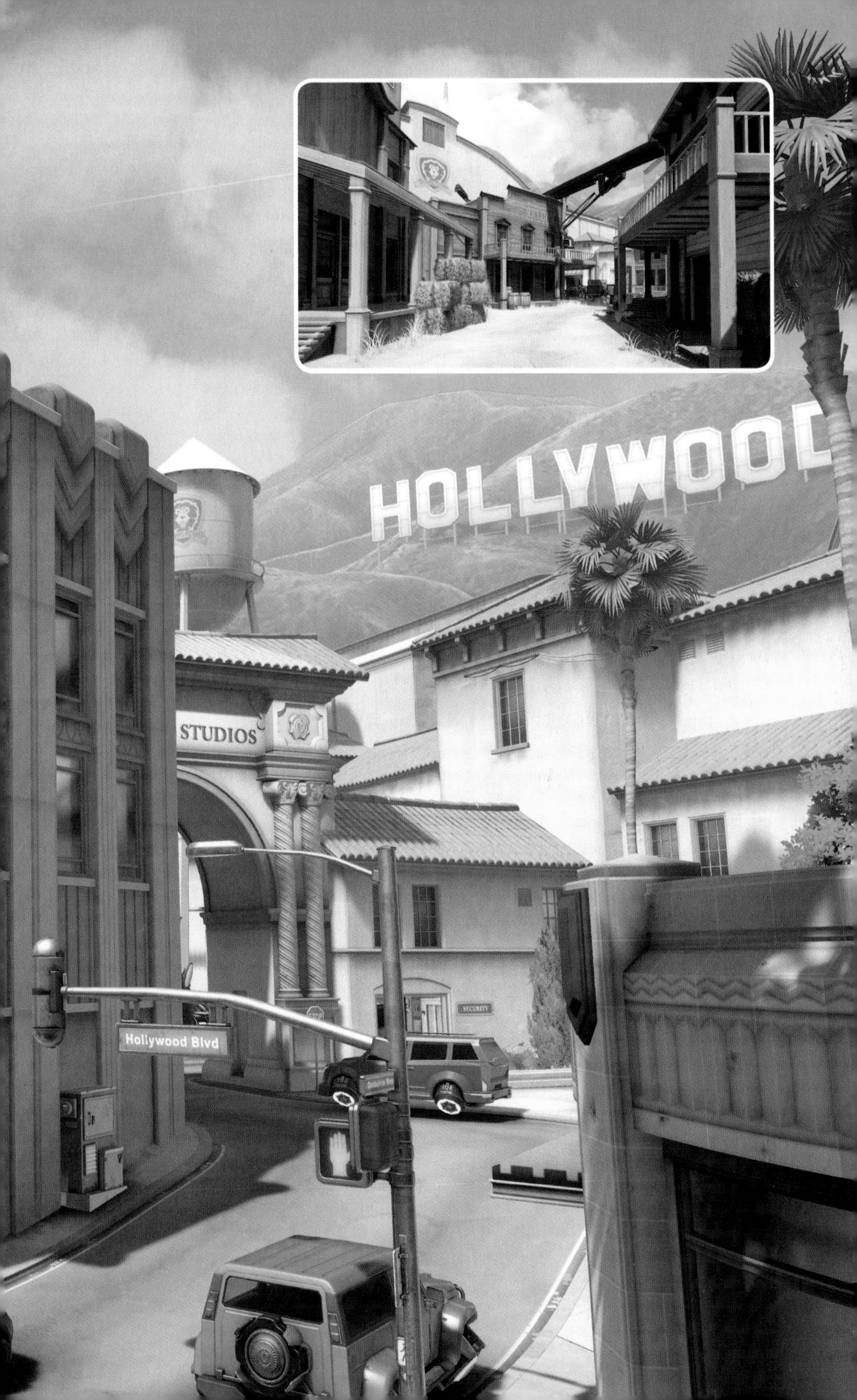
HOLLYWOOD
STUDIOS
SECURITY
Hollywood Blvd

MAP

KING'S ROW

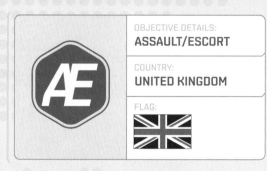

OBJECTIVE DETAILS:
ASSAULT/ESCORT

COUNTRY:
UNITED KINGDOM

FLAG:

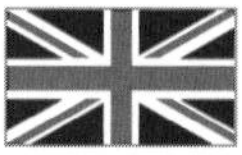

THE CITY BENEATH THE CITY

King's Row is a busy, thriving neighborhood in London—thanks to the labor of omnic robots. Those robot workers have been denied basic rights and are forced to live in a crowded city underneath the streets of London known as "the Underworld." Some humans support the omnics, but protesters recently clashed violently with police during a pro-omnic demonstration. Tensions are running high and like a powder keg, Kings Row is about to blow.

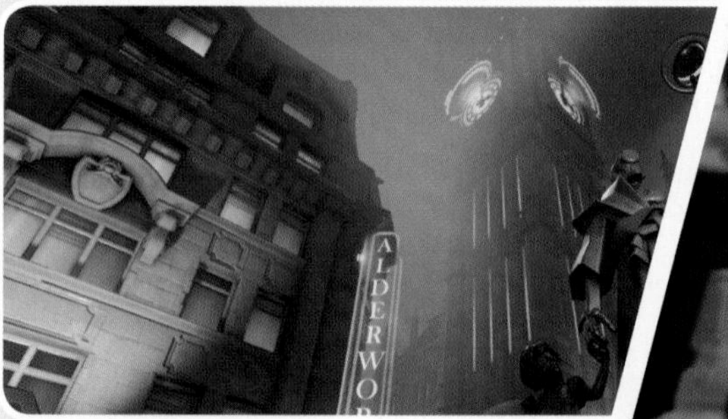

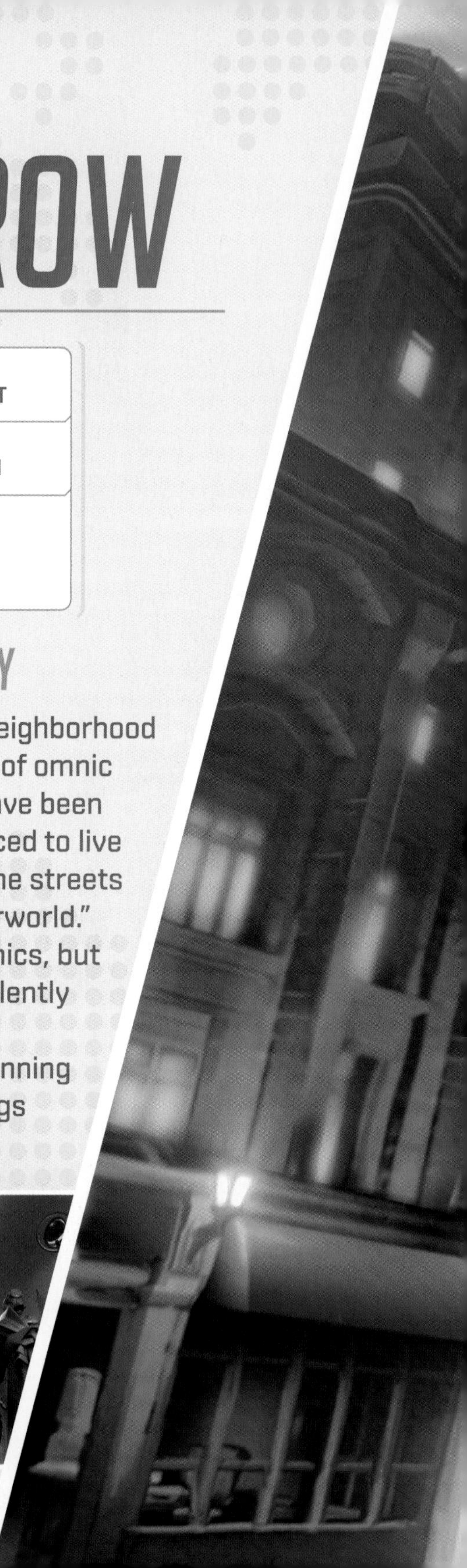

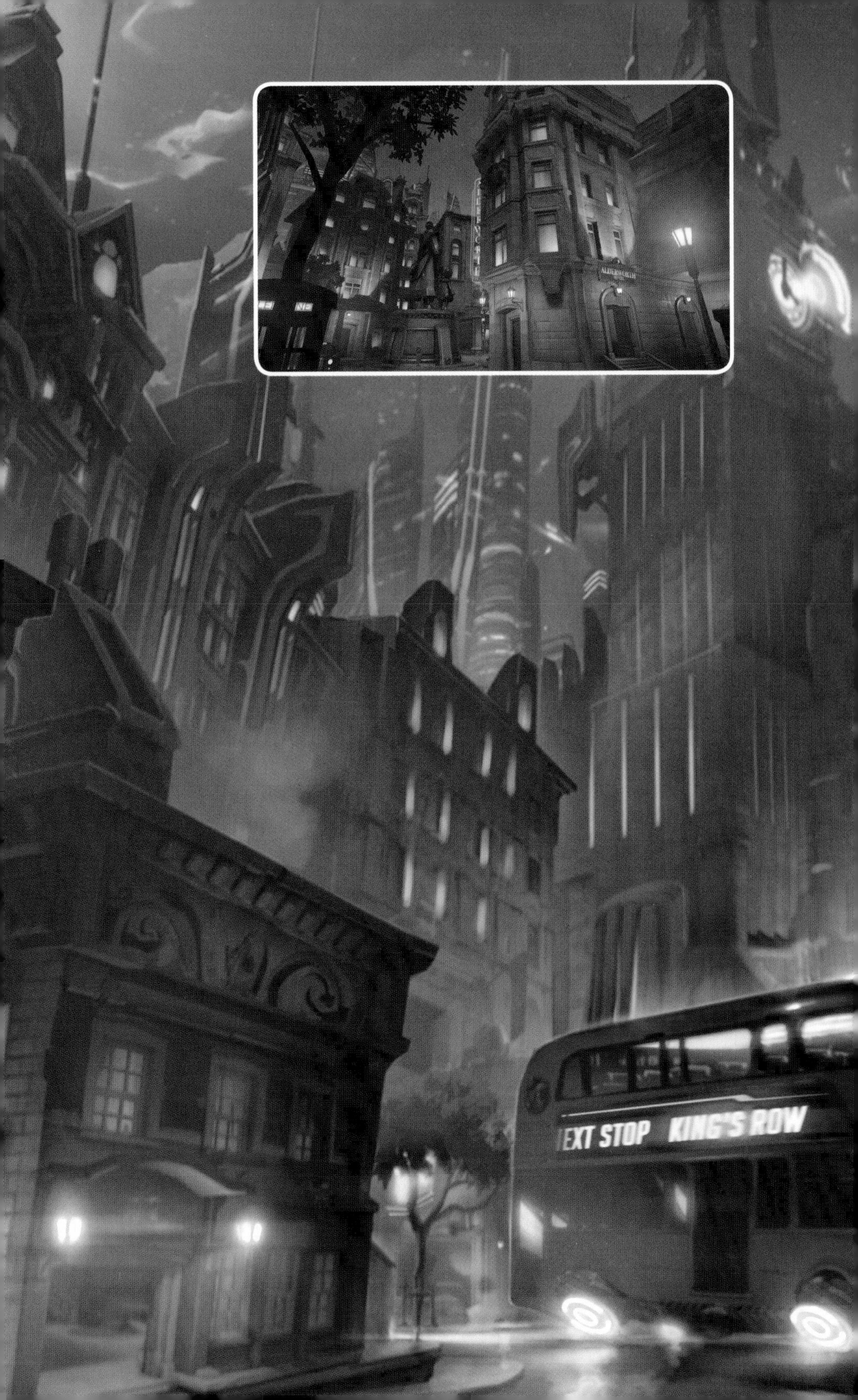
EXT STOP KING'S ROW

MAP

NUMBANI

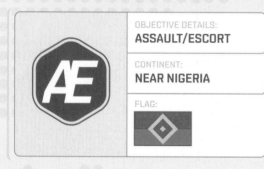

OBJECTIVE DETAILS:	ASSAULT/ESCORT
CONTINENT:	NEAR NIGERIA
FLAG:	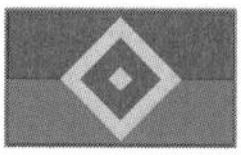

CITY OF HARMONY

Known as the "City of Harmony," Numbani is one of the few places on earth where omnics and humans live in perfect harmony. This collaboration has secured Numbani as one of the most technologically advanced cities in the world.

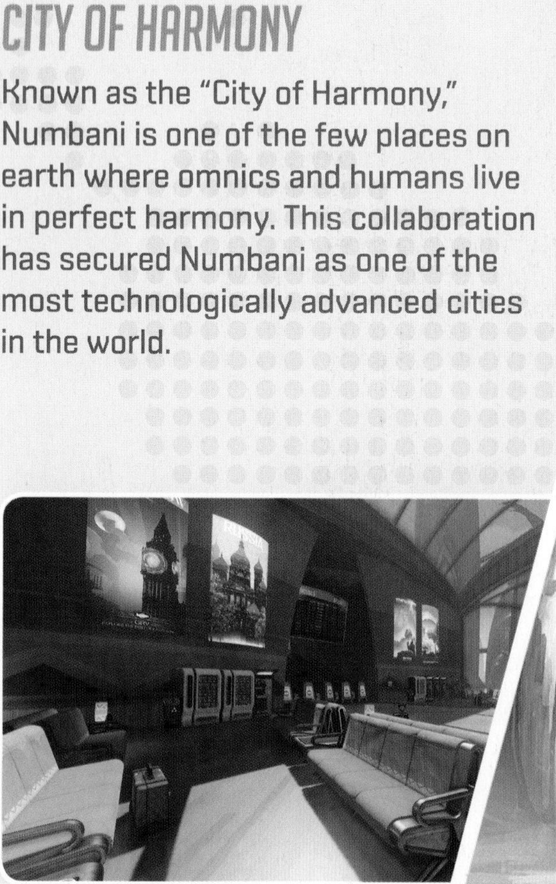

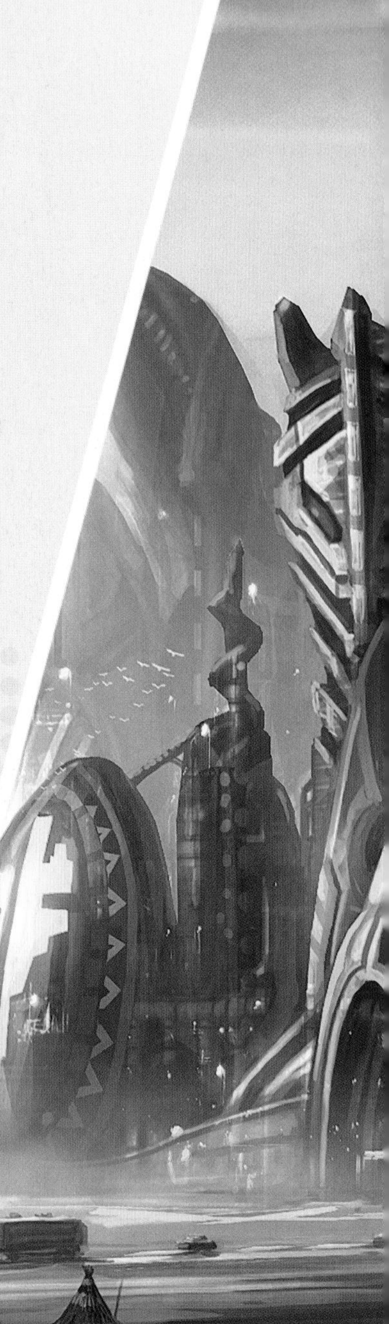

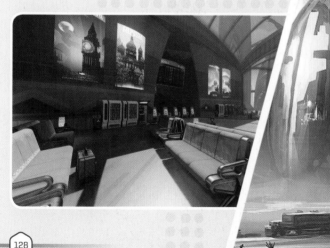

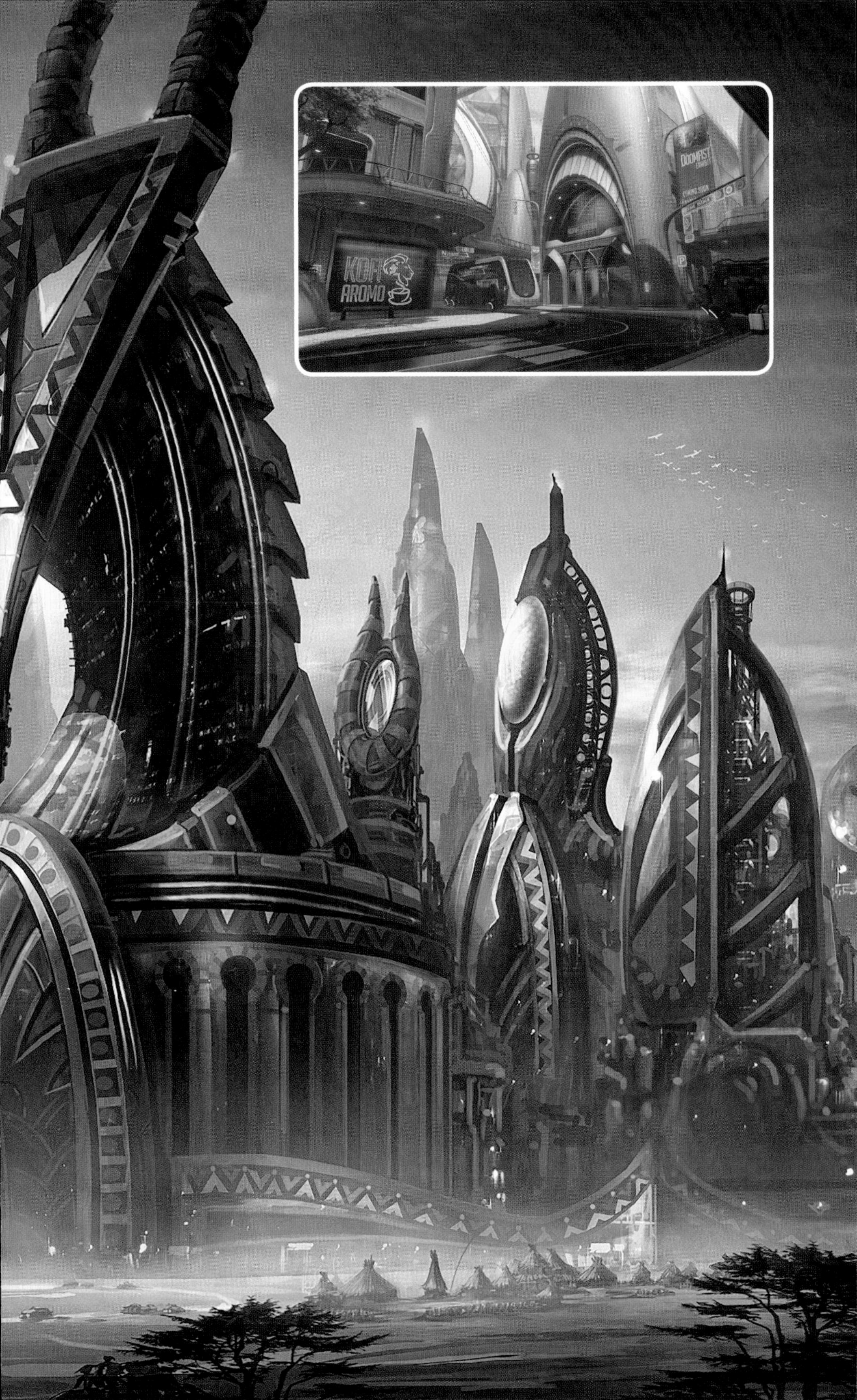

DOOMFIST
COMING SOON
KOFI AROMO
P

MAP

ILIOS

OBJECTIVE DETAILS:	CONTROL
COUNTRY:	GREECE
FLAG:	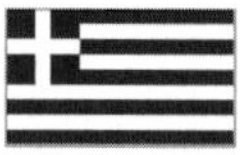

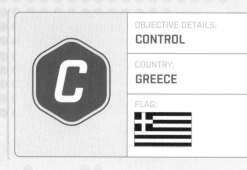

WELCOME TO PARADISE

This vacation destination is located atop a small island in the Aegean Sea. Some people come here to rest and relax, while others choose to explore the ruins scattered at the top of the island. Many ancient relics have recently been unearthed here—and Talon is poised to steal them.

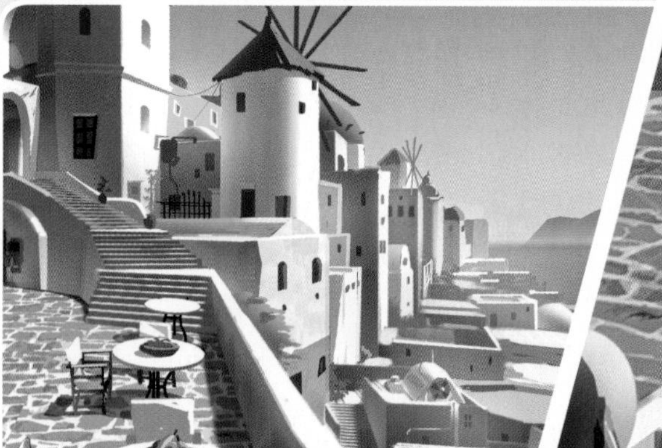

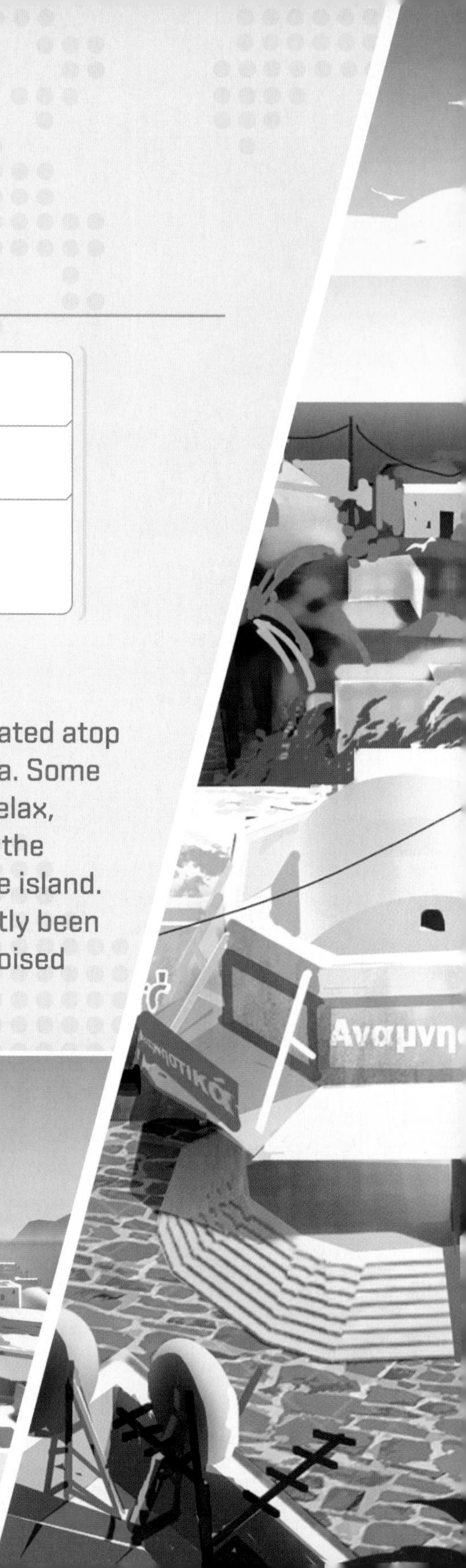

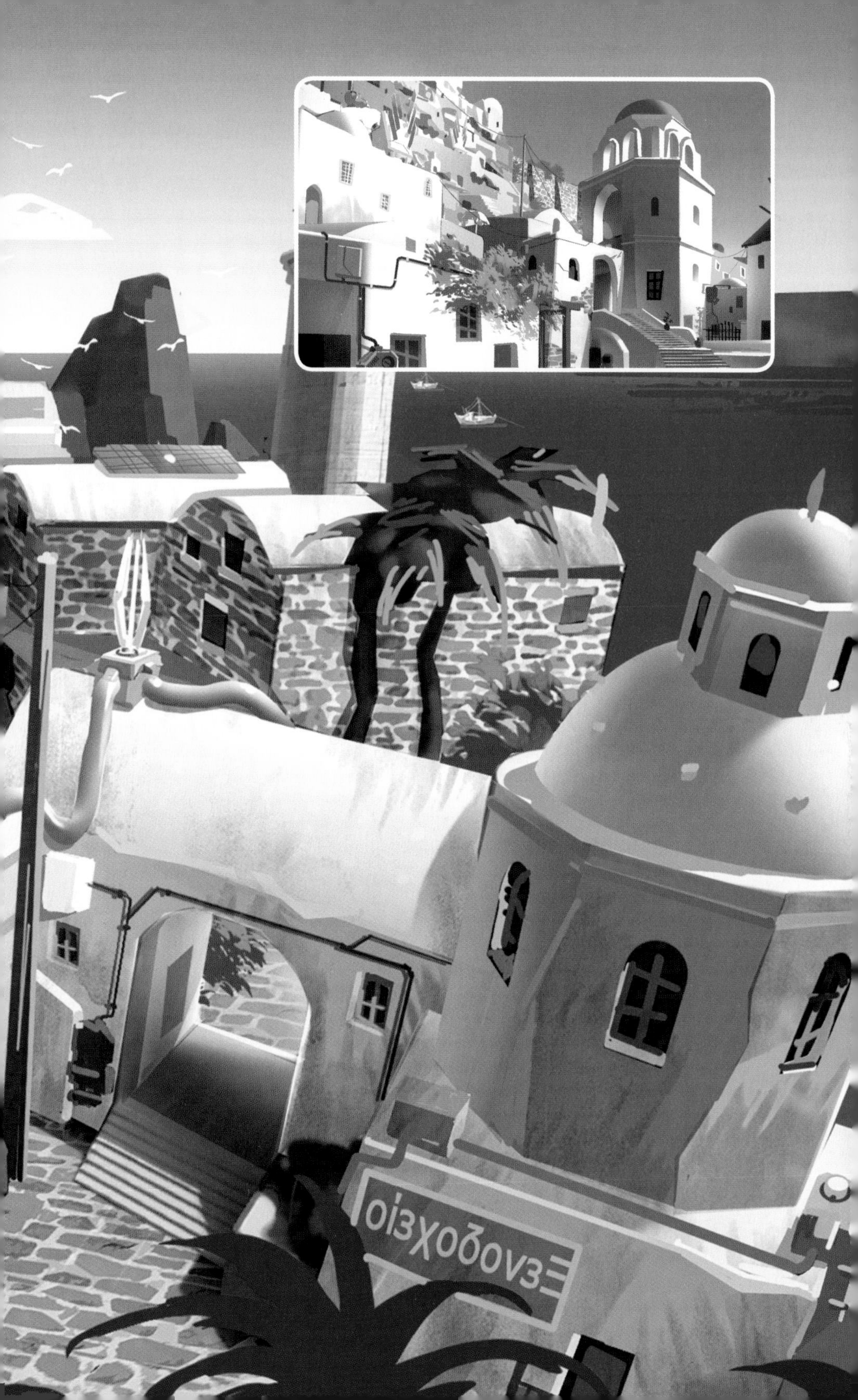

LIJIANG TOWER

	OBJECTIVE DETAILS: **CONTROL**
	COUNTRY: **CHINA**
	FLAG: 🇨🇳

SIGHTS ON SPACE

This tall, majestic tower rises up from the streets of a busy city in China, overlooking shops, gardens, and restaurants. The tower itself is owned by a company that is pushing the boundaries of space exploration. But what, exactly, does Lucheng Interstellar hope to find in the deep regions of the universe?

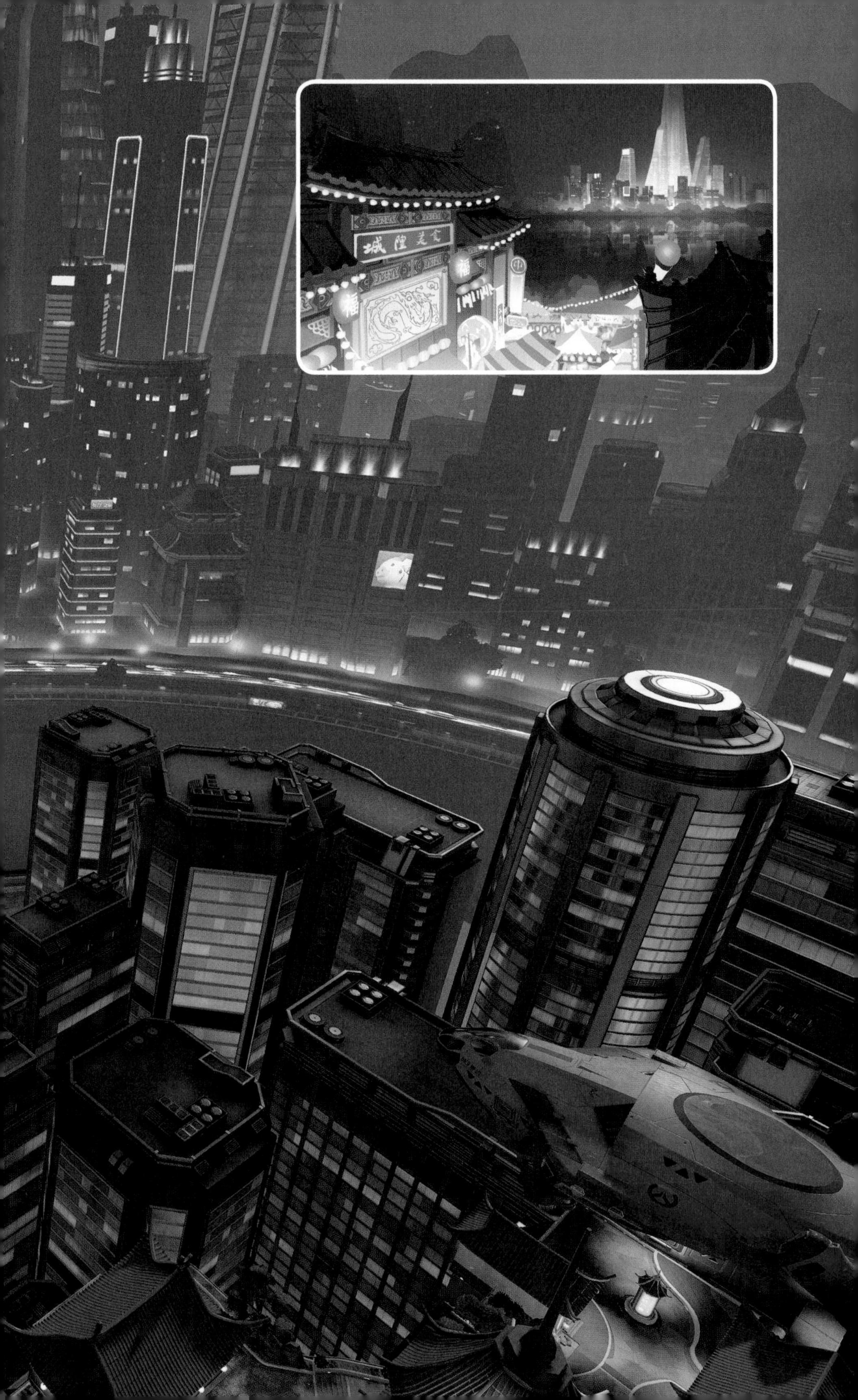
城隍美食

NEPAL

OBJECTIVE DETAILS:
CONTROL

COUNTRY:
NEPAL

FLAG:

WHERE SEEKERS GATHER

The country of Nepal has long been a destination for people seeking enlightenment. So years ago, when a group of omnics had a spiritual awakening, they came here and founded Shambali Monastery. Before his death, Tekhartha Mondatta taught them how to meditate on the meaning of existence.

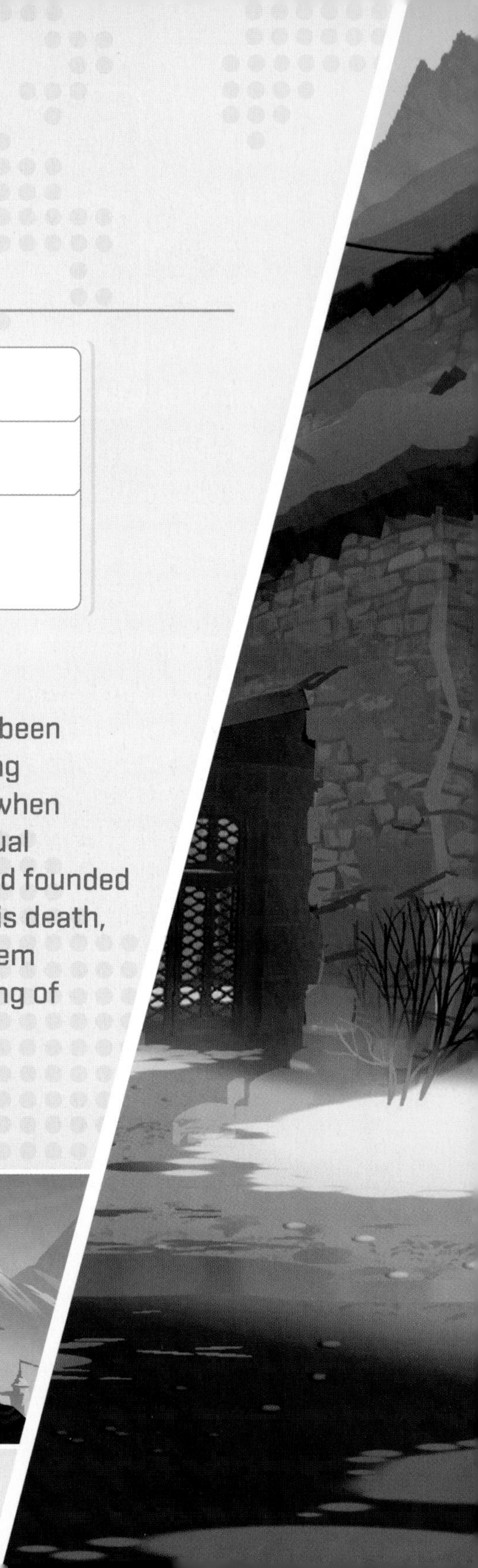

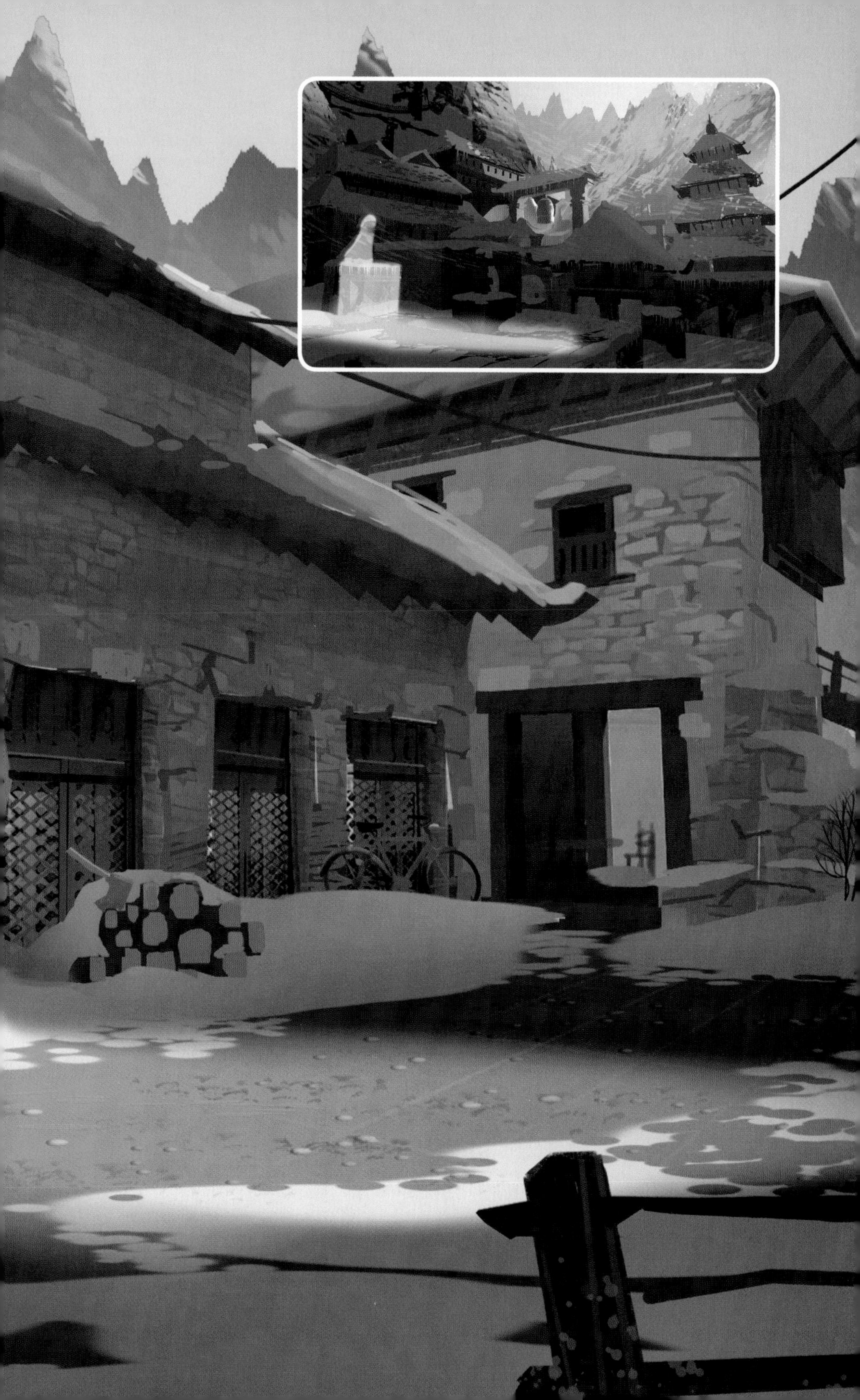

OASIS

	OBJECTIVE DETAILS: **CONTROL**
C	COUNTRY: **IRAQ**
	FLAG:

THE FUTURE BLOOMS

The safest. The finest. The most advanced. Oasis was designed for progress, to be a place where research and discovery could flourish without limit. The city was established by eight of the world's leading scientists, later bringing Moira O'Deorain into the fold as their Minister of Genetics. Oasis has the best restaurants, the tallest buildings, a library with everything ever written, and plenty of secrets that could change the world. Everyone wants a piece of this jewel, and many are willing to fight for it.

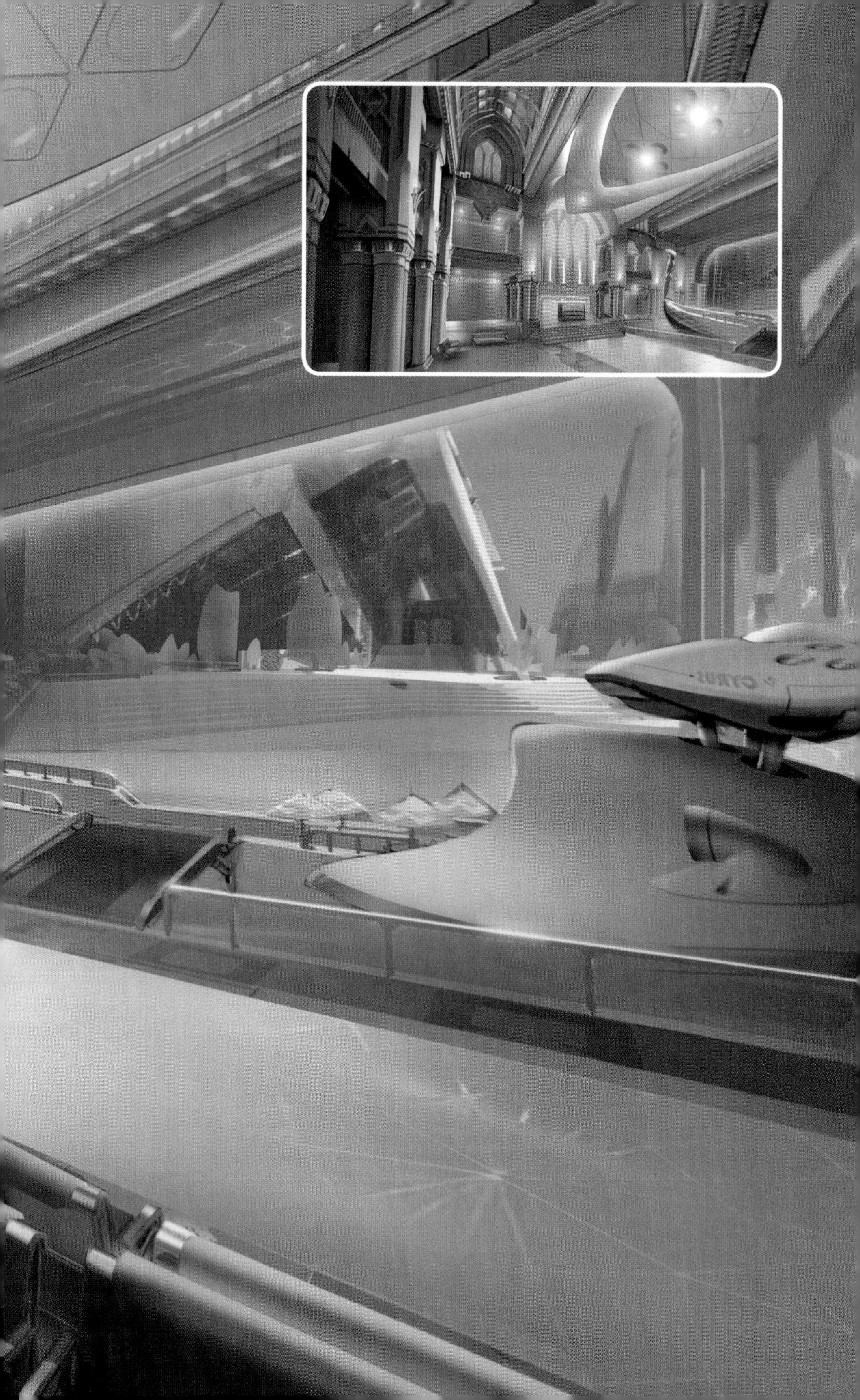
CYRUS

MAP

CHÂTEAU GUILLARD

OBJECTIVE DETAILS:	DEATHMATCH
COUNTRY:	FRANCE
FLAG:	

THE SPIDER'S WEB

This massive château is Widowmaker's ancestral home. The surrounding lake means it's the perfect hideout for someone who doesn't exist—and even here, Widowmaker barely leaves a trace. What else could be lurking in the shadows?

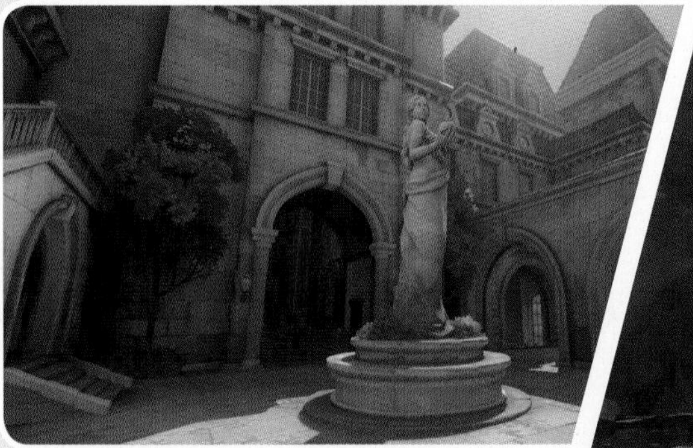

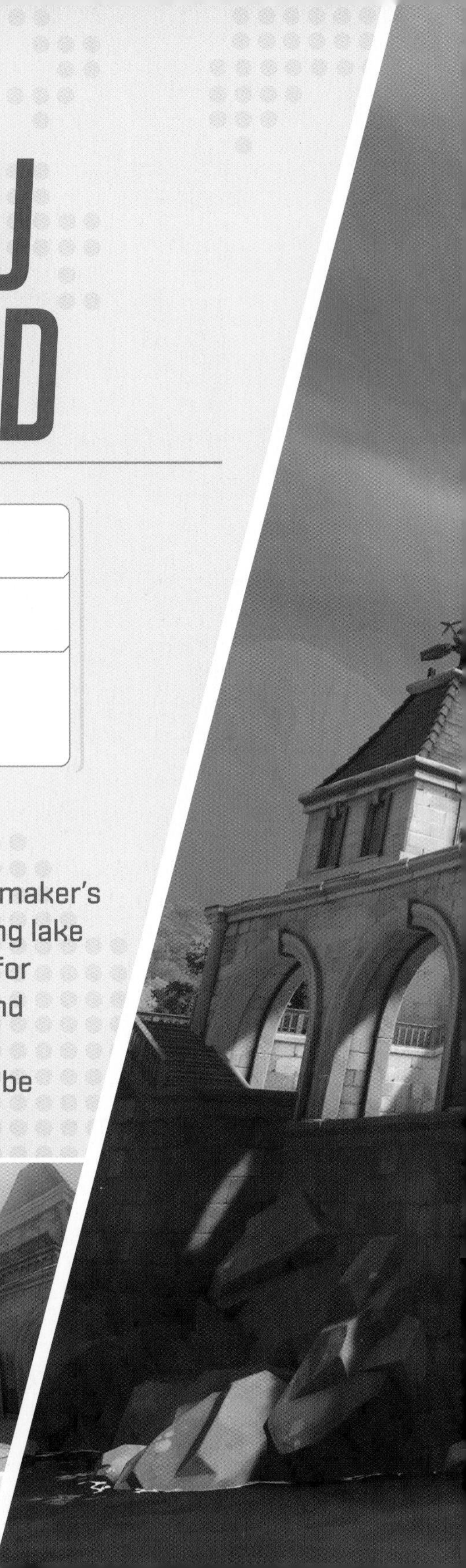

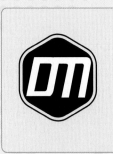

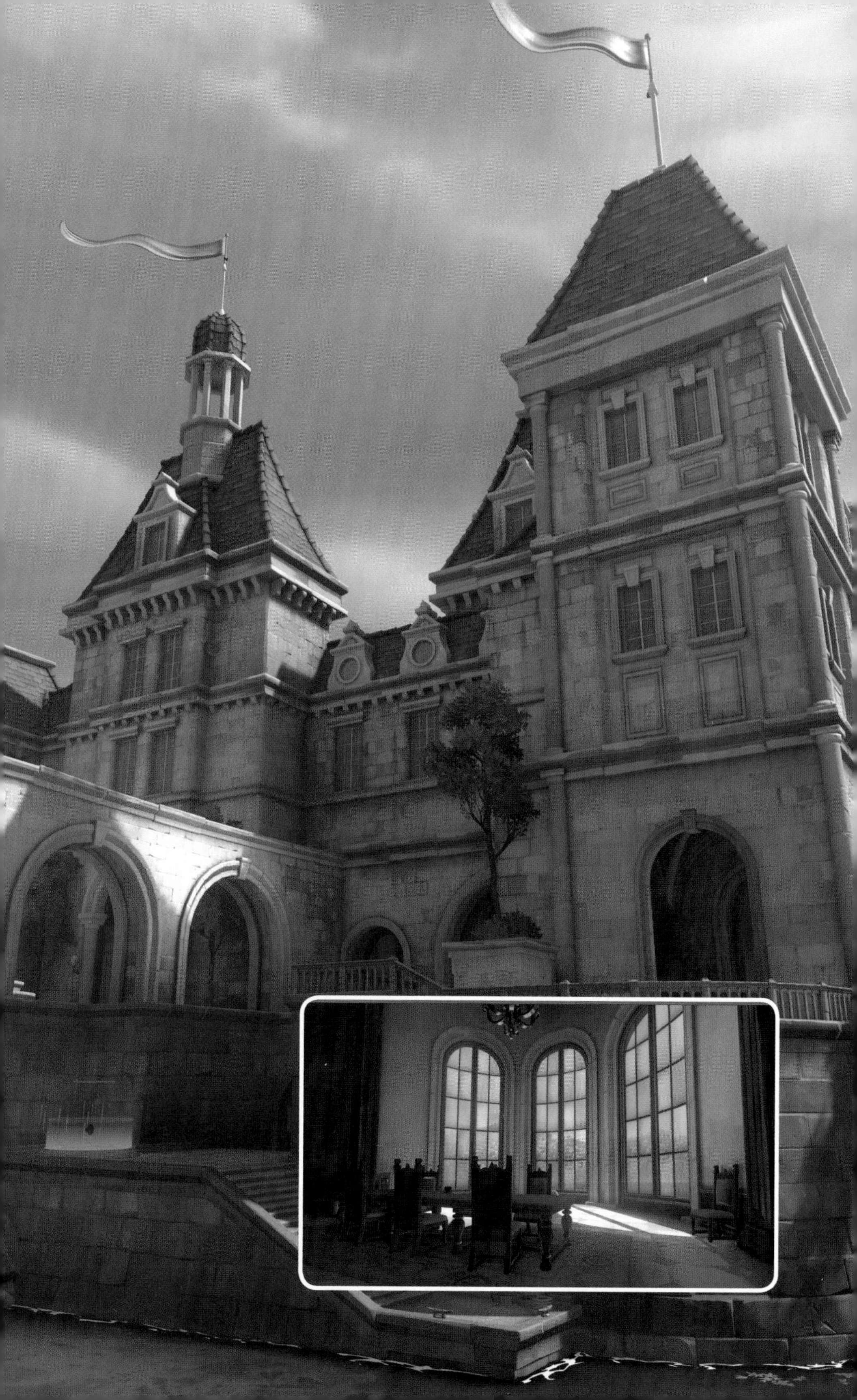

MAP

BLACK FOREST

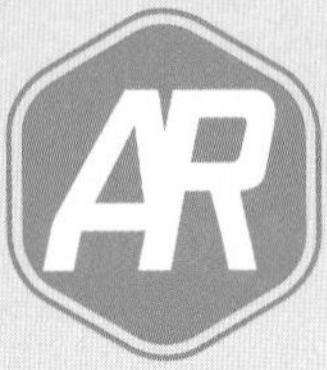

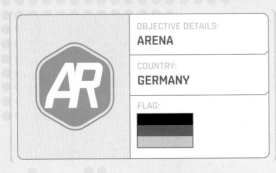

OBJECTIVE DETAILS:	**ARENA**
COUNTRY:	**GERMANY**
FLAG:	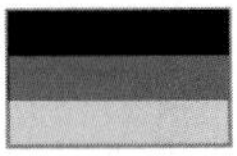

A NEW SEASON OF BATTLE

On the edge of Eichenwalde lies a dense forest, all but forgotten. Destroyed bastion units rest between the trees as a monument to the Omnic Crisis. Nature has been slowly reclaiming these buildings, but now the fight has returned and the forest is waiting.

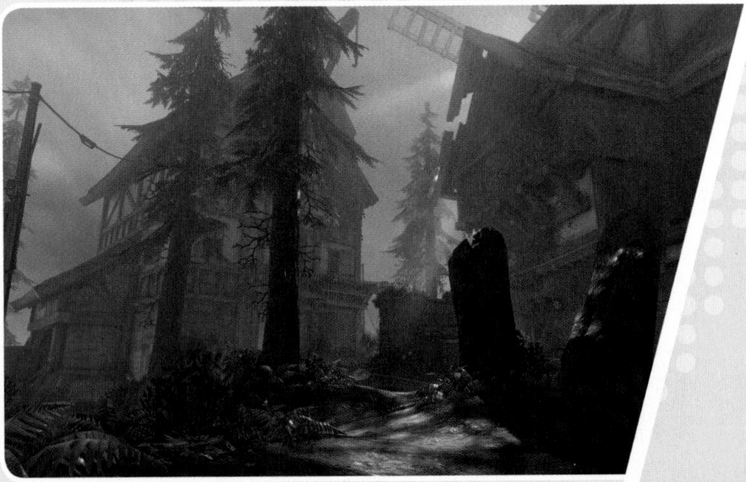

CASTILLO

	OBJECTIVE DETAILS: **ARENA** COUNTRY: **MEXICO** FLAG:

UNDER THE RADAR

This old fort on the Dorado coast may look beautiful and harmless on the outside, but there's a lot going on under the surface: the Los Muertos gang is active here, as is the infamous hacker, Sombra. All sorts of unusual people visit the Calaveras bar, where heists are planned and former heroes take breaks. It's a good place to escape . . . and to set a trap.

MAP
ECOPOINT: ANTARCTICA

OBJECTIVE DETAILS:
ARENA

COUNTRY:
ANTARCTICA

FLAG:

FROZEN IN TIME

While researching severe weather abnormalities in the region, an intense polar storm left this Overwatch station cut off from the outside world. Mei, a climatologist at the Ecopoint, awoke after nine years of cryostasis to find a different world, and a frozen base.

MAP
NECROPOLIS

OBJECTIVE DETAILS:
ARENA

COUNTRY:
EGYPT

FLAG:

CITY OF THE PRESUMED DEAD

This ancient ruin is covered in carvings and statues—monuments to the dead. Ana uses this area as a field base for her operations.

EVENTS

Even heroes like to have a little fun! Dive into the Summer Games, get spooky with Dr. Junkenstein, or chill out in Winter Wonderland. There is something special in every event! You can even experience the history of Overwatch from Tracer's first mission in Uprising to the Blackwatch capture-turned-escape in Retribution.

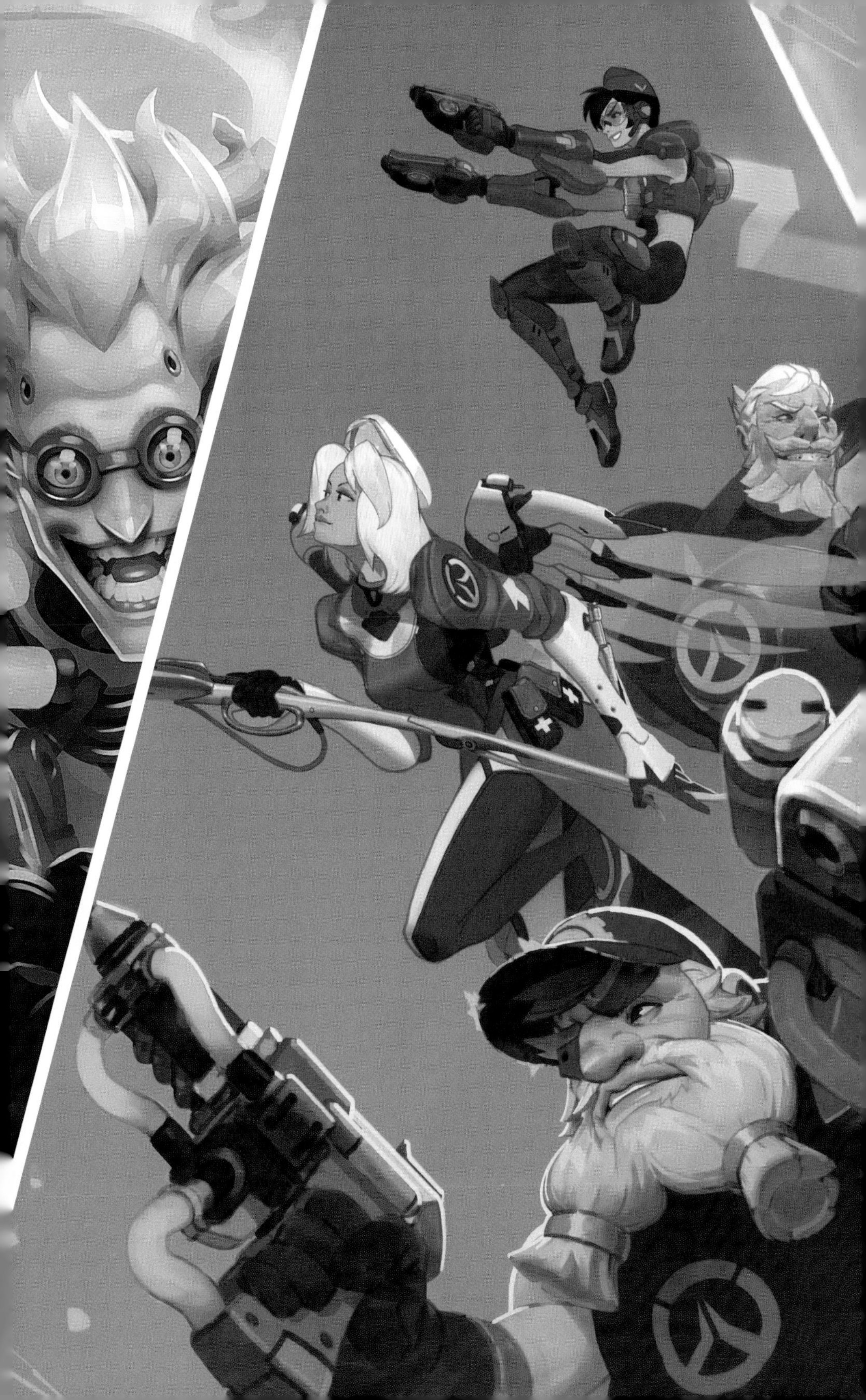

EVENT
ANNIVERSARY

Another year of Overwatch is always worth celebrating. Every hero has a new playing card spray, a golden icon of their logo, and they're all so excited, they're even dancing! (Roadhog and Junkrat will even high-five when they dance side by side!) Plus, there are a ton of new looks on display: Lúcio's playing jazz, Mei's studying bees, and Genji's straight out of a sentai show. Here are some of the prizes and outfits commemorating another year of saving the world!

THE WORLD NEEDS HEROES

OVERWATCH®
ANNIVERSARY

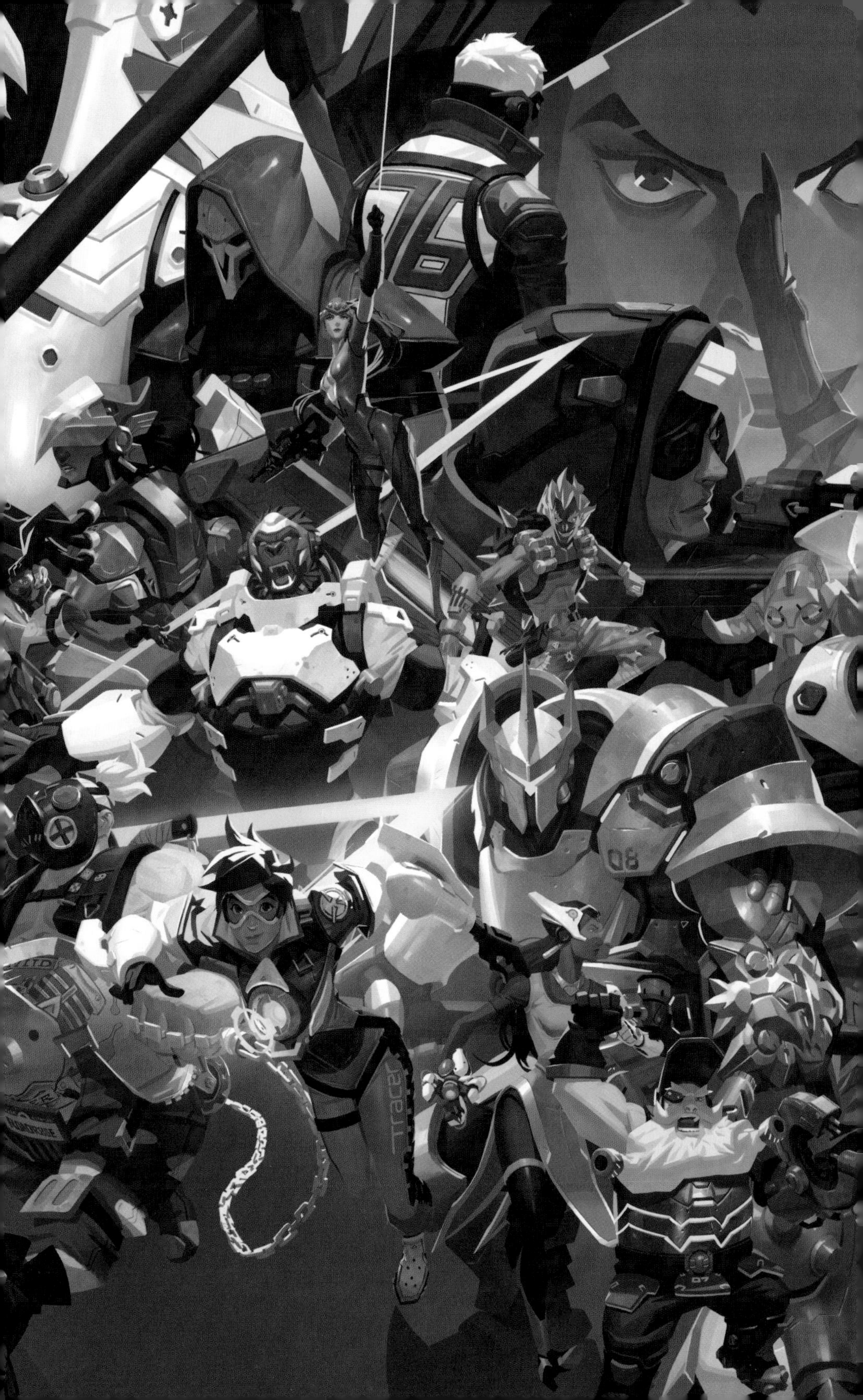
08
Tracer

EVENT

UPRISING

Tracer's first real mission was on her home turf in London. An omnic uprising began in King's Row when a rogue group of omnics known as Null Sector interrupted the groundbreaking ceremony of Turing Green, a new development meant to give homes to London's omnic population. They took Mayor Nandah and Tekhartha Mondatta hostage, leaving the city's officials powerless to stop them. Overwatch wasn't supposed to operate in the UK, but they couldn't sit back and let London fall without a fight.

New skins explore the past of Overwatch and Blackwatch—see how Genji and McCree looked when they were working undercover, Widowmaker's original Talon outfit, and Null Sector's Bastion units. Heroes who complete the mission especially well, or on the highest difficulties, can receive special sprays.

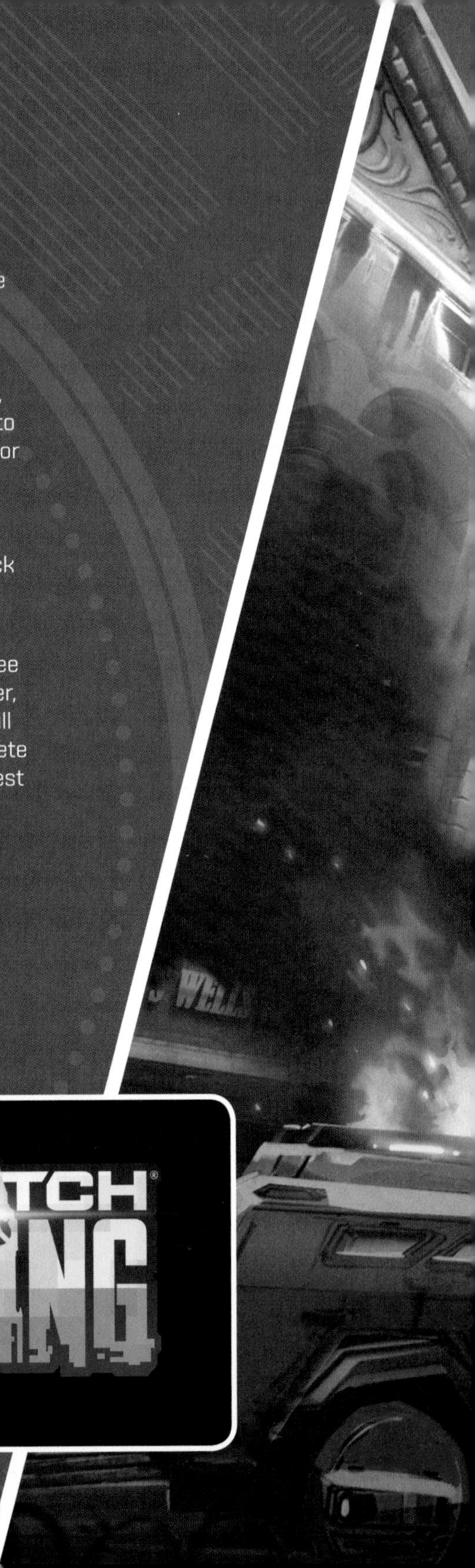

OVERWATCH UPRISING

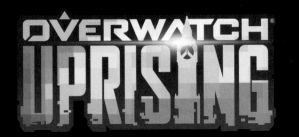

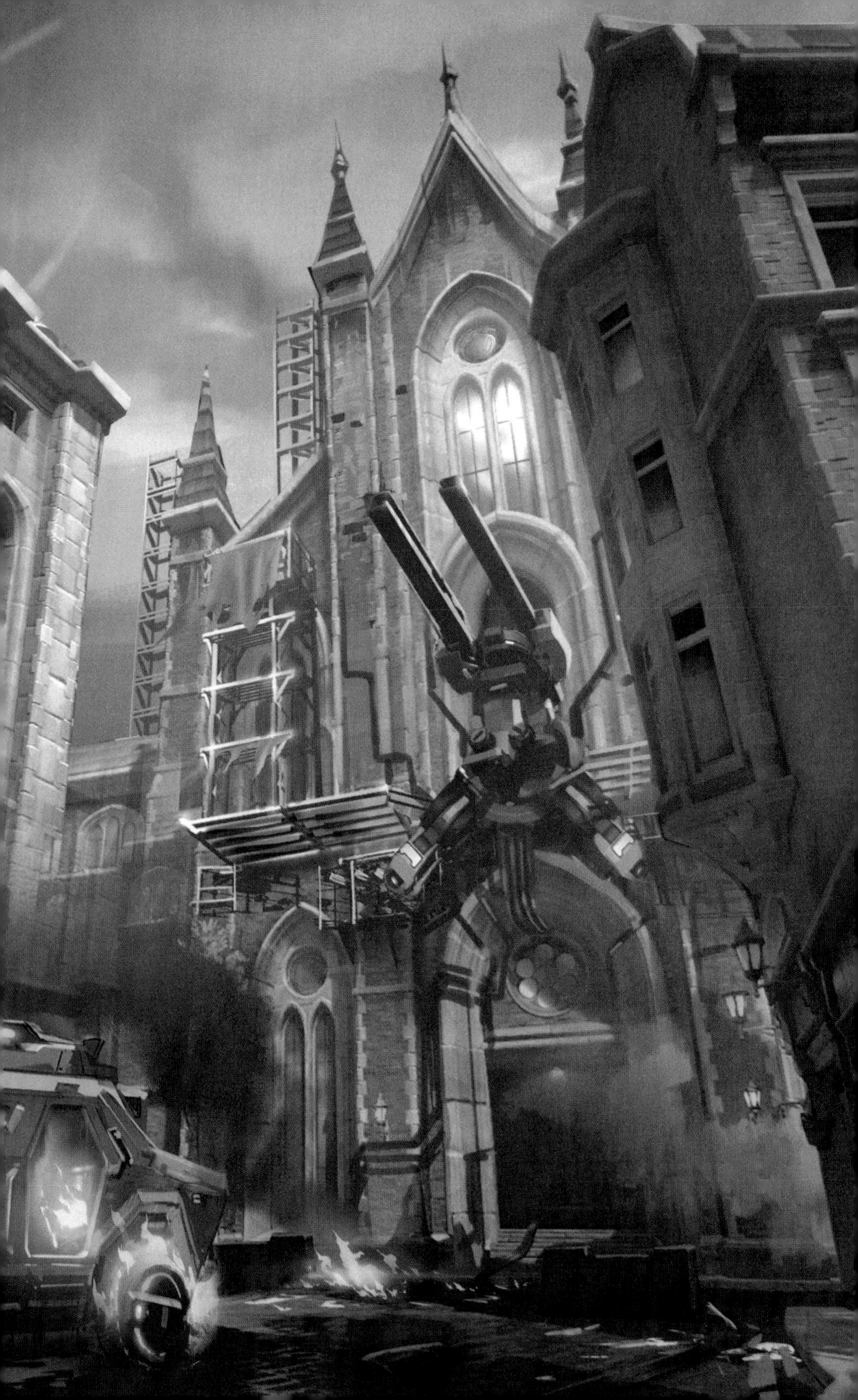

EVENT

SUMMER GAMES

The Summer Games are an annual tradition celebrating competition and sportsmanship! Lúcioball is the highlight of the season, where six Lúcios jam out to music while playing a futuristic version of soccer—play for fun with your friends, or compete for a high score in Copa Lúcioball! Check the new sprays for what event every hero is competing in, and their new skins to see what country they're representing. Some heroes may win gold medals for their victory poses, but all heroes have a specialty: Tracer sprints, Zarya lifts, and Soldier: 76 . . . grills.

OVERWATCH

SUMMER GAMES

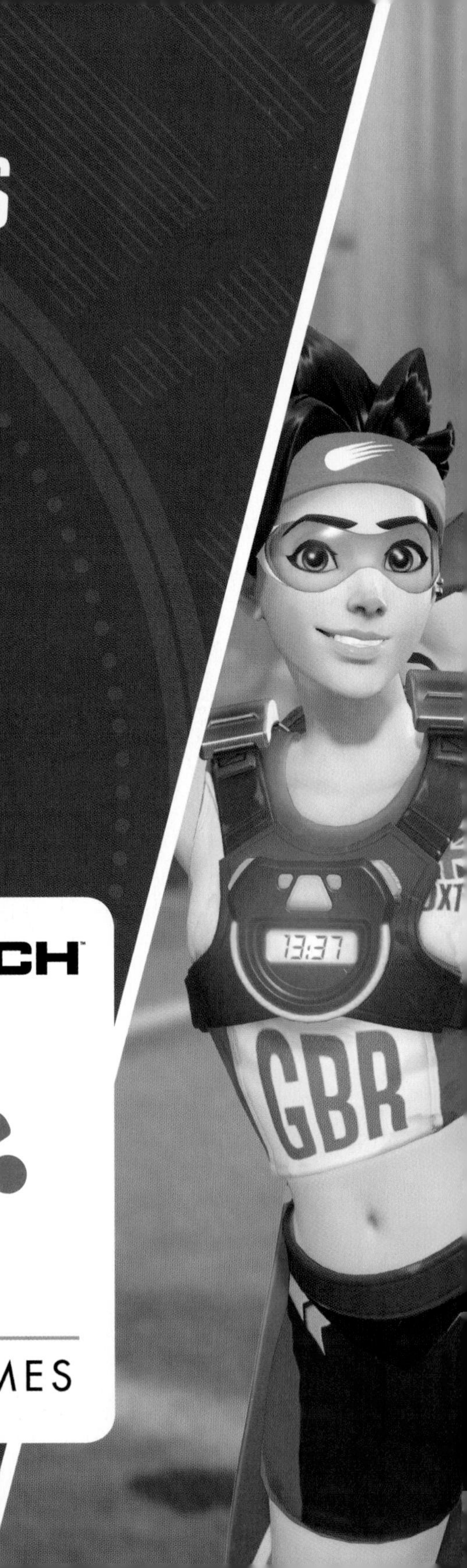
13:37
GBR

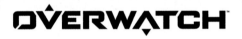

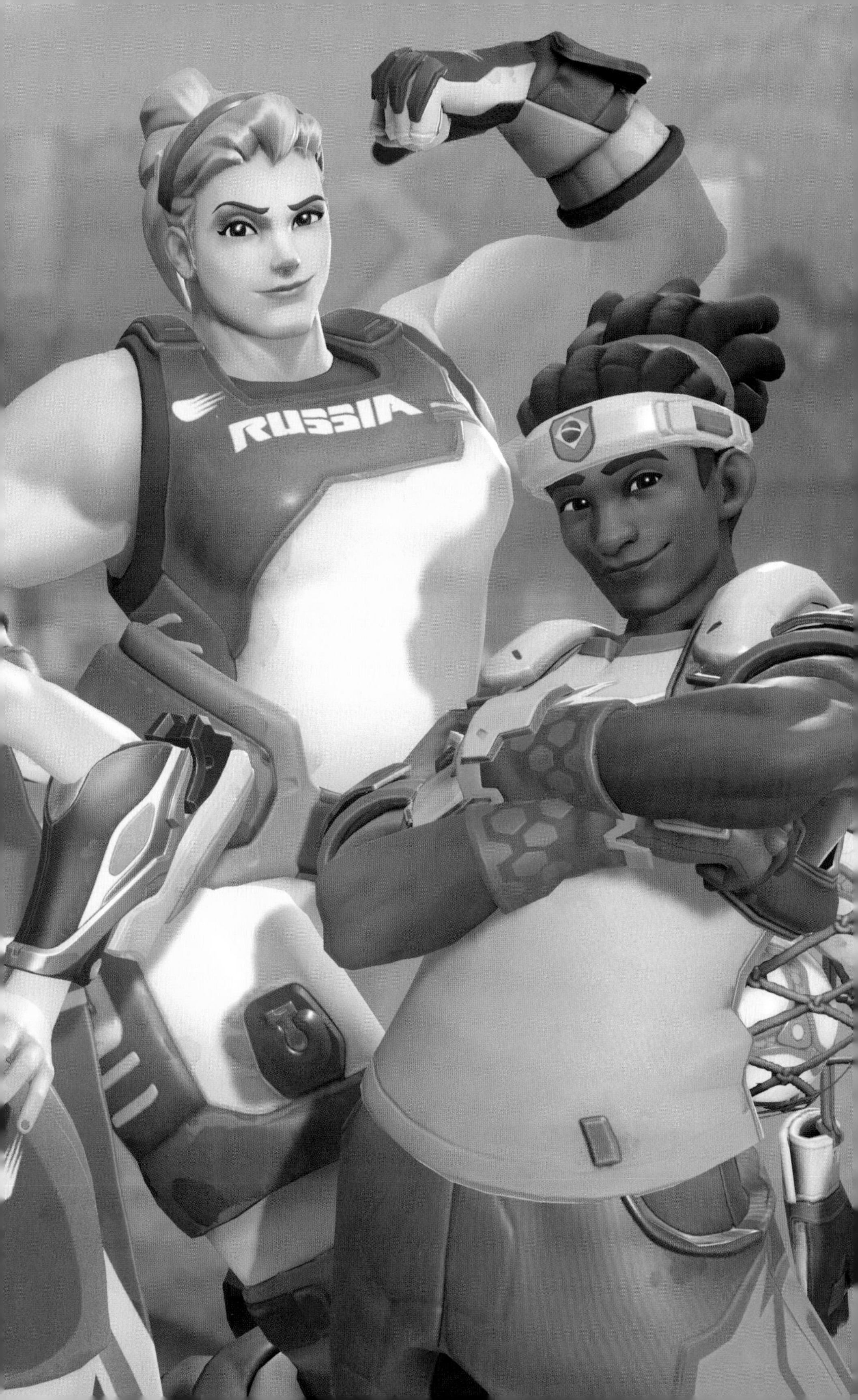
RUSSIA

EVENT

HALLOWEEN TERROR

Horror lurks deep in the Black Forest, in a town known as Adlersbrunn . . . or so Reinhardt says. After the local lord brushed aside all of Dr. Junkenstein's creations, the mad scientist sought out the Witch of the Wilds to make a deal for the spark of life—the final ingredient for his terrifying monster! His monster and an army of zomnics lay siege to the lord's castle unless four travelers can stop him! Join the gunslinger, the monk, the alchemist, the archer, and many others as they defend the castle gates . . . and look scary good while doing it. Special sprays imagine the Overwatch heroes as trick-or-treaters in Halloween costumes, and exclusive emotes let you play with pumpkins and give out candy. The most valiant protectors of the castle will be rewarded with sprays of movie posters, or cute versions of the featured villains. Can you survive Dr. Junkenstein's endless night?

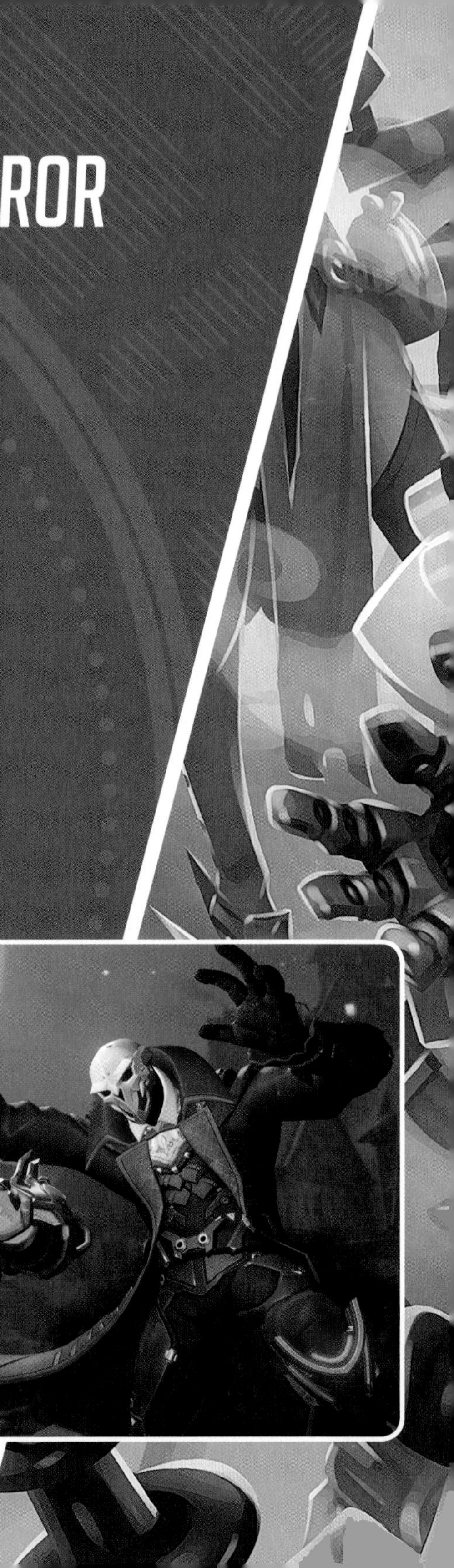

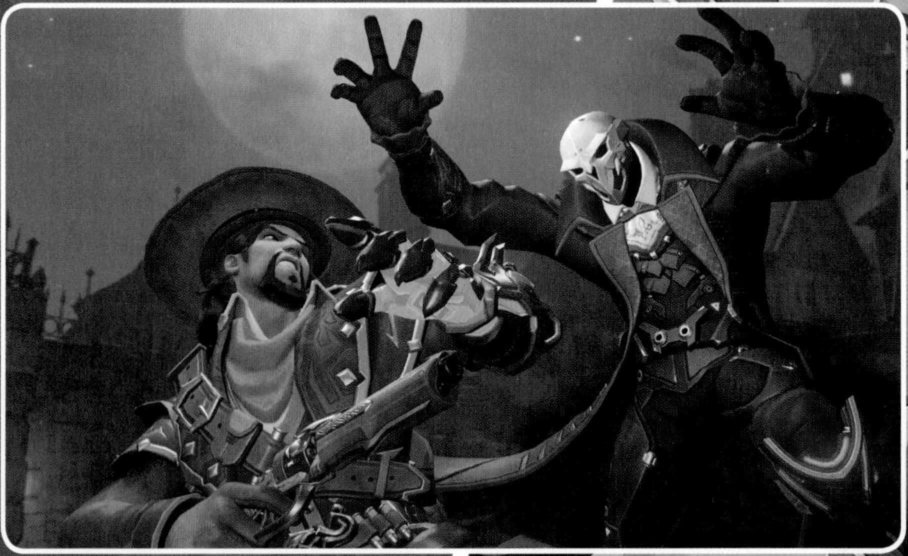

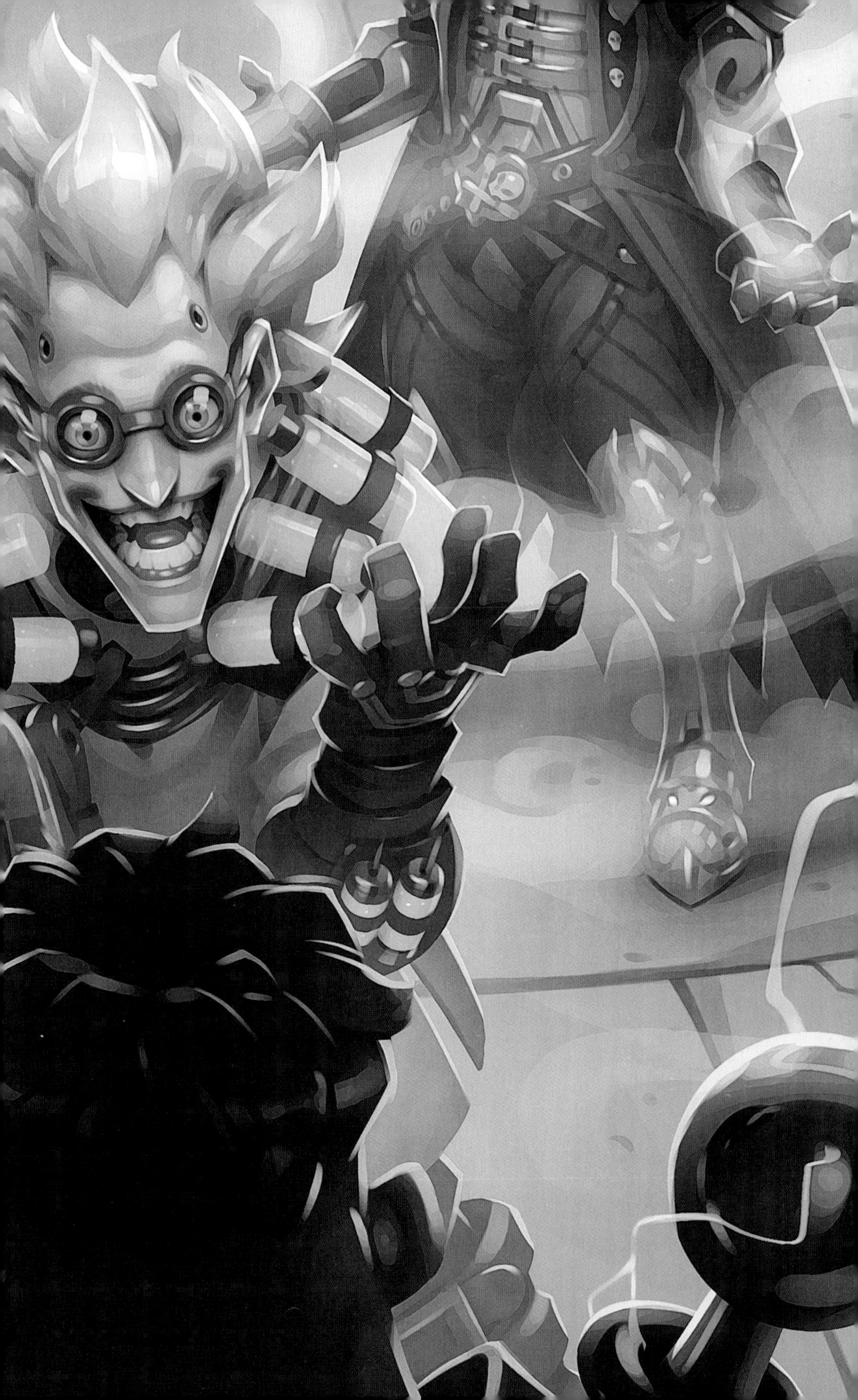

EVENT

WINTER WONDERLAND

Overwatch celebrates the holidays, too! A dangerous yeti has been spotted in Nepal, and a team of scientists are dropping traps and spraying ice to catch him and learn more about this mysterious creature! Mei's also hosting a big snowball fight, and there are all sorts of presents: winter and holiday-themed outfits, special highlight intros with mistletoe and snow, and even an emote where Orisa gets a brand-new puppy! (Of course, it's not cold everywhere in the world—Junkrat's ready for the beach.) The best snowball fighters and yeti hunters will receive sprays of special yeti hunter art and Overwatch snow-heroes!

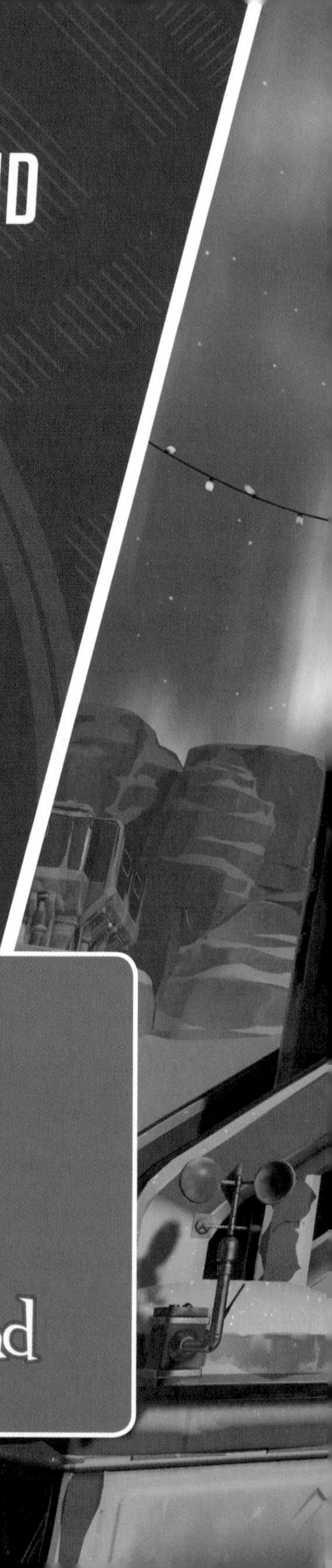

OVERWATCH

Winter Wonderland

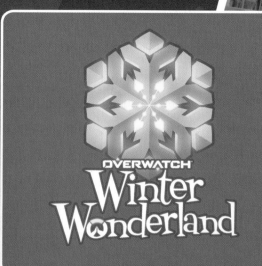

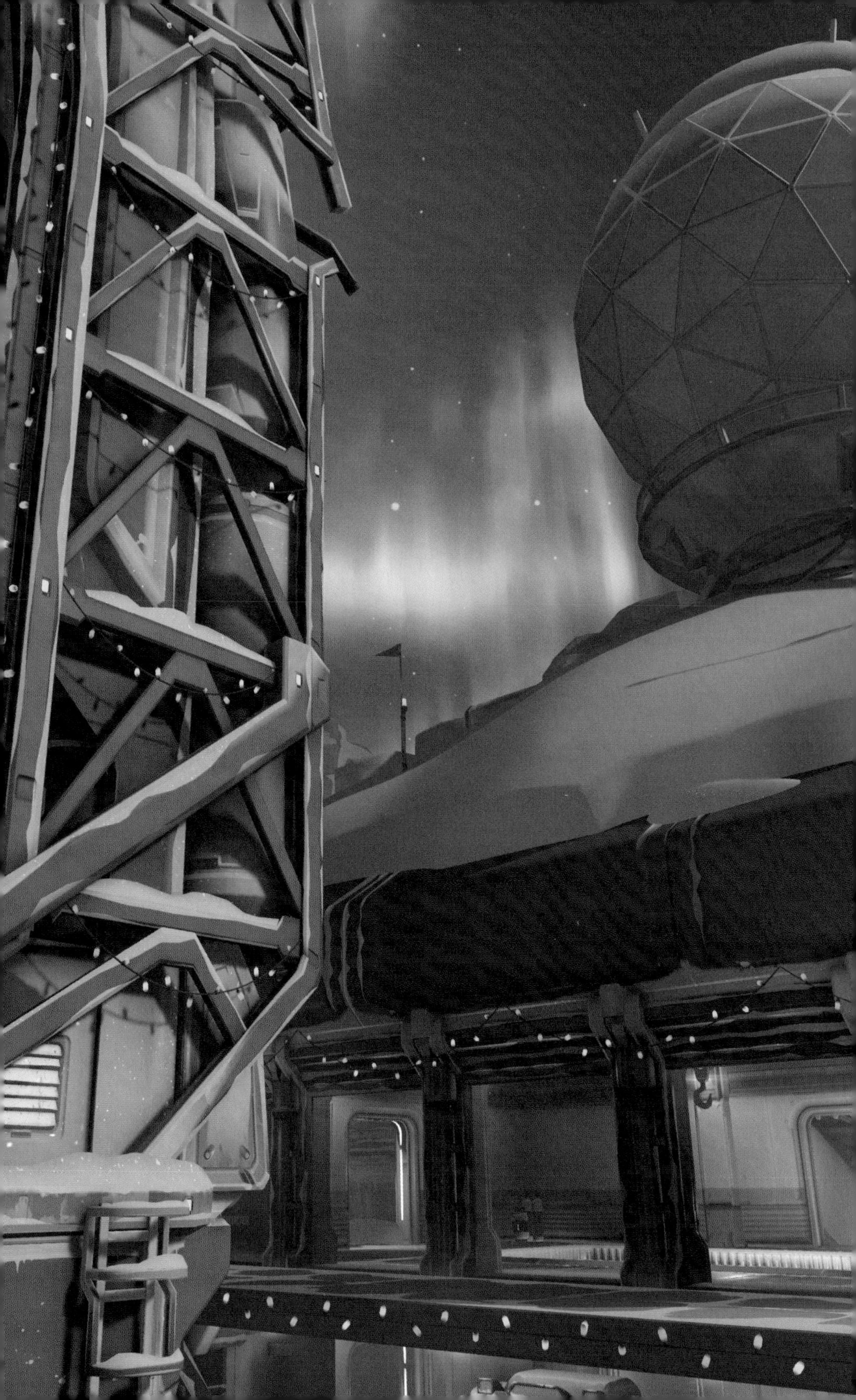

EVENT
LUNAR NEW YEAR

Enjoy the Lunar New Year with a game of capture the flag with Chinese zodiac flair, or join the heroes in a dragon dance with combinable sprays! Winston and friends dress up in outfits inspired by the Chinese novel, Journey to the West—a favorite of Winston's when he was a young gorilla in the Horizon Lunar Colony—and others celebrate in red and gold for the occasion. Earn special sprays by mastering your flag-capturing skills!

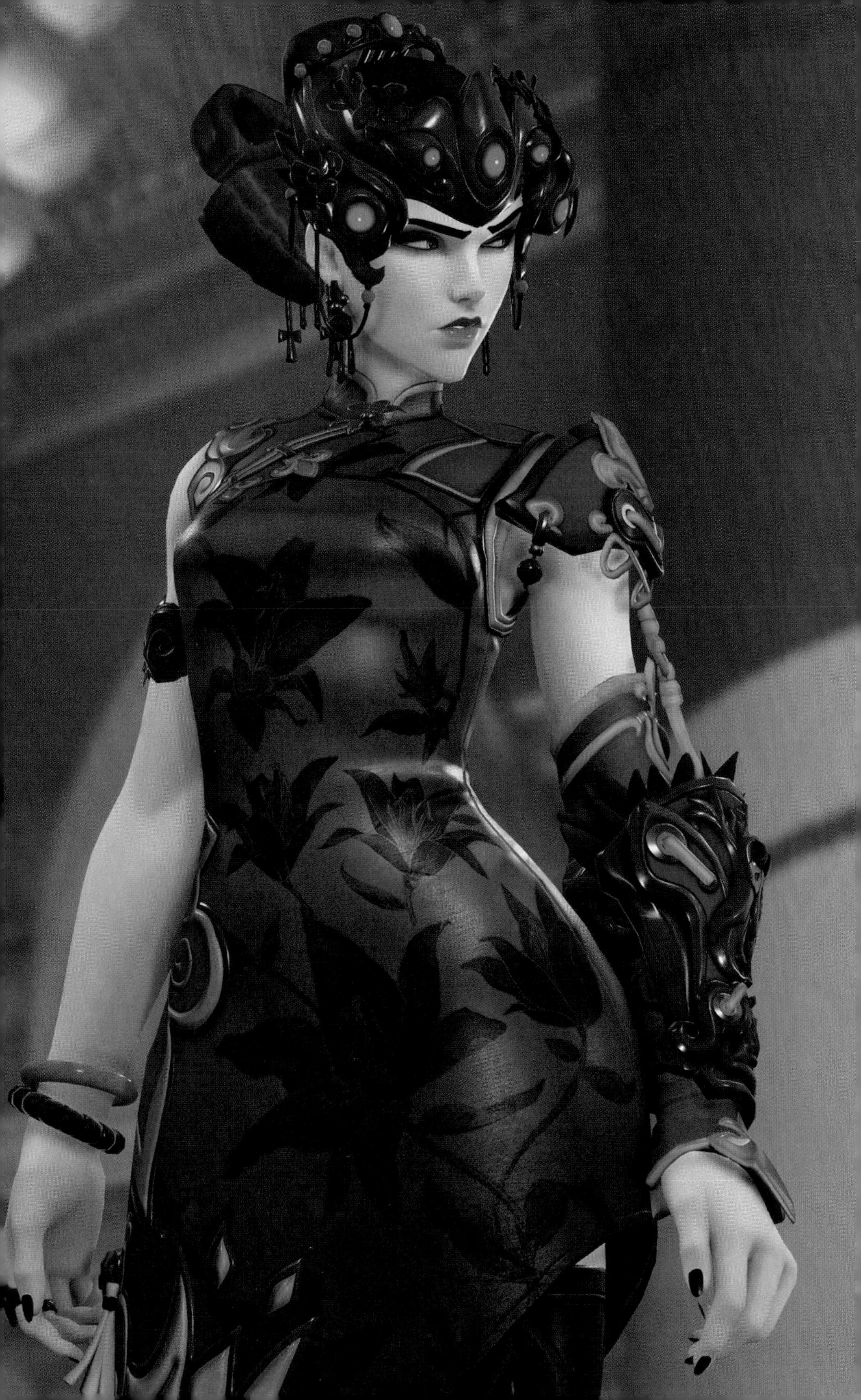

EVENT

RETRIBUTION

Nearly a decade ago, Talon launched an attack on an Overwatch facility. Overwatch needed to respond, but "officially" their hands were tied. Luckily, Blackwatch plays by its own rules. Journey eight years into the past as you take command of Blackwatch agents to fight in the streets of Venice. Objective? Capture a high-ranking member of the Talon organization! Fight for peace as Genji, Moira, McCree, or Reyes (later known as Reaper) in Story Mode or bring out your favorite hero in All Heroes Mode. But be careful: Talon will stop at nothing to protect its leaders.

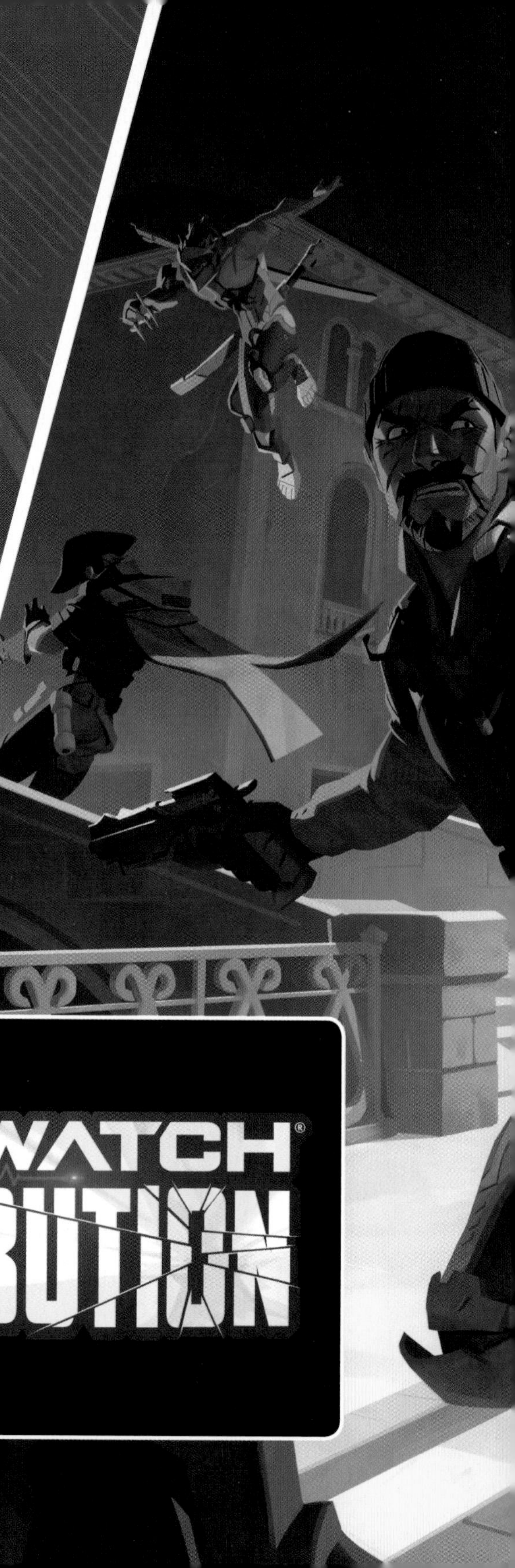
OVERWATCH®
RETRIBUTION

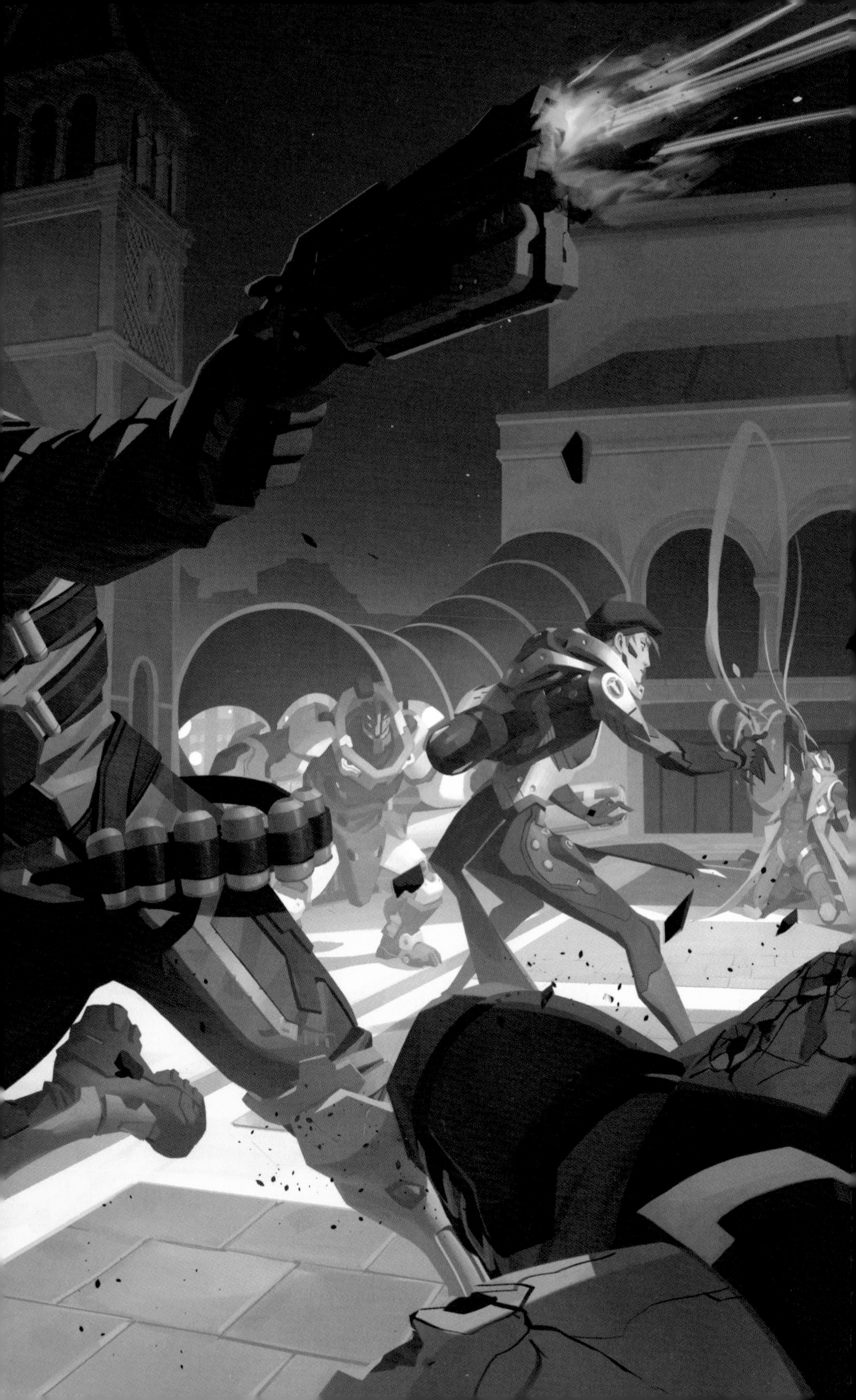

WHAT KIND OF HERO WILL YOU BE?

By now your mind is probably spinning with questions. Can humans and omnics really live in peace? Is Overwatch dangerous, or is it the only thing that can save the world?

There's only one way to figure out where you stand: Suit up. Grab some gear. Jump into the battle.

Find out what kind of hero you are destined to be!